LEAN TALES

James Kelman was born in Glasgow in 1946. His books include *Not not while the giro*, *The Busconductor Hines*, *The Chancer* and *Greyhound for Breakfast*, which won the 1987 Cheltenham Prize. His novel *A Disaffection* won the 1989 James Tait Black Memorial Prize and was shortlisted for the Booker Prize, and his collection of stories *The Burn* won a Scottish Arts Council book award. His novel *How late it was, how late* won the 1994 Booker Prize. James Kelman lives in Glasgow with his wife and two daughters.

Agnes Owens is the author of the novels *Gentlemen of the West*, *Birds in the Wilderness* and *A Working Mother*.

Alasdair Gray is a 61-year-old Glaswegian who lives by painting and writing things. He is now completing a collection of stories called *Teachers* to be published in 1995 or 6, and working on *The Anthology of Prefaces*, to be published in 1998 or 9, if he's spared.

BY JAMES KELMAN

An old pub near the Angel, and other stories
Three Glasgow Writers (with Tom Leonard and Alex Hamilton)
Short Tales From The Nightshift
Not not while the giro, and other stories
The Busconductor Hines
Lean Tales (with Agnes Owens and Alasdair Gray)
A Chancer
Greyhound For Breakfast
A Disaffection
Hardie And Baird & Other Plays
The Burn
Some Recent Attacks: Essays Cultural And Political
How late it was, how late

BY AGNES OWENS

Gentlemen Of The West
Lean Tales (with James Kelman and Alasdair Gray)
Birds In The Wilderness
A Working Mother

BY ALASDAIR GRAY

Lanark
Unlikely Stories, Mostly
1982, Janine
Lean Tales (with James Kelman and Agnes Owens)
Fall Of Kelvin Walker
Five Scottish Artists
Saltire Self Portrait 4
Old Negatives
McGrotty And Ludmilla
Something Leather
Why Scots Should Rule Scotland
Poor Things
Ten Tales Tall & True
A History Maker

James Kelman
Agnes Owens
Alasdair Gray

LEAN TALES

VINTAGE

Published by Vintage 1995

2 4 6 8 10 9 7 5 3 1

First published in Great Britain by
Jonathan Cape Ltd, 1985

Vintage
Random House, 20 Vauxhall Bridge Road,
London SW1V 2SA

Random House Australia (Pty) Limited
20 Alfred Street, Milsons Point, Sydney
New South Wales 2061, Australia

Random House New Zealand Limited
18 Poland Road, Glenfield,
Auckland 10, New Zealand

Random House South Africa (Pty) Limited
PO Box 337, Bergvlei, South Africa

Random House UK Limited Reg. No. 954009

A CIP catalogue record for this book
is available from the British Library

ISBN 0 09 958541 3

Papers used by Random House UK Ltd are natural, recy-
clable products made from wood grown in sustainable
forests. The manufacturing processes conform to the
environmental regulations of the country of origin

Printed and bound in Great Britain by
Cox & Wyman, Reading, Berkshire

Some of these stories have appeared before, as follows. James Kelman: *Busted Scotch, The Witness* and *learning the Story* were published in *Words*, 1977; *the same is here again* in *A.M.F.*, 1979; *In a betting shop to the rear of Shaftesbury Avenue* in the *Glasgow Magazine*, 1983; *Where I was* and *The City Slicker and The Barmaid* in *Three Glasgow Writers*, Molendinar Press, Glasgow, 1976; *Where I was* also in the *Fiction Magazine*, 1984; *Extra cup* (under the title *Mozambique*) in *Masque*, 1976; *Manufactured in Paris, The Place!* and *An Enquiry Concerning Human Understanding* in *Short Tales from the Night Shift*, Print Studio Press, Glasgow, 1978. Agnes Owens: *Arabella* was published in *Cencrastus*, 1980; *Bus Queue* in *Words*, 1978, and the *Fiction Magazine*, 1984; *Commemoration Day* in the *Edinburgh Review*,1984. Alasdair Gray: *The Answer* was published in *Words*, 1980; earlier versions of *A Small Thistle* in *The Glasgow West End News*, 1973 and in Polygon Press's *A Glasgow Diary*, 1980; *Portrait of a Playwright* in *Chapman*, 1981; *Portrait of a Painter* in *Cencrastus*, 1984; *The Grumbler* in the *Fiction Magazine*, 1985.

The lyrics on p. 165 from *Old Man River* (Kern/Hammerstein) are reproduced by permission of Chappell Music Ltd, London.

CONTENTS

Tim Kelman

James Kelman

Busted Scotch

I had been looking forward to this Friday night for a while.
The first wage from the first job in England. The work-
mates had assured me they played Brag in this club's casino.
It would start when the cabaret ended. Packed full of
bodies inside the main hall; rows and rows of men-only
drinking pints of bitter and yelling at the strippers. One of
the filler acts turned out to be a scotchman doing this
harrylauder thing complete with kilt and trimmings. A
terrible disgrace. Keep Right On To The End Of The Road
he sang with four hundred and fifty males screaming Get
Them Off Jock. Fine if I had been drunk and able to join in
on the chants but as it was I was staying sober for the Brag
ahead. Give the scotchman his due but – he stuck it out till
the last and turning his back on them all he gave a big boo
boopsidoo with the kilt pulled right up and flashing the
Y-fronts. Big applause he got as well. The next act on was
an Indian Squaw. Later I saw the side door into the casino
section opening. I went through. Blackjack was the game
until the cabaret finished. I sat down facing a girl of around
my own age, she was wearing a black dress cut off the
shoulders. Apart from me there were no other punters in
the room.

Want to start, she asked.

Aye. Might as well. I took out my wages.

O, you're scotch. One of your countrymen was on stage tonight.

That a fact.

She nodded as she prepared to deal. She said, How much are you wanting to bet.

I shrugged. I pointed to the wages lying there on the edge of the baize.

All of it . . .

Aye. The lot.

She covered the bet after counting what I had. She dealt the cards.

Twist.

Bust . . .

the same is here again

My teeth are grut.

What has happened to all my dreams is what I would like to know. Presently I am a physical wreck. If by chance I scratch my head while strolling showers of dandruff reel onto the paved walkway, also hairs of varying length. Tooth decay. I am feart to look into a mirror. I had forgotten about them, my molars; these wee discoloured bones jutting out my gums and lonely, neglected, fighting amongst themselves for each particle of grub I have yet to pick. Jesus. And my feet – and this mayhap is the worst of my plight – my feet stink. The knees blue the hands filthy the nails grimy, uneatable. What I must do is bathe very soon.

One certainty: until recently I was living a life; this life is gone, tossed away in the passing. I am washed up. The sickness burbles about in my gut. A pure, physical reaction at last. I feel it heaving down there, set to erupt – or maybe just to remain, gagging.

It is all a mystery as usual. I am very much afraid I am going off my head. I lie on pavements clawing at myself with this pleasant smile probably on the countenance. I have been this way for years. More than half my life to present has been spent in acquiring things I promptly dispose of. I seldom win at things. It is most odd. Especially my lack of interest. But for the smile, its well-being, the way I seem to regard people. It makes me kind of angry. I am unsure about much. Jesus christ.

Where am I again. London's the truth though I was reared in Glasgow. In regard to environment: I had plenty. But.

The weather. The hardtopped hardbacked bench concreted to the concrete patch amidst the grass. My spine against the hardback. My feet stuck out and crossed about the ankles. My testicles tucked between my thighs. I am always amazed that no damage is done them. I have forgotten what has happened to the chopper. The chopper is upright though far from erect. It lies against the fly of my breeks. And now uncomfortable.

Explanations sicken me. The depression is too real. A perpetual thirst but not for alcohol. Milk I drink when I find it. Smoking is bad. Maybe I am simply ill. Burping and farting. All sorts of wind. I should have a good meal of stuff. But even the thought. Jesus.

My hand has been bleeding. I cut it while entering a car. A stereo and one Johnny Cash cassette. My life is haunted by country & western music.

I have no cigarette in my gub.

And yet this late autumnal daylight. The spring in my step. Grinning all the while and wishing for hats to doff to elderly women. I am crying good-evening to folk. I might be in the mood for a game of something. Or a cold shower. When I settle down to consider a future my immediate straits are obliged to be conducive. I am grateful for the clement weather. Facts are to be faced. I am older than I was recently. And I was feart to show my face that same recently. Breakfast is an awful meal. If you dont get your breakfast that's you fucked for the day.

I cannot eat a Johnny Cash cassette.

Breakfast has always been the one meal I like to think I insist upon. When I have money I eat fine breakfasts. One of the best I ever had was right here in the heart of old London Town. A long time ago. So good I had to leave a slice of toast for appearances' sake. I was never a non-eater. Could always devour huge quantities of the stuff. Anything at all; greasy fried bread, burnt custard or eggs. Even with the flu or bad hangovers. A plate of soup at 4 in the morning. I cannot understand people scoffing at snails' feet and octopi although to be honest I once lifted a can of peasbrose from a supermarket shelf only to discover I couldnt stomach the bastarn stuff. So: there we are. And also food-poisoning I suppose. If I ever get food-poisoning I would probably not feel like eating. Apart from this

But not now. Not presently, and this is odd. My belly may have a form of cramp.

Immediately my possessions include money I shall invest in certain essentials as well as the washing of that pair of items which constitute the whole of my wardrobe in the department of feet viz my socks. For my apparel excludes pants and vest. An effect of this was my chopper getting itself caught in the zipping-up process that follows upon the act of pissing. Normally one is prepared for avoiding such occurrences. But this time, being up an alley off one of her majesty's thoroughfares, I was obliged to rush. ZZZIPPP. Jesus. The belly. Even the remembrance. For a couple of moments I performed deep breathing exercises aware that my next act would of necessity be rapid. And this was inducing vague associations of coronary attacks. My whole trunk then became icy cold. UUUNZZZIPP. Freed. It would not have happened had I been wearing pants. If I was being cared for pants would pose no problem, and neither would vests. Vests catch and soak up sweat unless they are made of nylon. In which case the sweat dribbles down your sides and is most damp and irritating.

My face looks to be ageing but is fine. A cheery face. It laughs at me from shop windows. The hairs protruding from my nostrils can be mistaken for the top of my moustache. The actual flesh, the cheekbones and red-veined eyeballs, the black patches round the sockets. Every single thing is fine. I am delighted with the lines. On my left – the right in fact, side of my nose has formed a large yellow head which I squeezed till the matter burst forth. I am still squeezing it because it lives. While squeezing it I am aware of how thin my skin is. I put myself in mind of an undernourished 87 year old. But the skin surrounding the human frame weighs a mere 6 ounces. Although opposed to that is the alsatian dog which leapt up and grabbed my arm; its teeth punctured the sleeve of the garment I was wearing but damage to the flesh was nil.

I bathed recently; for a time I lay steeping in the grime, wondering how I would manage out, without this grime returning to the pores in my skin. The method I employed was this: I arose in the standing position. The grime showed on the hairs of my legs though and I had to rinse those legs with cold because the hot had finished. I washed my socks on that occasion. They are of good quality. I sometimes keep them stuffed in the back pockets of my jeans.

The present is to be followed by nothing of account. Last night was terrible. All must now be faced. It has much to do with verges and watersheds.

Taxis to Blackfriars Bridge for the throwing of oneself off of are out of the question.

I have the shivers.

Reddish-blue blisters have appeared on the soles of my feet. They are no longer bouncing along. I can foresee. Nothing of account will follow. For some time now the futility of certain practices has not been lost on me. I shall sleep with the shivers, the jeans and the jumper, the socks and the corduroy shoes. I can forecast point A or point B: either is familiar. All will depend on X the unknown (which also affords of an either/or). The A and B of X equals the A and B that follow from themselves, not A and not B being unequal to not B and A. And they cannot be crossed as in Yankee Bets. Yet it always has been this way and I alone have the combinations.

I was planning on the park tonight. I left a brown paper bag concealed in a hedge near the Serpentine for the purpose. It will have been appropriated by now.

The trouble might well be sleep. I had a long one recently and it may well have upset the entire bodily functioning. This belly of mine. I must have slept for 10 hours. Normally I meet forenoons relatively alert.

Sheltering in an alley the other night, the early hours, in a motionless state. I should have been smoking, had just realized the cigarette in my gub as not burning where it should have been burning. As I reached for a match I heard movement. Two cats were on the job less than 20 yards distant. The alley banked by high walls. The cats should have been free from spectators and yet here was me, jesus. In a film I saw recently there was this scruffy dog and a lady dog and he took her out for the night down this back alley to meet his friends and these friends of his were Chefs in an Italian Restaurant, one of whom was named Luigi if I remember correctly. He brought out a table and candlesticks and while the dogs sat down the other friend came out with an enormous quantity of spaghetti and stuff. While they were tucking in out came Luigi again with a stringed instrument and him and his pal began singing an operatic duet.

This grass grows in a rough patch and cannot have it easy. The blades are grey green and light green; others are yellow but they lie directly on the earth, right on the soil. My feet were there and the insects crawled all around. A fine place for games. They go darting through the green blades and are never really satisfied till hitting the yellow ones below. And they dart headlong, set to collide all the time into each other but no, that last-minute body swerve. And that last-minute body swerve appears to unnerve them so that they begin rushing about in circles or halting entirely for an approximate moment.

I have to clear my head. I need peace peace peace. No thoughts. Nothing. Nothing at all.

Here I am as expected. The shoulders drooping; they have been strained recently. Arms hanging, and the fingers. Here: and rubbing my eyes to open them on the same again. Here, the same is here again. What else.

The Glenchecked Effort

This jacket had a glencheck pattern and I back centre vent, two side pockets and I out breast welt, two inside pockets and I in-tick. It was made to fit a 40″ chest and the arms of a 6′4″ gentleman. The buttons, two down the front and I on each cuff, were of dimpled leather. Inside the in-tick were ticket stubs and 4 spent matches; the inside pocket to the right contained a spotless handkerchief of the colour white, having parallel red lines along the border. The left outside pocket held eighteen pence in 2 pence pieces. It was a warm jacket, Handwoven in Harris read the label. It hung on a hook from where I lifted it neatly and stepped quickly outside and off. Though hanging loosely upon me it was a fine specimen and would have done much to protect me during the coming harsh winter. It should be stated that previous garments have afforded a more elegant finish but never before had I felt more pleasure than when surveying that person of mine while clad in the glenchecked effort.

I positioned myself to one corner of a rather quiet square to the right-hand side of Piccadilly looking south i.e. southwest. Two males and two females approached, all four of whom were of the Occidental delineation; each pair of eyes was concealed behind medium-sized spectacles with darkened shades. Can you spare a bloke a bob? I asked.

Pardon . . .

Proffering my right hand in halting fashion I shrugged my shoulders, saying: A bob, can you spare a bloke a bob?

They were foreign. They conferred in their own language. At intervals I was obliged to glance to the ground when a gaze was directed towards me. I shuffled my feet. Then suddenly a handful of coins was produced and projected towards me. Many thanks, I said, many thanks. I clicked my heels, inclining my head. And off they went. Upon depositing the money into the left outside pocket I lowered myself to the pavement; folding my arms I sat on my heels and thus rested for several minutes. A discarded cigarette then appeared in close proximation to my shoes. Instantly I had collected it. I sucked the smoke deep into my lungs, managing to obtain a further three puffs before finally I was forced to chip it away towards the kerb. I reknotted my shoelaces and rose to the favoured standing position.

An elderly couple had entered my line of vision, the progress of each being considerable abetted by the instance of two fine Malacca canes. With a brief nod of appreciation I stepped hesitantly forwards. Can you spare a bloke a bob? I quoth.

With nary a sideways glance they hobbled past me, their canes striking the pavement in most forcible manner.

You sir, I cried to a youngish man, can you spare a bloke a bob?

What . . .

Across the road I spied two uniformed fellows observing me with studied concentration. Slowly I turned and in a movement, was strolling to the corner, round which I hastened onwards. The skies were appearing to clouden. Yet my immediate prospects I continued to view with great optimism. Choosing a stance athwart a grassy verge I addressed successive pedestrians, but to no avail. A middle-aged couple had paused nearby, viewing my plight with apparent concern. Madam, quoth I, can you . . .

You're a bloody disgrace, she said, that's what you are; giving us a showing up in front of the English.

I'm really most dreadfully sorry missis, I gave as my answer, I have been disabled.

That's no excuse for scrounging! She turned to her companion: Have you ever seen the like?

I've a wife and two weans missis and I can assure you, having flitted down here in search of the new life I had the bad fortune to fall off a roof.

And would you look at the state of that jacket he's wearing! he's lifted it from somewhere.

I have not.

Maybe he's genuine, hazarded her companion.

Ha ha.

I am missis, I really am.

Oh you are are you!

About to retort I inadvertently sneezed. I tugged the handkerchief from my pocket; out popped a membership card to the British Museum. You see, I said as I swabbed at my nostrils, here's my membership card to the British Museum, since my fall I've been embarking on a series of evening classes with a view to securing a light post.

I think he's genuine, the man remarked and withdrawing a 50 pence coin from a trouser pocket he handed it to me.

You're too soft, cried the woman.

Now you're not letting me down? asked the man firmly.

Definitely not mister. Thanks a lot. I can assure you that . . .

Not letting you down! Hh!

Come on Doreen, he muttered then taking her by the arm, they continued on towards the very heart of the City. But I continued northwards. Soon I was entering the hallowed portals of our splendid literary museum. Moving briskly I proceeded beyond the lines of uniformed worthies at a pace I deemed seemly. Finding a more secluded room I occupied a chair at a table and settled for an indeterminate period. At length a bearded fellow who had been staring intently at the bibliographical pages of an handsomely bound volume, rose quietly and walked off. On the chair adjacent to his own lay an anorak, a plastic container, and a camera. Moments later I was strolling from the room, the camera safely secured in my inside left pocket. Entering a lavatory I continued to stroll, and passed into a vacant cubicle wherein I would remain for a lengthy interval. To occupy myself I examined each pocket and the gap between Harris Tweed and nylon lining, hoping against hope that I might discover other articles. It was not to be. Yet during my time in the cubicle no solitary voice of an excited nature had pierced my repose. There was much to be thankful for. I counted to three then pulled the plug and promptly unsnibbed the cubicle door. With practised eye I glanced to the washbasins before stepping forwards. I washed my hands. In the mirror I surveyed my glencheck jacket with undisguised satisfaction. Just then, as I prepared to dry my hands, an object attracted my attention. It was a knapsack. Slowly I turned, and in a movement, was strolling for the exit, uplifting the knapsack without the slightest check in my stride, and out through the doorway, allowing the door to swing backwards. In an instant I had considered the various uniformed gentlemen, their respective positions and demeanour, and was moving briskly, stepping into the magnificent surroundings of the vast entrance hall, then downwards onto the paved pathway to the iron gates, mingling with diverse individuals.

My getaway had been achieved with absurd ease. I was elated. You lucky bastard, I thought, you've knocked it off again!

The clouds were forming in puffs of the purest white. Surely a sign! Quickening my pace I crossed Russell Square, marching resolutely to the small grass park some two furlongs distant. While making my way to the rearmost bench my attention was drawn to a tearful urchin whose

ball was ensconced on top of a thorny bush. I reached for it
and gave it an almighty boot. The ball travelled high in the
air. I patted the little fellow on the head and off he
scampered in pursuit. When seated on the bench I sat for a
time before examining the contents of the knapsack. But at
last the moment had arrived; with a brief glance to the sky I
tugged at the zip, and could list the following articles:

  (i) One pair socks of the colour navy blue
 (ii) One comb, plastic
(iii) One towel
(iv) One pair swimming trunks of the colours maroon &
      white
 (v) One plastic bag containing: a) cheese sandwich
                                     b) lettuce & tomato
                                           sandwich
                                     c) slice of Madeira
                                           cake.

I smiled to myself and, withdrawing the camera from my
inside left pocket, deposited it at the bottom of the
knapsack. As I rose from the bench I chanced to glance
at '. . . God's fair heaven', and was reminded of these few
lines of the lyricist:

> Tell me – What is the meaning of man,
> Whence hath he come, whither doth go . . .

Slinging the knapsack over my shoulders with a mis-
chievous grin I walked onwards.

The Witness

As expected the windows were draped over with offwhite curtains, the body dressed in the navyblue three-piece suit, with the checked bunnet on the head. Drawing a chair close in I sat, smoking. I noticed the eyelids parting. The eyes were grey and white with red veins. The cigarette fell from my fingers. I reached quickly to get it up off the carpet. A movement on the bed. Scuffling noises. The head had turned. The eyes peering toward me. There was not a thing I could say. He was attempting to sit up now. He sat up. I placed a hand of mine on his right forearm, I was trying to restrain him. He wanted to rise. I withdrew my hand and he swivelled until his feet contacted space. I moved back. His feet lowered to the carpet then the rest of his body was up from the bed. He stood erect, the shoulders pushed back. The shoes on his feet; the laces were knotted far too tightly. I picked the checked bunnet up from where it was now lying by the pillow and passed it to him, indicating his head. He took it and pulled it on, smoothed down the old hair at the sides of his head. I was wanting to know if he was going to the kitchen: he nodded. Although he walked normally to the door he fumbled on the handle. He was irritated by this clumsiness. He made way for me. I could open the door easily. He had to brush past me. The cuff of his right sleeve touched my hand. I watched him. When he

got to the kitchen door he did not hesitate and he did not
fumble with its handle. The door swung behind him. I heard
her voice cry out. He was making for her. I gazed through
the narrow gap in the doorway. He was struggling with
her. He began to strike her about the shoulders, beating
her down onto her knees; and she cried, cried softly. This
was it. This was the *thing*. I held my head in both hands.

Are you drinking sir?

THEY had been seeking me for ages but being a devious old guy I managed to give them the slip on quite a few occasions. They found me in the broo. I was in there performing my song & dance routine, music from the 1st world war. At first I seemed not to notice them standing in the doorway then when I did I acted as though totally uninterested and my bravado had to be respected, not for its own sake so much as the effect it had on my pursuers. I turned my back on them and performed to those queuing to sign the register. Behind the counter the clerks looked slightly irritated although a couple of the younger brigade were smiling at my antics. But their smiles didnt linger, they continued working as though I wasnt there. I didnt bother at all, just carried on with the performance. Somehow an impression had been gained that no matter how erratically I might behave the clerks would never have me ejected. No doubt the reaction would be different had I become violent, or even explicitly abusive. Then suddenly, towards the end of a song, I lost concentration for a moment and appeared in danger of failing to perceive the course – but then I grinned briefly and continued the game. It was strange to behold. Nearby there were four youths sitting on a bench and they were stamping their feet and cheering and then one of them had flicked a burning cigarette end in my direction. I was dancing so nimbly that I scarcely seemed to interrupt myself while bending to uplift it; I nipped off the burning ash, sticking the remainder of it in an interior pocket of my greatcoat. Then I glanced swiftly at the doorway, whirled to face the counter; onwards I jigged across the floor, wagging my right forefinger at two young girls queuing at *enquiries*. I proceeded to address the chorus at them, the girls smiling their embarrassment, laughing lightly that they had no money, nor even a cigarette to spare. Yet still I persisted at them and the girls now having to avert their faces from me while I with the beaming smile, cutting my capers as though the doorway had never existed. And thank you sir, I was crying to a smallish fellow who had rolled me a cigarette, thank you sir. This distracting me from the girls and back again I faced the counter; but my sly glance at the doorway was unmistakable and I held the rolled cigarette aloft in my left hand, blatantly displaying it for their benefit. And I laughed at no one especially and again cried thank you sir, thank you sir, with both arms aloft now and waggling my hands round and round in preparation for the launch into my final chorus, but just at this point I made good my escape, and it wasnt till much later that they found me. I was in a stretch of waste ground near the river. I stared at them when they approached, but the stare expressed only the vaguest curiosity. My head lolled sideways, knocking the unbuttoned epaulette askew. They came forward and prodded my shoulder until my eyelids parted and my groan became a groan of recognition. Thank you sir I muttered thank you sir, and them, stepping back the way as though alarmed. But they werent alarmed, they were angry. And judging by the manner in which my gaze dropped to the ground I was trying to avoid witnessing it. And then they began talking to me in a language that was foreign. At length they stopped. I withdrew a halfsmoked cigarette from an interior pocket and held it to my mouth until being given a light. I inhaled only once on it, before placing it carefully on the ground; then I picked it up and stubbed it out, smiling in a very sleakit way. I glanced at them and said are you drinking sir? For a moment there was silence. When they began shouting at me there was an odd sense in which it seemed to have lasted a while but only now become audible. But to none of it did I react. I was not smiling, I sat there as though in deep concentration. Eventually there was silence again, and they stared at me with open contempt. It was obvious I was now getting irritated. I looked at them and glared, my eyes twitching at the corners as though I was about to say something but I didnt say anything, I just shook my head and grunted sarcastically; it was being made plain that I couldnt care less.

In a betting shop to the rear of Shaftesbury Avenue

Heh John! John . . . I grinned: How you doing?

He made to walk past me.

John, I said quickly, how's it going – I thought you were in Manchester?

What . . . He looked at me. My name's no John. He sniffed and glanced sideways, then muttered: McKechnie.

McKechnie! Christ. Aye . . . I thought you were in Manchester? How you doing man?

He looked away from me. I've no been in Manchester for years. And again he made to walk past, but I stepped slightly to the front.

Christ, so you left!

Aye, years ago. He sniffed, gazed round the interior of the betting shop. It was a poky wee dump of a place and with nearly quarter of an hour till the first race only a couple of people were about. McKechnie looked at them. He was holding a rolled newspaper in his left hand.

So how long you been here then? you been here long?

What . . . naw. He glanced up at the board to where a clerk had gone to scribble the names of the day's non-runners. He glanced across to the counter; the two women were eating sandwiches, sipping at cups of tea. Then he glanced back to me, and he frowned momentarily. He said:

Mind that wife of mine? I'm in for a divorce off her. She
wants the wean, but I'm getting the wean. Lawyer says I'm
a certainty. And these lawyers know the score . . .

Aye.

He nodded.

After a moment I said, Aye – these lawyers!

He nodded again. The door opened and in came a
punter, then another. McKechnie had noticed them and he
moved slightly. And then the knocking sound from the
Extel speaker and through it came the first betting show of
the day.

The other people were now standing gazing at the
formpages tacked onto the walls; up at the board the clerk
was marking in the prices against the listed runners, he held
a fresh cigarette cupped in one hand.

McKechnie unrolled his newspaper.

So you left then?

What . . .

Manchester, you left?

He nodded without taking his gaze from the newspaper,
not even raising his head. But he muttered, Aye – I went to
Sheffield.

Sheffield!

Mmhh.

Christ sake!

At this point a further betting show came through.
When it was over I said: Sheffield!

Mmm. He sniffed, still gazing at the racing page.

Did you never think of going back then? to Manchester I
mean – did you never think of going back?

What . . . He shook his head, and he grunted: Hard race
this.

I shrugged. Favourite cant get beat, it's a good thing.

Aye . . . He indicated the selection of one of the racing
journalists. That's what he says and all. I dont know but, I
hate backing these fucking odds-on shots. It's one to beat it

I want ... And he glanced at me, and added: Warrior Chief's supposed to be the only danger ...

Aye, it's got a wee chance right enough. Heh d'you ever see Tommy on your travels?

Tommy? His forehead wrinkled as he glanced at me again.

Tommy, christ, you must mind him – used to work in the building game. Carried the hod or something.

Aw aye, aye, I mind him. Subbied.

You're right! Hh! I laughed. That's right man – Tommy, christ: lucky bastard eh! must've made a real few quid, no having to pay any tax or fuck all.

McKechnie nodded; then he sniffed and indicated the comments on the race by the journalist. According to this cunt, Warrior Chief's the only danger.

Aye, it's got a chance. Heh, I wouldnt mind a start subbying somewhere myself, eh – that's the right way if ...

Hard race but, McKechnie muttered, a lottery, fucking lottery.

Another betting show was in progress and I altered my stance a bit, to be able to see the racecard in his newspaper. Then when it was over I said: What about yourself man, you working?

Who me ... He sniffed, he glanced up at the board, rolling up his newspaper at the same time. Hang on a minute, he said, I need a pish.

And he walked off immediately.

I went to the nearby wall; the front page of the *Chronicle* was tacked here and I read the post-mortems on yesterday's results. A couple of minutes before the *off* I looked up. I noticed McKechnie, he was standing right beside two old codgers who didnt look to have the price of a packet of Rizlas between them.

And it dawned on me: there wasnt any toilets in this fucking betting shop.

I crossed the floor. He had taken a brand new packet of

cigarettes from his pocket and was unwrapping the cellophane. He looked at me and extended the packet. Ta, I said. When we were smoking I smiled: To tell you the truth man, I never even knew you were married never mind in for a divorce!

What! christ, where've you been? Married – I've been married for years.

Hh. Who to? that wee thing back in Manchester?

He glanced at me: I was well married before I hit that fucking place. He sniffed. She thinks she'll get the wean but she's got no chance.

Good . . . I nodded. But still and all, sometimes . . .

Hang on a minute, I'm just . . . He turned and squinted at the formpage on the wall. Then he was edging along to where another punter stood and I could hear him mutter, This Warrior Chief's supposed to have a chance of upsetting the favourite . . .

I stepped over and peered at the form. Could do, I said, but the favourite's got a good bit of class about her. Won hell of a comfortably last time out and the way I heard it she won hell of a cleverly, a hands and heels game.

The punter was manoeuvring himself to write out his line in such a way that nobody would see what he wrote. Suddenly McKechnie thumped the page on the wall. That's the thing I'm feart of, he said.

Dark Lights?

Dark Lights. He nodded, and he grinned briefly. Dark Lights . . .

Hh.

Aye, he went on, they've just stuck it in here.

What?

Aye, fucking obvious.

I nodded. It's got a chance right enough. But you cant always rely on winning form out of *maiden* races; I mean this is the first time it'll have run in a *handicap*, and you know as well as . . .

Hang on a minute, he said. And he walked to a different wall, to where a youth was standing gazing at another formpage; I could see him begin muttering.

Then the runners were being loaded into the starting stalls and the youth strode to the counter to place his bet; and shortly afterwards McKechnie had scribbled down his own bet and was striding to the counter just as they were set to come *under orders*. And when the woman had returned him his change and receipt he went to the other side of the room.

It was no a bad night-life in Manchester, I said when I got there.

What . . .

The night-life – Manchester. Mind you, it's no bad here if you know where to go. Murder when you're skint but.

He nodded.

Aye, I said.

He sniffed: I've no been here that long.

What! christ, ach dont worry, dont worry man I mean you'll soon find your way about – once you get the hang of their fucking tube system. And then, when you've got a few quid you can always . . .

I'm going up the road the morrow.

Eh?

Edinburgh. I'm going to Edinburgh.

Edinburgh! Christ sake. Edinburgh . . . I nodded. Aw aye, I'll tell you . . .

OFF BRIGHTON: THEY'RE OFF BRIGHTON: RUNNING 2.17: AND ON THE OFF THEY BET FOUR TO NINE NUMBER THREE, FIVE TO TWO BAR . . .

The race was over the minimum trip and soon they were entering the final stretch; taking the lead at the distance the favourite won going away – exactly the style in which an odds-on shot should win.

A horse by the name of Lucy's Slipper ran on to snatch second place close home. Neither Warrior Chief nor Dark Lights had received a mention throughout the entire commentary.

But McKechnie was grinning all over his face. Told you, he shouted, I fucking told you – that favourite: couldnt get beat – a fucking certainty! I knew it.

I nodded. Trained at Epsom as well if you noticed. These Epsom runners usually do good here, the track, nice and sharp, fast. And . . .

The forecast! McKechnie was laughing and he elbowed me in the ribs: I've dug out the forecast!

What?

The forecast – I've dug it out, that Lucy's Slipper! a certainty for second place, I knew it, I fucking knew it.

Hh.

He winked. I'll tell you something: the shrewd money, all the shrewd money's down to it. Know what I mean? they've just stuck it in here – for the forecast. Fucking obvious. Think they're going to take odds-on on a single when they can lift five or six to one on a fucking forecast? you kidding!

Aye, eh.

Kept saying it all morning to myself: look for a forecast I says, look for a forecast, this favourite cant get beat, look for a forecast. McKechnie grinned and shook his head. And after a moment he glanced to the pay-out window. The youth stood there, holding a receipt in one hand. McKechnie walked across; he was still grinning; then I could hear him say: So you got it?

The youth nodded, and they began comparing notes on the following race in between congratulating each other on the last, as they waited for the weigh-in.

McKechnie copped the next three winners but the youth didnt return to the pay-out window. It had become difficult to tell where he was getting his selections; various people were going to the pay-out and McKechnie seemed to be in contact with most of them. He kept edging his way in and out of places, eavesdropping here and there. He had this peculiar kind of shuffle, dragging his heels as if his shoes were hell of a heavy – he probably kept a reserve fund stuffed inside his socks the bastard.

I went out for a breath of fresh air. I walked up and down the street a couple of times. Back inside he continued to dodge me but then I stepped right in front of him and said: A nicker, just a nicker, that's all, I'll give you it back man, honest.

Aw I cant, he said, no the now – I'm going to stick the lot on this next favourite. I'll weigh you in after but, dont worry, you'll be alright then – a nicker? Aye, no bother, you'll be alright for a nicker.

He about turned and walked to study a formpage, close in beside the two old codgers. Then just as the first show of betting came through on the next race I noticed him glance at me. Moments later he did a vanishing trick out the door. He probably thinks I didnt see him but I did.

Where I was

At least I am elsewhere. A wind like the soundtrack of a North Pole documentary rages underneath. I have absconded from my former abode leaving neither note nor arrears. I left arrears, I left no cash to discharge them. No explanations of any kind. Simply: I am somewhere else. No persons who knew me then or in fact at any time know of my whereabouts. Season: Midwinter. Equipage: To be listed, but boots as opposed to other things I may have worn previously. And also a leather pouch instead of my old tobacco tin. Jesus, and also a piece of cloth resembling a tartan scarf.

There are no lights. I am resting having walked many miles. I am well wrapped up; brown paper secured round my chest by means of the scarf crossed and tucked inside my trousers, a couple of safety pins are in there somewhere too. My health has got to remain fine otherwise my condition will deteriorate. At present I do not even have a runny nose. I stopped here because of the view. No other reason, none, nothing. I look down between mainland and island. Both masses ending in sheer drops, glowering at each other, but neither quite so high as where I am though maybe they are. Miles separate us. How many, I would be guessing. Rain pours. Sky very grey. The truth is I cannot tell what colour the sky is. May not even be there for all I know. And I reckon it must be past 10 o'clock. A car passed some time ago. A Ford it was but a big one. Expensive model.

Below, the tide reaches up to the head of the loch. No islets visible. My boots are not leaking. I laid out six quid on them. In the glen at the head of the loch are houses; I see lights there, and also opposite where I am a big house can be seen – white during daylight I imagine. A large dwelling house. It looks far from safe. Surrounded by tall, bent trees. A cabin cruiser tethered to a narrow jetty. Apart from all this nothing of moment.

Back a distance sheep were nibbling weeds. I saw them from thirty yards and knew what they were immediately.

I left the room in Glasgow recently and got here before the Ford car. There is something good about it all I cannot explain away. Not only the exhilarating gale blowing the dirty skalp clean. Nor the renunciation of all debts relating to the past while. Maybe it is as simple.

From here the road twists, falls, to a village where there has to be a pub. As pubs go it shall be averagely not bad. I wont stop. The place will be closed anyway. This afternoon I slept in a public convenience. Clean, rarely used by the smell of it. I should have invested in a tent. Not at all – a good thick waterproof sleepingbag would have been sufficient. I am spending money as I go but have a deal of the stuff, enough to be without worries for some time. If I chance upon a rowing boat tied near the shore I may steal it and visit the island across the way. Unlikely. I could probably swim it. The gap is deceptive but perhaps no more than two miles. Drowning. At one time it would have presented no problem. Never mind.

I enjoy this walking. Amble and race, set off at a trot, and once I ran pell-mell for quite a stretch – till a tractor saw me. Taking baby steps and giant steps, assume odd postures and if a car passes I shriek with laughter. Sing all songs. My jaw aches. My ears ache. Maybe the wind clogs them up.

Noises in my head. Sounding like a lunatic. But my nose remains dry. Probably impending bronchitis. Next time I waken with a bone-dry throat I shall know for sure. When I become immune to the wind everything will be fine. Immune to the wind.

Well stocked up on tobacco, always carrying cheese and whisky in case of emergencies; fever and that. The notion of buying a pipe. I have no room for useless piles of tobacco. I handrolled pipe tobacco in the past. Terrible stuff.

From Ardanruiach the road curves steeply through a glen owned by someone whose name escapes me. Stiff climb. Tired my knees in particular. For the eventual relief of walking with straight legs I firstly walked with bent ones, at the knees. Black specs in front or slightly above my eyes. The blood cannot be as good as the best. But the wind. I heard it all the time. Loud racket never dying. I thought of climbing a mountain. The real problem is rain. Whenever it falls I am affected. Soaks in knocking my hearing out. I am unable to look up for any length of time. It is damaging my boots and perhaps my coat. If my hair is plastered down over my brow in too irritating a manner water will drip down my sleeve when I push it up. Terrible sensation. The vehicles splash me. The face red raw; my nose must be purple, the constant drip drip from either nostril. Beads hang onto my eyebrows, cling at my eyelashes, falling from my chin down my neck – from my hair at the back down my neck it streams down my spinal cord, gets rubbed and rubbed by my trouser waistband into the skin at the small of my back. And no respite for my hands inside the coat pockets. The sleeves of this coat are far too wide so only my flesh actually enters each pocket, the wet cloth irritating my wrists, and tiny pools of water gathering within the nylon material. The rain spoils the walk but it brightens. Always brightens eventually. Then I see water on the leaves of bushes and I can skite the branch of a tree to see the beads drop. The road dries in patches, swiftly, sometimes I can sit on such a spot though not for long of course.

In the future I hope to sleep during the day, regularly. Apparently some folk do sleep on their feet the bastards. And I try striding with my eyes shut once I have noted the direction.

I enjoy night. Not dusk so much because I know pubs do business; possibly it gets easier when the days lengthen. I shall sleep all day perhaps. With this constant exercise four hours' kip wont be enough. And I shall be swimming when the water heats. Eating does not worry me yet. My money will run out. My best sleep so far was had in a hostel closed for the winter. Very simple to enter. No food but plenty of firewood which burned fine. I spread all my clothes on the backs of chairs in front of it. And washed both pairs of socks. And had a complete body wash which might not have been a good idea since two or three layers of old skin went down the drain. This explains why I am freezing. Unfortunately I appear to be really particular about clean feet thus socks although I dont bother about underwear, seldom have any. Up until the wash I was wearing each pair on alternate days and both when sleeping. They had a stale, damp smell. My feet were never wholly dry. Small particles stuck to the toejoints, the soles. I had to see all this during the changing process. In future I may steel myself if warmer feet can be guaranteed. And may even take to wearing both pairs daily, in other words keep them on at all times. Christ I wont be surprised if I catch the flu. I have acted very foolishly. No wonder tramps wash rarely. Yet what happens when the summer comes and I want a swim.

I considered staying in the hostel indefinitely. I could also have erected a sign for other wayfarers explaining how easy it was to break and enter, but did not. The reason reflects badly on me.

This day was bitter. Never warm inside the coat. That fucking wind went through me. Tried everything from walking sideways to hiding behind trees. All I could finally do was stride along punching my boots hard down on the road with my shoulders rigid, hunched up. This induced prolonged shivering but was the best I could manage. Every part of me cold, sick cold. Now and then I stopped for a swig of the stuff.

When the road closed onto the water again I cut off through the marsh and down to the edge of the loch or maybe it was the sea. There was land far out. An island? Amazing silence. Nothing but the waves breaking, lapping in over the pebbles. Where I was the wind was forgotten. Almost warm. I took off the coat and used it as a cushion on a dry rock a little way back. No fishing boats. I saw only small birds, landbirds, the country equivalent to sparrows I suppose. My mind got into a certain state. The usual blankness. A trance or something like it. Time obviously passed. Clear. I finished my whisky and chain-smoked. Staying put. No wish to walk the shore in search of a better position. The rain came later. Fine drizzle, spotting the water. I watched on for a bit then had to put the coat across my shoulders and shelter beneath the trees. But I remained for quite a while and might have pitched a tent there.

Extra cup

I was to wait in the waiting room, somebody would come to collect me. To pass the time I thumbed through the stack of industrial magazines, eventually dozing off until the door banged open. It was a clerk, clutching a sheaf of fulscapaper, he frowned and told me to follow him; he led me out the gatehouse, through the massive carpark and into a side entrance, along a corridor between offices then out, and across waste ground into another building where I followed him along the side of a vast machineroom into a long tunnel and out through rubber swing doors, onto more waste ground but now with rail tracks crossing here and there, and into another building via a short tunnel leading sharply down then up a concrete incline at the top of which we entered an ancient hoist with crisscross iron gates to go clanking downwards to a subfloor where the clerk questioned a youth on the whereabouts of a Mr Lambton, but received only a shrug in reply; on we went along a corridor, a deep thumping sound coming to the right of us and men occasionally appearing out of doorways and entering others, and we followed one of them outside and across more waste ground, bypassing one building and into another where we found Mr Lambton sitting on an upturned crate behind a big machine. He saw us but continued chatting to a dungareed man perched on a sort of balcony near the top of the machine, a rag covering his head he looked to be greasing the moving parts which were of course stationary at present. Then Mr Lambton ground out the cigarette he had been smoking and turned to say: What's up with you Eric? Something worrying you is there?

It's the new sweeperup, George.

New sweeperup?

The clerk sighed.

Mr Lambton laughed and winked up at the man on the machine then he glanced at me and nodded, and the clerk strode off. After a moment he continued chatting to the man on the machine. The man on the machine nodded now and then but never spoke. Eventually Mr Lambton said to me, You know the lay-out of this Block?

No.

I'll show you then eh! He smiled and got up from the crate; he yawned and stretched, and sighed before setting off. Every so often he would pause and indicate a machine, maybe telling me what it did in relation to a different machine. He led me outside and we walked round the building and he showed me the railway tracks and pointed out other buildings, occasionally denoting them by number. He knew a great many people and stopped to talk fairly often. Soon a bell was ringing. And I realized we were back where we had started, behind the big machine. Mr Lambton chuckled when he noticed me noticing this and he walked on. He opened a door and I followed him through rows and rows of wall-to-ceiling racks. We came upon a dozen men sitting either on upturned boxes or sacking on the floor; it was teabreak. An elderly man was pouring from a big urn. Mr Lambton called: Extra cup Bert.

Bert didnt answer.

Cup, extra cup – new man Bert, new man.

He glanced along at Mr Lambton and grumbled unintel-

ligibly, continued pouring tea then passed the cups out one
by one to the nearest seated man who then passed them
along to the others.

Alright? called Mr Lambton. And when he received no
reply he grinned at me, raised his eyebrows and walked
back the way we had come.

The elderly man didnt give me out a cup of tea but he
glanced at me as though I should understand there were no
extras to be had. Soon the bell was ringing and the men
rising, and leaving. Bert didnt move; he was sitting near the
urn, still munching a sandwich, gazing at the foot of the
racks facing him. I got up and walked along, and poured
myself the last of the tea, into one of the assorted cups left
by the men. Bert noticed and grumbled. Did you want it? I
said.

He didnt reply; he reached for a newspaper left by the
men and unfolded it, brought a spectacle case out from the
top pocket of his dungarees, and began reading. Then he
looked up: Sweeperup are you? You're supposed to help
me you know – dont suppose he told you that though eh!
Did he?

Aye, he said you'd tell me the score.

Hh! Bert shook his head and returned his attention to
the newspaper. A few minutes later he put the spectacles
back in the case and snapped it shut, put away the newspaper
and got onto his feet. He began collecting in the empty
cups and the discarded sandwich wrapping-paper. I helped
him. There was a brush leaning against a rack; I brushed the
floor. Leave that, he said. And he waved me to come with
him. We walked through the rows of racks in a direction
different to the one used by the men to exit, and arrived at
a small door which had two sections, the bottom and top
halves being separate. Bert unsnibbed the bottom half and
opened it very quietly, he peered out to the left and to the
right, then motioned me to follow him across the corridor
and into another room, but immediately inside here he cut

off to the corner, and I followed him up a short flight of stairs. When he glanced at me I saw the corner of his mouth twitching, then he frowned and opened a door. It was a tiny room with lockers and a long bench. He sighed and withdrew another newspaper from a pocket inside his dungarees and sat down, and took out his spectacle case; flapping the newspaper open he sighed again, began reading. About twenty minutes passed. He got up and walked to the wall to his left and moved a calendar; there was a peephole, he looked through it. Then we went back and he collected two brushes, giving one to me. Come on, he said. He led me about the building for a time but as we turned a corner the clerk appeared along the corridor and came striding towards us, gesticulating. You've to come with me, he cried: Mrs Willmott wants a word.

I turned to Bert but he wasnt there. And the clerk was striding down the corridor. I went quickly after him, out through the rubber doors and across the waste ground, and so on eventually into a building which seemed to consist only of offices, and into one with Mrs Willmott's name on the door. She was a young woman, sitting at a wide desk. The clerk closed the door behind me and she glanced upwards, but continued studying a sheet of fulscapaper then reached to a filing cabinet to take out another one, and after a bit she said, New sweeperup . . . Do you have your things? your cards and so forth.

No, sorry.

You dont?

No, sorry.

O for heaven sake.

I'm really sorry, I laid them out on the table last night all set for this morning but then I forgot to lift them because I was late and having to rush for the bus, it's because I'm

Well you must bring them tomorrow you know there is no excuse; if you dont you'll simply be obliged to return home for them.

Fine, I'll make sure, definitely; what I'll do, I'll stick them right into my pocket as soon as I get back the day.

A buzzer sounded. The door opened and in came the clerk, and he carried straight back out again so that I was to follow him. On this occasion he left me at the ancient hoist. Back in the right building the machines sounded as though they were being run down and sure enough it was dinner-break, and in the washroom the men were washing their hands and their wrists and crumpling the used paper towels into an empty crate. I walked along the corridor and into the room where the wall-to-ceiling racks were, just as the bell started ringing. Bert was spreading out the cups on the upturned crate he employed as a table. The men began arriving and taking their seats, opening their parcels of sandwiches and spreading their newspapers on their laps. Bert indicated a cup lying a little apart from the rest; it was for me. There was an old newspaper in the empty crate used for the rubbish. I sat reading this for a while. My belly began rumbling and eventually the man sitting next to me flourished his newspaper while turning a page as though I was to see he was having to endure it. Is there a canteen? I said.

He frowned. The man along from him turned and said, Canteen? course there's a canteen. Eh Reg! he called to another man farther along. That new canteen? Group 3 is it?

Group 2, 6 Block.

On the other side of me Bert snorted, and he leaned over to spit into the crate. Some of the men watched him; the one called Reg frowned slightly then added, Yeah, Group 2 – 6 Block.

There was a short silence. Bert gazed at the rack opposite where he sat, and he said: Group 5, the new canteen.

Bert's right, nodded another man, it's got to be nearer 5 than 3

Got to be nearer 5 than 3 . . . Reg glanced at him. What d'you mean it's got to be nearer, why the bleeding hell's it got to be nearer?

It was Bert replied. He called: Cause when they bleeding changed it Reg, that's why!

Reg shook his head.

You sure? said somebody but Bert didnt answer. He was munching a sandwich; he stopped at the crusts and tossed them into the crate, he glanced along at Reg and shook his head briefly. Then someone else began discussing the old canteen in relation to the new one and another joined in by relating this to why the new canteen had had to be built from scratch more or less, instead of just simply refurbishing the old one. A man got up and strolled along the row, pausing to read slips of paper sticking out from the articles stored on the racks. Bert nudged me and gestured at a newspaper lying on the floor and I handed it to him. Most of the other men were now leaving, as though going for a walk down the corridor to pass the time. When the bell did ring I lifted the brush to begin sweeping the place but I was finding a great deal of dust lying on the articles along the bottom racks and so I got an old rag and used it to give them a wipe down first. Bert looked in and said nothing, and went away again. Mr Lambton appeared later and he chatted with me for a bit on general matters to do with the building, finally saying I was to continue sweeping in the machineroom. I nodded. Once he had gone I carried on dusting the articles at the foot of the racks for a while, before leaving. I took the brush with me. Going along the corridor I caught a glimpse of Bert through in the machineroom, brushing between two big machines. He waved me in. I nodded and continued along the corridor and straight out, across the waste ground and into the next building, and so on until eventually I was in the one with the offices.

It's not the job for me, I said to Mrs Willmott.

I see ... she nodded. You havent given it much of a chance.

I just eh – well, I think it's best to make the decision now rather than hang on hoping I'll get used it.

She shook her head. I wont attempt to dissuade you Mr aaaa ... And she reached for the sheet of fulscapaper from the filing cabinet. Then she reached back into the filing cabinet and paused; she glanced at me: You didnt bring your things this morning?

No, I left them – remember? I was to bring them tomorrow morning.

Mm ... She nodded, closed the drawer and shifted on her chair. She looked at me, before studying the sheet of fulscapaper, and lifting a pen. Is this your address? she said while settling to begin copying it down on another sheet.

Yes but I'll be leaving.

O.

If you were going to send me something.

Well, she shrugged, the money.

Could you not just give me it just now?

She didnt say anything.

I'll probably be leaving the night, or early tomorrow morning, so ...

She clicked her tongue on her top teeth, shook her head and picked up the receiver of her internal telephone, and asked a Miss Arnold to come in. When Miss Arnold did come in she got up and went to meet her, and both of them went outside into the corridor, shutting the door behind them. About 10 minutes passed. Mrs Willmott returned alone, she laid a day's wages on her desk and put forward a receipt for me to sign. I did so, lifted the money and put it into my pocket. She sniffed and went to the door, opening it for me. Thanks, I said, taking the brush from where I had parked it against the wall.

I had to return to the building where I had been working

to get my jerkin. Bert wasnt about. I laid the brush near to the upturned crate he used for the rubbish then I left immediately.

learning the Story

I once met an old lady sitting under a bridge over the River Kelvin. She smoked Capstan full-strength cigarettes and played the mouthorgan.

The moon was well up as I had passed along the footpath listening to the water fall at the small dam beyond the old mill. Aye, cried the voice, you are there are you! If I had spotted her before she had me I would have crept back the way I had come. Aye, she cried again. And rising to her feet she brought out the mouthorgan from somewhere inside the layers of her clothing, and struck up the tune: Maxwelton Braes Are Bonny was the name of it. Halfway through she suddenly stopped and she stared at me and grunted something. She sat down again on the damp grass with her back against the wall at the tunnel entrance; she stared at her boots. Very good that, I said to her. From her shopping bag she pulled out the packet of Capstan full-strength cigarettes. She sniffed. And I felt as if I had let her down. I always liked that tune, I told her. She struck a match and lighted a cigarette. She flicked the match a distance and it landed with smoke still rising from it. Drawing the shopping bag in between her raised knees she inhaled deeply, exhaled staring at her boots. Cheerio then, I said. I paced on beneath the bridge aware of my footsteps echoing.

The old lady wore specs and had a scarf wrapped round her neck. Her nose was bony. Her skirt may have showed under the hem of her coat. When she was playing the mouthorgan she had moved slightly from foot to foot. Her coat was furry.

Getting there

I stayed with the lorry and bypassed the dump. Down the A74 the driver was turning off into the weird Leadhills so I got out. I remained on this side of the road. A van. The driver wasnt going far, not beyond Lockerbie. I went. I spotted an inn in the distance and told him to stop, I felt like a couple of pints. Four customers including myself. Moving to a table within earshot I tried to concentrate on what they were saying but difficult to make heads or tails of, not just the accents.

I still had money. I had enough to rent some accommodation in the inn for the night and get rid of the beard and the grime and the old skin before returning up the road.

The man refused me a room. Full up. I was really surprised. I had expected a refusal of course but at the same time hadnt. He said the rooms were all taken. Aye. May his teeth fall out and his hair recede the bastard, saying the rooms were all taken yet allowing me to stay drinking his beer. I was being sociable, a bit sorry for them, not wanting to hurt their feelings by leaving too early for christ sake. Enough. I had to vanish in England. And I didnt have to walk. I had enough for a fucking bus. Or a train maybe. But the lift came almost at once and soon I was crossing the border.

The Appleton Arms. Pint of bitter and a pastie with mustard. A husband and wife behind the bar: no bother the bed and breakfast sir. The outside lavatory with an ancient bicycle parked against the washbasin. Upstairs to immerse for twenty minutes in the grime and old skin then out for a smooth shave, and then back into the bath again till finally emerging in the pink. The desire for newly suiting, never seen nor heard of, outside of books by bad authors; the freshly pressed lined underwear and silk pyjamas, the valet to disrobe one, the smoking jacket velvet Jackson yes, hock'll do ably with the old cheese & water biscuits and invitations to the chambermaid.

The bed was soft, sagging in the centre, but I slept amazing and woke in fine fettle, in plenty of time for breakfast which was sadly meagre but good cups of dark red tea with plenty of toast to atone.

Waiting halfway up the sliproad onto the M6 I allowed three lifts to go by, attempting to explain that it had to be London or bust. Springtime in old King's Cross. But I could see the drivers' faces tightening into huffs. I feel bad about that, three probables vanishing from the paths of other wayfarers.

Then the rain of course.

So aye, Bristol? Aye, yes, Bristol's fine mate. Maybe the M4 or something.

Very snug inside the big artic, the driver's cassette blasting it out and no need to gab but just enjoy the ride down the safe inside lane, the drone of the windscreen-wipers while the rain, battering hard down on the cabin roof.

Fuck the M4. I liked Bristol on sight. Something about the place. Yet I couldnt remember having passed through before. As though last time along I maybe missed it. But I had been heading northwest, detouring via Wales and according to maps the passing through Bristol is inevitable. That's a strange thing.

Windswept Weymouth and nothing to add except I still had money.

A bad time aboard. Pounding waves. Passengers having to heave out their guts here there and everywhere; the mess on the saloon floor, it streaming about, the bits of meat and veg amongst the Guinness-type froth but the grumpy barman stood me a pint when he saw I wasnt getting affected. I told him a yarn about working on the boats off Cromarty – in fact it must have been down to the time spent plying the Glasgow buses over cobbled streets, those boneshaking old efforts probably ensuring I can never be seasick again. And so pleased with myself I would have ordered a three-course meal if the cash had stretched.

. . .

An old guy had been tethering a group of rowing boats, down on the beach, to the side of a wee pier; then he sat on a deckchair up by a green hut which was advertising fishing tackle for hire. Going over to him and saying: I want your job ya old bastard.

. . .

This island. And so long to accept the warmer weather as a fact. It bringing out a great many people, all young-looking for some reason maybe to do with the summer looming ahead. The jeans and T-shirts and sandals or trainers. Even on the concrete promenade my feet are comfortable.

The clouds are not in sight.

In a delicatessen I could buy 2 ounces of cold spiced sausage and rolls. Narrow streets and pavements and all of the tiny shops. The promenade is very long and straight. Word of an old castle. The rest of it to be explored. In a pub later on I was sitting at the bar, eavesdropping on the chat of three girls who were sipping at blackcurrant & Pernod; and the sensation of being offered the opportunity. I could have explained the present predicament. But there was nothing to be said then till finally it was too too late, and it was getting dark, the rain probably drizzling.

Staying in the bar, my back to the wall – yet still content –
the feet outstretched beneath the table and tucking them
under when someone walked by, with apologies articu-
lated that I might be reasonably understood; clearing the
accent to please, in other words: in a good way but.

The barmaid roused me. It had to be around 11.30 p.m.

I knew all about the police here. Throw you off the place
at the slightest excuse – unfixed abodes the especial cause.
Twice in ten minutes I had to go down an alley to piss. Yet I
still wasnt too worried, it was so very dark, so very quiet,
and neither strollers nor stray animals. A patrol car rolled
by. I had the smoke cupped in the palm of my right hand.

Now the rain.

Out onto the promenade I cut smartly across, down the
stone steps to the sands immediately below the big wall;
right along quickly, to the farthest point, and up, retracking
to the third last shelter. I had to take this chance I think
though well aware it was obvious, unsafe. I sat on the bench
in the side exposed to the Sea, elbows on knees and hands
propping up the head. The rain belting down, like a storm,
the incredible noise. I was probably trying to sort things
out about the dump and being here instead but I dont
remember doing any of that at all, just entering a kind of
daze, a kind of numbness, literally, having to get up and hop
about to regain sensation proper. And the rain blowing in,
having to huddle into the side of the wall, escaping the wind
but the draughts, the draughts were just not, they were
too much – not too much, they were just, they were like
the wind, sudden blasts. And this strange experience of
hearing a clock strike. I had no idea of time, I had sixteen
pence in my pocket. Then later, later on, through the
blackest greys a little bit of red showed in snatches; enough
for the luck to be hitting on. I knew it. A certainty. No need
to hop.

. . .

The tide was out. I walked the sands a furlong or so, the boots squeaking then squelching. Sand worms. Red veins. So so tiny, thin. The first time I ever saw them though I had often looked at the mound of twirls they left dotted about. Amazing. What are they like at all, the red things. And sitting on my heels gazing back to the promenade, the row of villas, guest-houses and hotels. And back at the Sea, two boats an inch apart on the horizon.

the paperbag

What was the point anyway, there didnt seem to be any at all. I footered about with the newspaper, no longer even pretending interest. It was useless. I felt totally useless – I was useless, totally. I crumpled the newspaper in both hands, watching it, seeing the shapes it made, the way its pages became.

I would go on a walk; that was what to do. I uncrumpled the newspaper and rolled it into a neat sort of bundle, to carry it in my right hand, and then began walking. O christ but it was good to be alive – really. Really and truly. I felt magnificent. Absolutely wonderful. What was it about this life that made a body feel so good, so absolutely fucking wonderful. Was everybody the same. Now I was chuckling. Not too loudly but, no point worrying folk. A woman approached, her message bags not too full, preoccupied, the slight smile on her face. Where else could it be? Her eyes. Her eyes could be smiling. Is that possible. I was chuckling again. And then the mongrel appeared. I recognized it right away: a stupid kind of beast, even how it trotted was a bit stupid – plus that something about it, that odd look it could give – as though it was a fucking mule! Mule. Why did I think of that, mule. Well it was a beast and it was stupid-looking – or rather, it behaved stupidly, the way it looked at folk and didnt do as they desired, they wanted it off the pavement out their road but it never went off the pavement out their road, it just carried on trotting till sometimes they even had to get out of *its* road. Amazing. Imagine giving it a kick! Just going up and giving it a kick. Or else poisoning it. Taking it away on a long walk and then dumping it – maybe on a bus journey right out the other side of the city, pushing it off and shutting the door, leaving the thing yelping in astonishment. What'll happen to me now! Christ sake the dirty bastard he's pushed me off the bus and shut the door and I dont know where I've landed!

Imagine being a dog but – murder! people taking you wherever they like and you dont have a say in the matter. Here boy, here boy. I would hate to be a dog like that, getting ordered about by cunts without knowing what for, not having a genuine say on the matter. Horrible, really fucking horrible. And then getting put down for christ sake sometimes for nothing, no reason, just for doing what dogs do. Biting people!

Crazy, walking along the road thinking about such stuff. Absolute fucking nonsense. Mongrels by christ! But that's what happens. And thinking of that is better than thinking of nothing. I would say so anyway. Or would I? The trouble with being useless is this thinking; it becomes routine, you cannot stop yourself. I think all the time, even when I'm reading my newspaper. And the things I think about are fucking crazy. Imagine going up to somebody and saying Hey, have you ever felt like screwing the queen? Just to actually say it to somebody. Incredible. This is the kind of thing I can think about. I cannot help it. I didnt always think like it either. I used to think about ordinary things. Or did I? I find it hard to tell.

Then she was coming towards me but I didnt notice properly till there we were having to get out each other's road. Sorry, I said and I smiled in a hopeful manner. I was lost in abstraction . . .

And then I smiled coyly, this coyliness compensating for the use of the long word, abstraction. But everything was fine, everything was fine, she understood. It's okay, she replied, I was a bit abstracted myself.

And of course she was! Otherwise she'd've fucking bumped into me if she hadnt been careful to get out my road while I was getting out of hers!

Then she had dropped a paperbag and was bending down to retrieve it; and once she had retrieved it she opened it and peered inside.

And so did I!

I just fucking stretched forwards and poked my head next to hers – not in any sort of ambiguous way but just to peer into the bag same as her. She glanced at me, quite surprised. Then we smiled at each other as though in appreciation of the absurdity of my reaction. And yet it had been a true reaction. Normally I'm not a nosey person. But having said all of that I have to confess that it maybe was a bit ambiguous, maybe I was trying to get a bit closer to her because it should be said that she was nice, in fact she was really nice. The way she was standing there and then bending to get her paperbag etc., the smile she had, and above all that understanding, how she had eh o christ o christ, o christ and there wasnt anything I could say, nothing, nothing at all because I was without funds, absolutely fucking without funds. So after a wee moment I smiled, an unhealthy smile – even at the actual instant it was happening I was thinking how it would be to have a blunderbuss whose muzzle I could stick my head into and then pull the trigger.

It was a surprise to see her still standing there. How come she was still standing there the way things were. I didnt even know her. I had never seen her before in all my life. I said: Eh d'you live eh roundabout? But she didnt reply. She was frowning at something. She hadnt paid the slightest attention to what I had said. And no wonder, the things I say, they're always so fucking boring, so fucking boring. Why am I the most fucking boring bastard in the whole fucking world? Her cake was bashed. Inside the paperbag was a cake and it had become bashed because of falling on the pavement. I could have mentioned that to her. That was something to say, instead of this, this fucking standing, just fucking standing there, almost greeting, greeting my eyes out. I was just standing there having to stop myself greeting like a wean, looking at her, trying to make her see and by making her see stopping myself and making everything fine, everything fine, if she would just stay on a minute or two and we could maybe have a chat or something – just a couple of minutes' chat, that would have worked the oracle, maybe, to let her see. Because after all, she hadnt been put off by the way I had peered into her bag; she had recognized it as a plain ordinary reaction, the sort of thing that happens out of curiosity – a bit stupid right enough, the way a kid acts. And yet she hadnt been put off. Not even as a person had I put her off. She smiled at me, a true smile – there again, it had happened at the point of departure

for yes, that moment had indeed arrived and was gone now, gone forever. And so too was she, trotting along the pavement, away to a life that was much better than this one. If I could run after her and clasp her by the hand.

I had unrolled the newspaper and was glancing at the back page, an item of football news. I could just have run after her and said Sorry – for having almost bumped right into her and making her drop the paperbag. But what was the point of it all? it was useless, totally fucking useless. I crumpled the newspaper in my right hand then grabbed it from there with my left, and continued the walk.

Old Holborn

He was pounding away on the guitar and mouthorgan as if it was 1968. A sad sight during this overcast morning in central December. I had been coming along the pavement, caught a glimpse of something just off the kerb – silver paper, poking out from under a half brick. Then this music. Dear god. He paused to take a tobacco pouch out from his jerkin pocket. Bad time of year for this game, I said, eh? this weather! fucking murder.

He didnt say anything, he spread the tobacco along the rice paper.

Carols, I said, it's carols you should be giving them. This time of year man that's what they're fucking looking for, carols.

Could be right jock, he said.

Jesus christ the accent! What a relief hearing a London voice man where you from?

London's right.

Well well well, eh – heh what's that? I sniffed. Old Holborn a mile.

Yeh jock. He licked the gummed edge and handed me the pouch while bringing out a box of matches.

I rolled one quickly then said: How long you been here?

Half an hour.

I nodded; he handed me the box of matches. When I inhaled I went into a fit of coughing, it ended in a bout of the sneezes. Always the same. I gave my nose a wipe. That first drag man, I said, it's always the same. Nectar but. Bad for you as well so they say. Hh – makes you think right enough.

He was looking up the road. A tin box lying to the side, by his feet. I nudged it; about thirty pence maybe. Christ sake, half an hour too!

Yeh, bleeding hopeless jock . . . He began to footer with the musical instruments and then launched into a dirge of some kind. No wonder he was skint. Not a bad guitarist but the song was rotten and he couldnt sing very good. The pedestrians marched past. I lifted the tin box. He looked at me.

It's alright man, I'll do your collecting.

He didnt answer, continued the singing. A middle-aged man with rolled-up brolly approaching.

Couple of bob for the singer jimmy eh? I stood in front of him, holding the tin box beneath his chin and into it he dropped a ten pence piece. Easy business. Next along came a couple. Heh jimmy, I said, the singer – what about the singer? Eh missis? something for the singer?

The purse snapped open and she dropped in some copper stuff while he chipped in with another ten pence piece. The next miserable bastard carried on marching, his ears purpling when I shouted. In this game you can get to the point where you're wanting to strangle some cunt; it's best not to take it personally. Savage glares and leave it at that. Once or twice I was having to catch myself up from chasing some of them. While he was continuing with the singing. Young boys and lassies were the best; they thought it a good laugh, maybe because of the accent. But they usually came across and the tin box soon rattled in the healthy manner. Then he stopped; the singing had deteriorated. He brought out the pouch.

Can you sing jock?

No me man I'm no up on that country & western stuff – Dell Shannon I'm into.

Folkrock, he said, frowning. I dont sing that country crap.

Aw.

Dell Shannon . . . he nodded.

I always forget the bastarn words but. I've been trying to sing that *Runaway* for years.

He shrugged, glanced across the road; a post office with a clock in the window. He started strumming the guitar in an absentminded way. I cleared my throat and began to sing, and he stopped strumming immediately. Fucking hell, he muttered.

Naw, I said, I usually just remember the words when I hear the thing getting sung. Heh what about *Kelly*? d'you know that *Kelly* at all?

He scratched at his ear, glanced up and down the street for a period, before shifting the glance into my direction, not really looking at me. What about Dylan, he said, you've got to know some Dylan.

Course.

Right then jock, on you go, I'll pick it out . . . He sniffed, glanced at a well-dressed woman who passed. He sniffed again. Alright?

Aye, fine . . . I began straight in on that one *The Hard Rain's Gonna Fall* but tailed off long before entering the second verse; I tried to keep it going by repeating the opening. He continued strumming, but without even bothering to blow the mouthorgan. Fucking hopeless. No point. I stopped singing. Look, I said, we were doing good with me just collecting. Eh? Better off sticking to that. You do the singing and I'll hold the box – at least we'll be getting a fucking wage out it!

He shook his head.

How no?

He shrugged, started picking away on the individual strings. It sounded fine.

You just do that then.

No good jock, they dont want to know.

Well at least give it a fucking try man I mean if

Much I got in the tin?

Nearly two quid – heh! fancy a pie and a pint?

Just had me breakfast jock.

Breakfast!

Yeh.

Hh.

He turned away and gave a sharp rasp on the mouth-organ and launched into another fucking dirge.

Tell you something, I said, I've no eaten for days – days! A tin of fucking sardines! And you talk about breakfast! Breakfast by fuck.

He nodded, still involved in the music. I grabbed the tin up from the pavement and then he stopped and shook his head briefly. I put it back down. He continued playing.

What's up?

He didnt reply.

Heh, what's up man?

He paused to say: Leave it out jock.

Leave what fucking out, you'd still have thirty fucking pence if it wasnt for me.

Yeh, he said immediately, that's the problem jock, too heavy. Ten more minutes from you and the Man'd be here sticking me for extortion.

What?

He nodded.

Well I'll tell you something for nothing, I said, I'm due a couple of bob off you . . . I had reached to tap the tin box with my right foot. Then I bent to lift it. At least fifty pee.

Take a pound.

Fifty's plenty.

Take the bleeding pound jock, for christ sake.

Okay then. I'm really starving man honest; listen, you want me to get you anything? ½ ounce of Old Holborn or something?

I got enough.

Pint of milk or something?

He shook his head. He continued with his singing.

Okay then ta. I'll be back shortly . . .

I didnt go back of course — doubtful whether he would have been there anyway.

O jesus, here come the dwarfs

When the dwarfs appear everything is at an end. All you ever fixed. The lot. All gone. On the Thursday night they are there. The process of rapid disintegration then follows. Until that point problems do not exist. Problems? what are they at all! no such things. Afterwards there is nothing else.

Dwarfs never have anything fixed, plans have not been laid down, there are no 'eventualities'. They have nothing whatsoever. Yet they come and they take over. And they look at each other as though joined at the nose, while the feet are being cawed from the very ground you walk on. Nothing can remain the same. Tents will have started collapsing. Those previously occupied are mysteriously empty. Dustbins have been overspilling their contents into the long grass. Television sets explode without causal explanation. And the swimming pool is become infested by insects and wee dods of animal shite. Moles. Moles are burrowing beneath groundsheets apparently. All the things, they all stop working. Continual reports of blocked toilet bowls and sinks; and a pile of pots has been found behind the kitchen area, these pots used to be fine but are now food encrusted beyond repair; and the smells, all the smells, now encroaching throughout the walking area. And into this same walking area come farm animals, bleating. And the site-shop seems to have ceased trading: the wee woman from the village no longer arrives first thing in the morning – that great wee woman who always gave you the cheery nod and allowed you the couple of grocery items plus tobacco on tick till wagesday no problem if the coast was clear.

All gone. All of it.

Yet though holidaymakers may grumble the dwarfs will remain silent. Dwarfs dont grumble. They just smile, are humble, are thoughtful to others. They go dashing around endeavouring to help, ostensibly existing for your especial convenience whereas the reality: you are being set fair for a corner wherein the possibility of laying down your life is advancing. Do not believe in their smile. It is not happy-go-lucky. They have arrived in the pub on Thursday evening because tomorrow you get your wages. When first you bear witness to the voices your puzzled but immediate response is to fuck off home to the tent. This you will not do, having some vague notion that by remaining aloof you must influence events; thus you stand there, awaiting the barman, gradually becoming aware that a cloud of staggering proportions has settled above your head. It is all over. Chance could have reaped a future as secure as this. Aye, of course your defences were down. A Thursday evening. You are tired out, just managed to tap Pierre for the price of a couple of pints, enough to see you through the evening in a quiet way.

With determined nonchalance you will carry your pint to the dominoe table to sit on the fringe of the onlookers. But the nodded greeting to such as Emil or Jaques was perfunctory, you are totally preoccupied by something you arent quite able to grasp. Then you are amazed to realize that some sort of inflexion of the voices at the bar was giving you to understand that you were supposed to be charging across the room crying: Welcome dwarfs welcome! It is incredible. You lean forwards, place your pint on the ledge beneath the table, rest your elbows on your

knees, attempting to devote your complete attention to
the game of dominoes. But this is not the weekend, it is
Thursday evening and the bar is not full to bursting with
exuberant holidaymakers. Voices echo. The dwarfs know
fine well you can hear them. It is what they intend. They
intend that you hear them, that their voices can and must
be heard. At this stage you are not quite admitting your
quandary and are willing to indulge in such internal asides
as: Am I hearing things! hoping against hope that the
consequent ironic smile about your mouth will be noticed.
But so what if it is? And why are you in this position in the
first place? Is there anybody there to answer such questions? How come you are having to ask them? What the
fuck is it? What is going on? Maybe you are hearing things
after all. Thursday night, you've been tired out, too knackered even to cook yourself a proper meal, you just washed
and came straight down the pub; maybe you're fucking
hallucinating. No matter, for by this time you are unable to
contain the pressure – your belly, it has been churning –
the beer giving you heartburn, the tobacco maybe, burning your lips and causing that dryness in the mouth and
you're having to tighten your lips and close your eyelids,
trying to suppress the rage. It is rage; you are raging, you
have lifted your pint but your hand is shaking and you slam
the pint glass down onto the table and jump to your feet
and go marching across to deliver the most bitter diatribe
ever heard in the pub. But the dwarfs are just sitting there,
occasionally drawing their noses together. Are they naïve?
Is that all it is? How can you tell? You cannot tell. There is
no surefire way of knowing. And you are sitting at their
table. Here you are on a chair adjacent to theirs. And the
questions are coming at you from all angles and if you dont
put a stop immediately you are seconds away from giving a
moment by moment account of all, all the things. Those
pauses occurring in the conversation. Aye, you were about
to speak. You must be alert, you have to sit there saying

nothing, turning pauses into longer pauses. Or questions into questions: you can turn questions into questions. Tax them on their existence, on their experience, their expectations — above all else their expectations. What precisely is it they are demanding of you? What is it that you are to be having done? Well for starters: consider the things you never classed as problems because of your studied attention to possible eventualities — the things you classified under the banner 'impossible'. Not only have the dwarfs encountered such things as problems, they have surmounted them. Apparently without having realized it. They havent even realized those things were problems, they just fucking went ahead and got beyond them. And they are gaping at you, at your irritation. They have no comprehension of its cause, and will look to each other as though joined at the nose. Meanwhile you do not feel a mug. Somehow you are given to understand that you yourself are the one individual present who genuinely is aware of the central ins and outs. Only you know the truth, that you are a fucking mug, that you have never known anything, nothing, nothing whatsoever. It is odd. You will sit for a moment, gazing into space, then jump up and rush to the dominoe table to collect your pint and your tobacco and matches, and back with the dwarfs you . . . Back with the dwarfs? Aye, exactly, of your own volition. It really is fucking incredible. You will look at them for signs of guilt but why should there be? Do they have cause for guilt? It was you returned to sit beside them. You stare at them, and discover that the pint you are holding contains a fresh quantity of beer; it's not the same pint at all — you swallowed the remains of your first in a gulp and the dwarfs have bought you a new one. There is no deceit. Everything is out in the open and being accomplished fairly. They are actually insisting that they dont want a drink in return. They dont want one. They maybe know you are skint because it's a Thursday evening and are quite rightly opposed to you letting yourself in for taking favours from the barman. He's a taciturn old bastard and you hate having to ask for credit even though it's in his own interest, which is why you prefer tapping Pierre although it means that extra 20 per cent on the loan, but there you are, and across at the bar a few folk are waiting to be served – unusual in itself considering the day of the week it is – which makes it difficult to signal the old cunt and when finally you do he comes over and will make it necessary to raise your voice so that almost every customer in the fucking place is now aware you've been asking for tick, and for that reason alone you're somehow obliged to add to your order at the last minute; you call for whiskies as well as the beer. Now obviously the dwarfs didnt want any fucking whisky and neither did you and there is no satisfactory explanation as to why you will have done it, but you will have fucking done it and that's that. Down on the table you thrust the drinks, right under the dwarfs' noses, not able to say a word. If you so much as glance at them you will end up having to punch them, you will kick fuck out them, you will smash a bottle across their bastarn skulls. What you do is settle on your chair and stare at the whisky, eventually shuddering in anticipation of that horrible boke ahead, when the first drop of whisky hits at your tastebuds, all the time knowing how the dwarfs will gulp at theirs and express an honest relish of the flavour. Moments later you have invited them back to the site.

The possibility of spare tents. Who was mentioning that in an absentminded manner? The very question must send you into a reverie on the nature of dualism. Meanwhile, the dwarfs are trying to stop themselves bouncing up and down on their chairs. Their studied, unclamorous display of thanks cannot be properly described. Yet you will recognize its truth. The dwarfs mean no harm. Nor is there any side to them. They make their feelings manifest in the only way they know. You attempt to lay the blame on their shoulders but know fine well that it is all down to you. It is a total waste of time. It is a fraud. Everything is a fraud. Every last thing is a fraud. And on you go for the next few minutes inventing different ways of saying the same thing, till finally your head develops its own release and suddenly the noises of the pub bring you back to reality: you leap up off your chair and shout it is time to be going! if you dont leave at once the tents must no longer be available! The dwarfs will look at each other behind your back, indicating the drinks on the table and whether they swallow what remains or not can never be known for you are already outside the door, gasping at the fresh air, clawing for the stillness of the evening, those quiet, distant sounds of the countryside after dusk.

The doors bang open, and click shut; the dwarfs are beside you, waiting in silence, gazing over the fields in the direction of the site, enjoying the scene, its tranquillity. Now you will tell them the tent can be théirs for one night and one night only because as far as authority is concerned yours is less than fuck all if truth be told and you are really only doing this as a favour for some reason or another you're not quite sure except that you cannot take any chances because the camping site proprietor is a funny kind of cunt who takes instant dislikes to people for no apparent reason. And come morning they must bolt the course at all costs — either that or they'll have to seek an interview with the man himself because you'll have nothing more to do with it. Sorry, but that's that. You carry on talking like this, any kind of rubbish will do, just so long as it offers the slim possibility of them deciding against the site. And without warning you march off down the lane, clattering your boots to keep from hearing their footsteps behind you. And what about their fucking goods and chattels you're thinking. Surely they've fucking brought something with them! Are they just going to come straight down the lane after you without even having to stop off and collect a bundle of suitcases from beneath a fucking bush! What is it with these dwarfs you're thinking. What in the name of christ is it all about? The went-befores! This is what you're looking for. But there arent any went-befores. Nor is it a simple matter of faith in you as the kind of total stranger who doesnt mind putting oneself about on behalf of a fellow human being. Not at all. What is it then? Fuck knows, you dont have an earthly. Maybe they are Christians you think, who can tell with dwarfs. And then, as though wafting on the breeze one matter-of-fact voice is remarking to another on some remote question such as the itness of the stars and since you will have come in at the end and not really heard you'll toss out some sort of daft comment such as the funny thing about stars is you never hear anybody remarking on them in a specific sense but only as some kind of vaguely collective unity viz O look at the stars – but never O look at that particular star up there to the right hand side of the bastarn moon. And then the reply, the reply you receive. Have you never heard of the Pole? Or the Plowe? What about the Plowe? The Plowe by christ! But you have been so tightly, so tightly, so – knotted, so tightly knotted up inside that you havent a fucking clue about the Plowe at all until they spell it out as p-l-o-u-g-h and then you remember all about the fucking thing but in so exasperated a fashion you will demand to know why it is called the Plough and not just plain ordinary plough plural since there is a fucking cluster of the bas- tards – jesus christ you're shouting why do they not simply say there's Plough instead of fucking the Plough. And before you know where you are you're off and charging home to the tent. Home to the tent. What a fraud. This tent was never home. You only labelled it home for some fanciful notion you had about watering holes and final resting places. In fact, this tent in which you are currently dwelling is situated on a camping site you have yet to admit is falling down about your ears. Aye, precisely, the camping

site has been disintegrating: you were ignoring it, probably
hoping the problem would go away. But the very presence
of the dwarfs is enough to establish the reality. And for
some reason you will now go off at a tangent, raving at the
dwarfs on the subject of necessities; of the need to keep
tents clean, of not smoking under canvas, of rolling up one's
walls in the morning to let in the fresh air because everybody knows there's nothing worse than stuffy tents at the
height of summer. Not so bad if you are on your tod as the
likes of yourself but hopeless when there's more than one
sharing. And what about the needs of the third party. On a
camping site a great many people live and all it requires is
one bad apple and the whole place takes a nosedive.
Consider for example tidiness: it isnt a question of being
fucking neat, it all has to do with hygiene. If you forget to
clean your fucking pots and pans you wind up getting mice
and rats and christ knows what else. The same applies to
the swimming pool. You go walking about all day in the
middle of fields in your bare feet and then jump in for a
swim and what happens? fucking obvious. And holidaymaking weans just run about here, there and everywhere,
and there's no point telling the parents cause they just fucking look at you, and the same applies to chucking food
away into the long grass, as if it's going to disappear. That is
the kind of thing that happens. This is why you have to be
tidy. The chores must be done. It is necessary. You glance at
the dwarfs to see whether they are appreciating the point.
They will be walking beside you – not exactly parallel
because they dont like being forward, a couple of steps to
the rear they will be. And they pause significantly while you
unbolt the fence into the walking area. At this point you
know you've been talking a load of rubbish. They will enjoy
doing the chores. Chores shall be done without a grumble.
It isnt that dwarfs enjoy chores. In fact they do not do
chores because chores do not exist. Chores? what are they
at all! They just see themselves as performing a lot of wee

actions. They perform this list of wee actions they see as necessary if ever they are to become fully fledged campers. Jesus christ. And now you glimpse your tent, away to the rear of the field, where you had figured isolation a certainty until the day the first holidaymaking family had arrived and pitched their tent next door, under the misapprehension some sort of prearranged order had been given. Behind you the hinges of the gate creak as the dwarfs footer around, letting you hear that they are well up on country matters and are bolting the lock on the fucking fence. The door of the Ladies Washroom opens and out steps a mum. She will be a young mum and this is the end of her second week, she leaves on Saturday morning. She always wears a thin summer dress and goes about barelegged and has taken on a great tan while her husband has remained a peely wally white no matter how often he lies out in the sun on that inflatable rubber mattress. And even so, the most she has ever given you is a nodded good morning or good evening without once saying hello. And here she is bestowing a beaming smile on the dwarfs and all they do is grin idiotically. There's no fucking point any longer. You pause a minute in case she thinks you're following her and then wave your arm in the direction of the tents, before leaving the dwarfs to take their pick. And you walk by a roundabout path to your own tent, knowing that come a certain stage they should be unable to see you in the dark. And even if you're fucking luminous, so what? The dwarfs have arrived and there are empty tents, the game is up. Your part is at an end. From hereon you have become redundant. You are no longer required. They see that you have no authority. They must do as they please, they can come or go and stay or leave. What they do has become their own affair. Aw jesus you think, they're off my back at last; and inside the tent you bury yourself beneath a pile of blankets and just manage to set the alarm before falling completely asleep. It is Thursday night after all, and you've

been tired out, up since half five in the morning and out
working a 12 hour shift in the fields. Not even the dwarfs
can keep you awake.

The next day is very strange indeed. Unfathomable
matters are somehow in motion. Things are taking place
slightly beyond arm's reach. It is funny. Out in the field you
are smiling to yourself quite frequently. It is no surprise to
discover you have had a bad morning. The frenchmen are
frowning; you arent picking your fair share of the crop. But
there again, your back and shoulders are more knackered
than usual and once you've had your dinner you'll make it all
up in the afternoon session. But you will find yourself
lagging behind yet again. You were in a reverie. What the
hell was it about? You cannot remember; it is all hazy,
something to do with green fields and blue skies and
walking down to a sandy beach, arm in arm with a young
woman dressed in a summer dress, a bikini on underneath.
Now that you dwell on it you vaguely recollect having
listened in on the conversation you both were having.
What was it about? It was probably important. Up ahead
the lorry has arrived and the frenchmen are carrying the
crop across to it – Emil and Jaques are already there and
loading. Normally you would be there also. You like to be
first and to be seen doing the heavy work. Fuck it you're
thinking, you cannot be bothered today. Yet this is Friday.
Glorious Friday. Of all the days this is the day, the one you
get weighed in with the wages and see yourself fixed for
another week. Even forming the words makes it seem
ridiculous. Your trouble is you're a dreamer. You have
been carrying on as though things are remaining the same.
But even in the act of admitting this to yourself you are
aware of the smile lurking about your mouth. The truth is
you dont fucking care, you arent really bothering. If you
were bothering why are you here when you could be home
guarding your interests? The farmer would have given you
the day off if you had asked. In fact, you preferred to come

in and spend the day picking spuds; you knew it would allow your brain to take off, it would allow you the opportunity of ignoring the dwarfs – an opportunity which you werent slow to accept. Ah well you're thinking, that's it all fucking finished now, and thank christ for that. Aye, precisely, that's what you are thinking at this very point. You will be doing nothing whatsoever. You will be stuck in the middle of a field doing nothing whatsoever. Meanwhile the frenchmen are nudging each other and wondering what is going on. And meanwhile the dwarfs are on the camping site wreaking their own particular form of havoc. A group of holidaymaking dads is discussing the dreadful condition of the place, the dreadful amenities being offered, the dreadful state of the swimming pool into which their weans are plunging, these bastarn television sets always conking out; supposedly sturdy tents that keep collapsing, a plague of moles and field mice and all the litter abounding among the long grass and hedges surrounding the cooking area. On and on it goes, their list, lengthening; the whole fucking site is a shambles. In the background the dwarfs are nodding deferentially because they are somehow linking you with the carry on and doing their best to stick up for you, they dont fucking realize you arent the fucking proprietor and it doesnt have anything to do with you in the first place except insofar as you were attempting to be a permanent resident, you were referring to the dump as home, charging around with your head stuck in the grass, lapsing into reveries connected with watering holes and final resting places, while all about you things were disintegrating. The dwarfs were only a reply. And yet, you will say, if they hadnt arrived it wouldnt be happening. They are to blame. While you were at work they've been charging around the site sowing seeds of discontent among the holidaymakers. Not by intention – granted, there is no malice, okay, you can accept that but still and all, still and all: they have come and they've taken over. They did not know what they were doing. They probably thought they were just being polite when chatting to the dads about the semi-detached villa on the outskirts of Burnley. They couldnt comprehend that this would result in a dialogue, that the holidaymaking parents would wind up getting together, comparing notes on their so-called camping site and its so-called amenities which are rubbish when you consider what is being offered across on the west coast at little or no difference in cost.

And now you are aware of why you have not been working properly this morning. Even your reveries were fraudulent. It was always there; you were always thinking about it – your thinking was just at so deeply set back a stage that you werent aware of it. This is why you lagged behind the frenchmen, the gaffer frowning at you, wondering if you really are up to it after all. You havent enjoyed the morning. Normally a Friday is good but today has been terrible, you are suffering; and meanwhile a deputation is being formed by the holidaymaking mums and dads, to march right in and confront the camping site proprietor first thing tomorrow morning. And this camping site proprietor ... Camping site proprietor! what a joke. Because he owns a camping site he gets labelled that. He knows next to nothing about camping sites. The whole kit and caboodle would have collapsed weeks ago if you hadnt been dropping hints via the wee woman from the village – between the two of you you kept it going. And now she's fucked off and left you to it. But what more could be done you're saying, what more could be done!

That is for you to say. But you will be aware of a peculiar diffidence on the part of the farmer when collecting your wages later. He seems not to want to look at you. And the frenchmen hang back, waiting for you to leave before going to collect theirs, as though they dont want to be tainted by the bad luck surrounding you. Well, maybe that's a bit strong but such an inference could be drawn. And your face will be red; you'll want to walk off immediately, preferably without comment although you'll attempt a matter-of-fact cheerio, before strolling to the side of the bar for a quick wash at the outside tap. You have decided against returning to the site; you're heading straight for the pub. Fuck it you're thinking, I feel like a drink. And the way you've been suffering you're entitled to one. The fucking dwarfs! You smile to yourself, amazing how they can come and just take over! Funny. Just when you think you've got everything fixed, then bang, finished, all gone, all of it.

You have been walking now. You have been walking for quite a while. You have walked way beyond the pub; a car whizzed by, and as its sound decreased you became aware of it and thus of yourself there, way beyond the pub, you were walking, just walking. Now here you are. What will you do? will you go back to the pub or continue walking; you could be in town in another half-hour – even less should a bus appear; on this part of the island buses appear infrequently but more often on Friday nights and the weekend; or you could thumb a lift, or just walk the whole way. It is a nice day, a nice day for walking; also the kind of day you enjoy being on the site, having returned home from work and cooking a few spuds, lazily, not bothering too much; the cries of the weans from the swimming pool and the play area, the holidaymaking parents sitting outside their tents relaxing after the evening meal, music quietly in the background, from the radio or cassette recorder: Friday night. And you will return to the pub; you still have to weigh in Pierre with the couple of quid you borrowed. And anyway, you arent really dressed for town, still being in the working togs – different if you had gone home first and had a decent wash and shave and so on. In fact, this carry on about going into town, it is familiar. You have been meaning to go into town much more often.

You pause, keeping in to the side of the road as a pair of cyclists pass, then you take out your tobacco and sit on the grass by the side of the ditch. Aye, you were meaning to go into town more often. Just the time it takes, getting back to the site and washing and eating and getting yourself ready and then having to hoof it down the lane to the junction and wait for a bus, usually finding you had just missed one or something, so you nearly always stepped across the road and into the pub. It was handy – too handy! You smile wryly; you stop it at once, rising immediately and striding back to the pub. But it is annoying you're thinking, this not making it into town more often. You'll need to make more of an effort in future. The local's all very well but a change is as good as a rest and so on. Seeing the same old faces all the time – especially that cunt of a barman who seems in the wrong job altogether. What is it with him at all the way he serves people? If he doesnt like serving people how come he works in a fucking pub! that superior smile on his face all the time. No wonder you . . . Jesus christ, that couple of quid you borrowed off him. But it wasnt off him you borrowed it, it was the brewery; he just makes you feel that way, that's why you hate getting tick in the place. Fucking dwarfs. Fucking bastarn dwarfs, those fucking bastarn dwarfs coming here by christ you're fucking sick of them. Wee bastards. What is it with them? the way they look at each other all the time, christ – incredible, it really is incredible, the way they come and just take over. And they're probably out looking for you right now you're thinking. Of course they are. It's because they are loyal and thoughtful to others. They want to advise you of the goings on up by at the site. It isnt a question of them not wanting you to think they're working behind your back because that never occurs to them because they arent, they are entirely above board and out in the open. They want to fill you in on what has been happening. Amazing they'll say, these poor holidaymakers, we never knew it was as bad as it is, really dreadful, Tommy Jackson – he's from Burnley you know, a nice fellow, lovely wife he's got and a couple of smashing weans – he was telling us about the amenities, really fucking dreadful so they are, did you know? Did you know! what a joke. What a fucking joke. No you say, I didnt. And they look at each other as though joined at the nose. They are standing by where you are sitting; they have their pints in their hands. One of the holidaymaking dads realized they were skint and offered them a couple of quid till they landed their first job. They didnt ask. And one of the holidaymaking mums has been feeding them all day – after the chores they've been getting through she thought they deserved it. They were really going at it hammer and tongs, you should've seen them, charging about here, there and everywhere cleaning up the site, mending fuses and getting all sorts of insects out the swimming pool. They even fixed an appointment with the fucking camping site proprietor for tomorrow morning's deputation. Aye, they just marched right up to the door and chapped it, and the cunt answered. According to rumour he's about to offer them the job of running the site shop but they will refuse; they'd prefer the wee woman to return and unless he's any objections they're going to charge down to the village first thing Monday morning and drag her back if need be. And they seem hopeful; they reckon she must listen to reason. And you know fine well she will listen to reason; not only that but she'll invite them in for their fucking breakfast. It really is funny. In some ways you have to admire them. Do they have something special? What is it they've got? because they've definitely got something. There's Pierre telling a couple of the frenchmen to squeeze up so the dwarfs can sit down next to you and be able to watch the dominoes. And they do want to watch the dominoes. They're trying not to seem too keen in case you're offended but back where they come from they used to play the game regularly and aye, when somebody asks if they want to sit in, aye, they will, if nobody's got any objections.

You have to hand it to the wee bastards. You shake your head, smiling. In fact you'd probably quite like them if you werent so fucking . . . so fucking – so fucking what? You are frowning; you glance sideways. There they are there right beside you, taking the spectators' part in the game as energetically as any of the frenchmen, grinning and yapping and gesticulating away, and now smiling at you because you smiled at them but they dont really realize you are smiling at them, they probably think you're just glad to be alive. And two of the holidaymaking dads have entered and are trying to attract the dwarfs' attention – Billy and Dan, they're supposed to be meeting the dwarfs for a pint but now when they spot them here with the locals they feel a bit sheepish and dont want to be pushy although at the same time they're secretly proud to know them. In a couple of minutes one of them'll arrive with the pints he has bought them; he'll walk with determined nonchalance to place them on the shelf beneath the dominoe table and pause a moment, to study the game. Then, after a decent interval, a dwarf will glance upwards and say: Ta, and return his attention to the next dominoe being played. Then almost at once he will say: O – how's your wee boy? is his knee any better? This wee boy cut his knee earlier on; he fell in the long grass, landed on a bit of broken glass or something, a nail maybe. Aw he's fine now, says the holidaymaker, last I saw he was plunging into the swimming pool. Then he gives them a friendly grin and a brief nod at the game, and returns to his mate at the bar who is waving and smiling. It is all a load of shite you're wanting to yell across, dont fall for it. But for one reason or another you will not do that. You dont have the energy for a start. But aside from that, aside from that you feel more inclined to burst out laughing. You clear your throat, move your shoulders, you sip at your beer, calming yourself down – it would be pointless doing anything daft. Aye, suddenly you find yourself aware of the possibility. It's because the place is so crowded you think. There arent even enough seats to go round. Friday night of course, the start of the weekend, and it is always busy. A great many holidaymakers are here, from different parts. Quite a few have stepped off their boats. You spot them immediately by the way they dress but even without that they cant be mistaken, the way they stand there gabbing so loudly just to let everybody know. They seem to think they own the fucking place. The ordinary holidaymakers are fine; it's these weekend boat sailors you're opposed to – another reason for making more of an effort to get into town in future. You have turned to the dwarfs and begun telling them about this. They nod. They are not a hundred per cent interested. In fact, they are genuinely interested in the game. You will pause and they dont realize you arent speaking. No wonder; what you were saying is boring, even to yourself. You smile ruefully. Emil smiles back at you. He is one of the players and he thinks you're smiling because you've spotted the bad dominoe he laid down; his smile is also rueful and he shakes his head and says something in french, all set to lose the game.

When it ends you go for another pint and ask for a whisky as well, and as an afterthought you get whiskies for the dwarfs because they already have fresh pints lying. The barman looks at you. There is something about the look, a puzzled quality, and not just to do with the additional drinks. For a moment you think you've been misjudging the man; maybe he just has that kind of face and he isnt really a taciturn old bastard. How would you like to be cooped up here all day you're thinking, and having to serve these fucking boat sailors! It's no joke. When he returns to give you your change you smile and he ignores you and wins again. You are definitely going to start going into town, starting from tomorrow, as soon as you finish your work you're going straight home for a wash and a shave and a change of clothes. No question. And there can be no excuse either because Saturdays you only work half the day. You glance quickly at him before lifting the tray of drinks: he's staring into space while pouring a pint for somebody. Even if the job's as bad as that you're thinking, it's useless taking it out on the customers, far better just leaving. If you had a job like that you would just leave, you wouldnt start taking it out on people; one of these days somebody's going to stick one on the old cunt's chin and nobody'll jump in to give him a hand, least of all you – in fact, it'll probably be you sticking the one on him! The thought makes you grin, then laugh quietly; you clear your throat, but continue grinning. The dwarfs look at you, smiling politely. Aye you say, and begin telling them about a funny thing that happened while picking spuds recently. A lot of funny things happen in the fields and you mention a few of them. They show interest. All in all you say, there's a lot worse jobs than picking spuds – being out in the fresh air and that, there's a lot to be said for it. Even if jobs were plentiful you reckon you would probably prefer the one you have. Of course there isnt much of a choice nowadays. There used to be but not now. The dwarfs nod. You're glad to see they appreciate the point because quite a few folk land on the island thinking the farmers'll be queuing up to offer them work. The same applies to fixing yourself with a roof. A great many cunts come here thinking it's straight-forward, but it isnt, it's nowhere near straightforward; it used to be, but not now. If you dont get things fixed then you're bang in trouble; it's a question of knowing the ins and outs; you have to consider the eventualities, sort out what is possible and what is not possible. Take yourself for instance: when you came here you had your eyes open, none of that romantic shite about tropical paradises, you knew you would have to graft, that it was down to you to make things work because one thing you've learned in life and that is if you want to do something then do it yourself because no cunt's going to do it for you. That's a fucking beauty! That could make you laugh aloud. You dont. What you will do is raise your pint glass and sip slowly, gazing at

the dwarfs over the rim. And they are gazing back at you.
They are next on at the dominoes and are wanting to
return their attention to there but are unsure whether
they should continue listening to you. And they make their
decision; they continue gazing at you. They are expecting
something. You are to speak. What are you to say? They
are waiting for you to say something. What is it you . . .

O jesus.

It'll be a beautiful summer's evening outside. One of
those where you get that amazing expanse of sky and then
when it darkens a shade you see the stars, an infinity of
them. It always looks special when you're on an island and
standing looking from the middle of a field; the sky, it's like
a blanket or something. This is what you say to the dwarfs,
about the sky at night, it looks like a blanket or something,
with thousands and millions of shining stars and each
moment you witness the thing another one explodes into
life. It is amazing. Yet so many people dont even bother
looking at the stars. They come to a place like this and go
walking about with their head stuck in the grass. The
dwarfs arent like that. They genuinely appreciate the value
of things, same as yourself. If you have any criticism to make
of them it has to do with their naïvety. It isnt so much that
they are naïve in the ordinary sense – otherwise they
wouldnt be here and making a go of things as well as they
are – it is more to do with faith or something. The way
they look upon you for instance; you can understand why
they regard you as highly as they do but all in all you'd
advise against it in future.

Christ, you stop talking; you shake your head, there's a
lump in your throat. You stare at your whisky, not wanting
to be seen. The dwarfs have coughed and shifted on their
chairs so they cannot see you without turning their heads.
They are good people. They are thoughtful and they are
fucking loyal, you dont care what anybody says. And yet it's
funny how it happens you're thinking, and you smile then

offer them your job. You're not a hundred per cent certain the farmer'll take them on because there was only one of you but you reckon they could do a lot worse than give it a try, and once he sees how well they get on with the frenchmen ... well, you're sure it'll be okay. There are other problems – well, not really problems, more to do with irksome chores; things like the deputation. The most important thing to remember is the camping site proprietor himself: whatever you do you must not put the jitters into him. He's so fucking incompetent and so fucking aware of being incompetent that at the slightest show of being thought incompetent he'll run for cover, he'll close down the site and head for the mainland. You've seen cunts like him before and so have the dwarfs, there's no real need to tell them, you just thought you'd mention it. O, and the holidaymakers, there's quite a bit to be said about them and you start in on that for a time, until gradually the dwarfs are turning their heads from you; the game of dominoes currently in progress is due to finish any minute. And anyway, what you are saying is fairly boring – not completely boring because it must be of some value; but all in all, all in all ... And it's hell of a noisy in this place – Friday night, the jukebox going constantly and the boat sailors seem to have bribed the barman into turning up the volume; a couple of the females are now dancing a bit while the males are sipping at their half pint shandies. It wont be long now till you apply the method. This is it: a dwarf will rise to his feet to go to the bar and while manoeuvring his way through he will accidentally rub against one of the dancers and one of the males will pass a comment. One thing leads to another. The upshot is that you, being the tallest member of the present company, will challenge the tallest boat sailor to go to the boxing games. At this a great tumult shall occasion. People are on all sides of you, many of whom you recognize, as though trying to paw at you. They are excited by the prospect ahead. You hear them discuss this that and the next thing with some of the female boat sailors trying to play matters down but the males arent letting them; they want to prove themselves – although they act as if they own the fucking place they are in reality very insecure and hate it when they enter an out-of-the-way pub like this only to receive cheek from taciturn barmen and have their females ogled by the regulars. You can hear what sounds like holidaymaking parents attempting to pacify them but to no avail, and then an indistinct voice is calling for a more sporting contest, something less violent, maybe a swim or some fucking thing. Great you shout, and make a lunge at the tallest boat sailor: Me and you outside in the fucking Ocean ya bastard! And this does the trick. The silence lasts for several moments before the tumult continues – it appears to be a kind of vote. It is a vote. A great cheer goes up when a voice calls: Carried! And then by your side you feel hands tapping your shoulder in a furtive way; it's the dwarfs; they are attempting to dissuade you. At first this seems a contradiction, a paradox maybe, you arent sure, there isnt time, you look at them. No they cry, you shouldnt be going out swimming on a night like this with all that beer and whisky in your belly. Out my road you shout, out my road. And a couple of holidaymakers are there also, including a young mum in a summer dress who looks very worried, her hand to the side of her mouth, clutching a hankie. For christ sake! Too late, too fucking late you're shouting, too fucking late. You're just wanting out there, nothing else matters, nothing. Where's that fucking boat sailor who insulted your wee pal the dwarf? that's what you're wanting to know. He's waiting outside with his cronies. And you might've known, the cunt's got a pair of swimming trunks. Ah well. And there's the frenchmen laying bets – Pierre's making a book – and glancing with interest as you go charging down the beach with the dwarfs scurrying alongside, trying to keep up. The boat sailor's there already with a couple of his mates; one of them's testing the temperature for him and he's saying: Not as cold as when you swam the fucking channel Bertie! Aw good, says the boat sailor, glad to hear it. But you're straightening your shoulders and marching right past him, way beyond him, and the Ocean's lapping up by your ankles and you pause a moment to kick off your working boots. You can hear indistinct voices from the shore. Is it cheers you wonder. Who cares you say, and when the water comes up beyond your knees you immediately plunge in and begin a hectic breastroke in a direction sou' sou'-westerly.

Manufactured in Paris

Whole days you spend walking about the dump looking for one and all you get's sore feet. I'm fucking sick of it. Sweaty bastarn feet. I went about without socks for a spell and the sweat was worse, streams in my shoes. Shoes! no point calling them shoes. Seen better efforts on a – christ knows what. Cant make you a pair of shoes these days. More comfort walking about in a pair of mailbags. A while ago I was passing a piece of waste ground where a few guys were kicking a ball about. On I went. We got a game going. Not a bad game. I kicked the stuffing out my shoes but. The seams split. Everybastarnthing split. Cutting back down the road with the soles flapping and that. And I had no spare pairs either by christ nothing, nothing at all. Then I found a pair of boots next to a pillarbox. This pair of boots had been Manufactured in Paris. Paris by christ. They lasted me for months too. Felt like they were mine from the start. I had been trying to pawn a suit that day. No cunt would take it. We dont take clothes these days is what they all said. Tramped all over the dump. Nothing. Not a bad suit as well. This is a funny thing about London. Glasgow – Glasgow is getting as bad right enough. They still take clothes but the price they give you's pathetic. I once spent forty-eight quid on a suit and when I took it along they offered me three for it. Three quid. Less than four months old by christ. A fine suit too, 14 ounce cloth and cut to my own specifications. The trimmings. That suit had the lot. I always liked suits. Used to spend a fortune on the bastards. Foolish. I gave it all up. It was a heatwave then as well right enough but an honest decision nevertheless.

The Place!

Deep water. I want to float through breakers and over breaststroking across uplifted by them. This is what I need. And upon the deep open sea. Freshwater wont do. Where are the breakers in freshwater. None. You dont fucking get them. I want to be by a sheer rockface. The steep descent to reach the sea where at hightide the caves are inaccessible by foot alone. I have to startle birds in their nests from within the caves. At hightide the rockplunge into the deep. That is what I want. That. I can swim fine and I can swim fine at my own pace and I have no illusions about my prowess. I'm not getting fucked about any longer.

There is a place I know on the coast. I cant go there. It is not in reach. The remains of a Druid cemetery close by, accounts for a few tourists. The tourists never visit the Place. Maybe they do. But it isnt a real reason for not going. There are real reasons, real reasons. My christ what a find this place was. I climbed down a dangerous part of the rockface. Right down and disregarding mostly all I know of climbing down the dangerous parts. Only perhaps 25 feet. The tide was in. I wanted to fall in. I wanted to dive in. I did not know if it was safe to dive in. If there were rocks jutting beneath the surface. So I did not want to dive in. I wanted to fall in and find out whether it was safe for diving. But if I fell onto submerged rocks I might have been killed so I did

not want to fall in at all for fuck sake which is why I clung at
shallow clumps of weedgrass, loose slate; and it was holding
fast, supporting me, the weight. I kept getting glimpses of
the caves. Impossible to reach at hightide unless by swimming. When I got down to where I could only go I saw the
rocks in the depth and had to get away at that moment
seeing the rocks there I had to getaway at once and each
grain of matter was now loosening on my touch my toes
cramped and I had to cling on this loose stuff applying no
none absolutely no pressure at all but, just balancing there
with the toes cramped in this slight crevice.

A Nightboilerman's notes

The bunker faces outwards, away to the far corner of the ground surface area. When it requires replenishing (twice nightly) I push the bogey out into the corridor and through the rearmost swing doors, down the steep incline onto the pathway by the canal, along to where the coalmountains pile some thirty yards from the embankment. It is good to walk here, the buckled rattle of the bogey wheels only emphasizing the absence of noise. The Nightoutsideman has charge of this area. I used to envy him. His job has always seemed so straightforward in comparison to this one of mine. He sits on his chair to the side of his hut door, gazing to the sky or to the canal. I walk past him but he doesnt look across, not until he hears that first strike of my shovel into the coal, when he turns and waves.

It takes 4 bogey loads to replenish the bunker. I could manage it with 3 but the incline up into the factory is too steep to push the bogey comfortably if fully laden. And there is no need to rush. This is a part of the shift I like. Once the 4th load is in the bogey I leave it standing and go over to have a smoke with the Nightoutsideman. We exchange nods. I lean my back against the wall on the other side of the hut door from him; sometimes I lower myself down to sit on my heels. Due to the configuration of warehouse and factory buildings there is never any wind here (a very very slight breeze, but only occasionally) and the canal is still, its water black, grey foam spreading out from its banks.

He will have been waiting for me to arrive before making his next cigarette. He used to make one for me but I prefer my own. I strike the match; while I am exhaling on the first draw I flick the match out onto the canal, watching for its smoke but there never is any; if there is I havent been able to see it. He raises his eyebrows, a brief smile. He smiles a lot, speaks very rarely; he just likes to sit there, watching the things that happen. Most of the buildings are unoccupied during the night and their differing shapes and shadows, the shades of black and grey, red-tinged. Now and then he will gesture at the sky, at the bend in the canal, sideways at one of the buildings, to the one where jets of steam suddenly issue from escape pipes, and to high up in the same building, at the large windows where headlike shapes appear frequently. I never quite grasp what he is on about but it probably has to do with plain truths, and I nod, as though acknowledging a contrast. Then when I finish the smoke I flick the dowp out onto the canal, listening for the plop which never comes (which never could come, not in any canal). I wait on a few moments, before going to get the bogey. I like this last push up the incline, that rutted point near the top where the wheels seem to be jamming and the bogey halts and

                    I cannot hold it any longer! All my strength's gone! The load's going to roll back down and crash into the canal!

                    and then I grin; I breathe in and shove, continuing on up and through the swing doors into the corridor, still grinning.

I have charge of the boilers. Their bodies are situated in the basement and their mouths range the ground surface area, shut off by solid square hatches with set-in rings. The floor is made of specially treated metal plating so that although it is still very hot it is never too hot such that it is impossible to walk upon when wearing the special boots (metal studded, and perhaps the uppers are of a special substance?). When I arrive with the 4th load of coal I wheel the bogey past the bunker and go straight across to begin stoking. I have a crowbar to insert in the rings to wedge up the hatches which settle at an angle of 100°. With the hatch raised the heat and light from the boiler is tremendous and I have to avert my face while stoking. Asbestos gloves are there to be used but I work without them, simply taking care not to touch the metal parts of the shovel. It is habit now and I cannot remember the last time I burnt my hands. There is an interesting thing that a child would like to see; this is the coaldust dropping from my shovel during the stoking, it ignites simultaneously to touching the floor so that countless tiny fires are always blazing, and it looks startling (diamonds that sparkle). Then I have finished and kick down the hatch, and that thud of impact separating the loud roaring of the open boiler from the dull roaring of the closed boiler that I can never quite anticipate. And I move onto the next. Finally, when I have finished them all, I wheel off the bogey to its position by the bunker then return with the wirebrush to sweep clean the floor of the ground surface. Coalbits will be lying smouldering or burning nearby the hatches; I sweep them straight across and into the water trench next to the basement entrance. Towards the end of the shift I rake out the trench and use what is there on the last stoke. Whenever I forget to do this the trench is full when I come in next evening. The Dayboilerman is responsible. This is his way of reminding me not to do it again.

From a distance the entrance to the basement re-

sembles another boilermouth but it is set away to the side
of the ground surface, and its hatch is permanently raised.
There is a step ladder going down, the top of which is
welded onto the inside panel of the hatch. I enjoy descend-
ing. I grip either side with both hands, sometimes scurrying
down to break the existing speed record, other times I go
stepping very very slowly, very deliberately, as though
engaged upon ultra serious business to do with submarines
or spaceships. I can be standing watching myself from way
over beyond the bunker, seeing my head sink from view,
vanishing, wondering if it cracked against the edge of the
metal plated floor but no, always I just avoid that by the
briefest margin possible, gglullp. gone. Then I poke out my
head again. Or maybe remain exactly there, just beneath
the surface, counting 25 and only then will I reappear, and
back down immediately.

Nowadays I appreciate no tasks more than those that
have me down in the basement. It did use to have its
frightening aspects but my imagination was to blame. The
black holes is the best example. I would step past them and
pretend they were not there, or if they were, that I was
not particularly bothered by them. This was daft and I knew
it was daft but I was just working out a method of
conquering myself. At that time I was having to actually
force myself to enter the basement. I would say inwardly;
these black holes, they are ordinary black holes, ordinary in
the sense that they are man-made, they only exist because
of the way the walls have been designed. (They also exist as
they do because of the effect the lighting system has on the
boilerbodies: permanent shadows.)

The basement is a sealed unit, built to accommodate the
boilers; the only entrance/exit is by way of the step ladder.
Firstly the boilers were sited then they built the basement,
and the rest of the building. It took me a while to

understand that fully. And when I had I think I was either
over my fear or well on the road to it. It was pretty bad at
the time. I had to force myself to sit down beside them, the
holes, facing away from them, not able to see them without
turning my head. I would sit like that for ages, thinking of
horrible things, but not being aware of it till later, sometimes much later, when walking home. One morning the
Dayboilerman found me. It was a terrible shock for him.
The sound of his boots on the steps of the ladder had
reached me but could scarcely correspond to anything I
knew so that I wasnt really aware of it beyond my thoughts.
Then he was there and his eyes staring as though seeing a
ghost, seeming about to collapse with a heart attack. Yet
he had been looking for me. I hadnt clocked out at the gate
and the timekeeper had asked him to check up. So he was
looking for me and when he found me reacted as though I
was the last thing he expected to see sitting there. He told
people I looked like a zombie. A zombie! But eventually it
made me realize he had never managed to conquer himself.
He must have been really nervous, terrified about what he
might find.

The switches for the basement lighting are on the wall
behind the ladder so they can be turned on before reaching
the bottom, but they are supposed to be kept on permanently. I think the reason for this has to do with the idea
of one man being down and then another man coming
down without realizing the first is there, and returning
back up and switching the lighting off, leaving the first man
in total blackness. That would be a horrible thing to
happen, particularly to someone new in the job. But I have
to admit here and now that I do play about with the
switches, sometimes leaving the lighting off during the
times I'm away from the basement. I think about how it all
looks down there, different things. Also, there is that
incredible sensation when switching them back on again

later. I go stepping off the ladder with my back to the inner wall, facing away from the shaft of light above, right out into the blackness. Occasionally I will walk 3 or 4 (5 at the most) paces until that feeling of narrowness has me stock-still and trying to reflect on a variety of matters, maybe wondering how it would be having to work in such conditions forever (a miner whose lamp keeps going out?). And I continue standing there, thinking of different things, then slowly but surely I notice I am moving back the way, sensing the approach of that strange feeling of being buried in cotton wool and I am turning to reach for the switches calmly, not panicking at all, getting my bearings from the shaft of light high above at the entrance. And the lighting is immediate throughout the basement, and the noise of everything now audible apparently for the first time, that deep deep humming sound.

The boilerbodies dominate the basement. I can stand watching them. They are large, their shadows rigid but falling on each other (it can seem as though your eyes are blurring). There is a complex of narrow passageways between them, just wide enough for a man to walk, carrying a crate of cinders and a rake and shovel perhaps. I used to think a bogey might be adapted to fit the passage-ways but this is not at all necessary; it is possible the idea only occurred to me because of movable objects — I thought it would be good to have one. There are 4 tools: 2 crates plus a rake and a shovel. There are also 2 pairs of boilersuits, 1 for the Dayboilerman and 1 for me; they have to be kept in the basement, if we want to wear boilersuits on the ground surface we have to order different ones for the purpose. I also keep a towel down here which I find necessary. Although the atmosphere is not stifling it must be akin to tropical. I think of equatorial forests full of those peculiar plants, gigantic ones, with brightly coloured buds the size of oranges hanging down the middle, and that

constant dripping. But there isnt any dripping in the basement, nothing like that. There is water in the trenches of
course, which surrounds the bottom of the boilerbodies.
Cinders fall through to here somehow and I rake them
out and carry them in a crate to the foot of the ladder,
dumping them into the other crate which I will carry up
later on, for eventual use in the last stoke. I enjoy carrying
the crate between the boilerbodies. I take different routes
and go quickly or slowly, sometimes very very slowly,
studying my boots as they land at that point on the
passageway nearest to the trench. Even though I work
naked I continue to wear the boots. I once tried it barefoot
but the edges of the trenches get quite slippy when I'm
raking the cinders out; also a daft thing, I was being
continually tempted into the water, just to dip my feet (but
if I had succumbed to that I would maybe have gone in for a
swim!).

The trenches are narrow and they slope in below the
bottoms of the boilerbodies so that cinders can become
stuck, and stuck fast, there seems to be a great many
crannies. I know most of them through having used the
rake so often. This part of the job is good, the raking noise
and my own silence, that clung of the rakehead below the
surface of the water on the sides of the trench, the scraping
noise of its teeth in the crannies. I could have expected
both that and the sense of touch to grate on me but they
dont, perhaps because they come from outside of me
altogether. I work silently, and in silence. It is an important
point. The idea of the work noise is funny, how it would
appear to somebody (not the Dayboilerman) poking his
head down the ladder, seeing how all the objects and
everything are so stationary, just taking it for granted for a
spell while not being conscious of anything else, not until
that moment he has become aware of something, of an
unexpected noise, rhythmic, and I couldnt be seen from

there because of the shapes and shadows, only the clung
and scraping sound; after a moment the person would
react by snorting, maybe giving himself a telling off for
being so daft, and then he would climb back up and out as
quickly as he could, trying to kid on he wasnt bothered by
it.

But nobody from outside ever comes down into the
basement. Firstly the ground surface area needs to be
crossed and it cannot be crossed without special footwear.
If anybody wishes to attract my attention they either shout
or batter the floor with a crowbar. It happens only rarely
and I seldom respond since it is always to advise me that the
pressure isnt being maintained. This I discover myself
sooner or later because of the safety precautions. I might
be wrong not to respond. I sometimes wonder whether to
ask the Dayboilerman what he does. But his perception of
the job will differ radically from my own. It cannot be
avoided, he is on constant day and I am on constant night,
we each have our own distractions. Yes, I can still be
distracted; in some ways it is essential to the work; but I
cannot be distracted against my wishes. If I think of things
they must be things I wish to think of.

I used to make myself sit by the black hole farthest from
the entrance; it lies on the same side but to reach it I have
to walk to the wall opposite the ladder then follow the
passageway there, right around and into the corner. I
would bring the boilersuit to sit on and the towel to lean
my back on against the wall; then I lit a cigarette. Smoking is
frowned upon down here but I've always done it; I really
enjoy it, finishing a particular part of the work and sitting
down quietly and lighting one. Sometimes when I sit down I
leave the cigarettes and matches beside me for a while
before smoking; other times I'm smoking even before
sitting down. One thing I used to do in the early days, I used

to push the matches and cigarettes inside the hole. I sat there for a long period afterwards, till finally I knelt and withdrew them without looking in, just using my hand to feel around.

There is nothing extraordinary about these black holes, they are cavities and short tunnels. I found them of interest because they had never been seen into since the factory's original construction. I still find the idea quite interesting. When I first found them I thought they were just inshots, little gaps, and I sat by them not bothering. Then one night after sitting a while I suddenly was kneeling down and peering in and I couldnt see anything, nothing at all. I struck a match and the light scarcely penetrated. It was really funny. Then I had to push in my hand; I discovered the wall, and then a tunnel veering off at a tangent. I could have brought in a torch or a candle, and a mirror maybe, but I never did. If I remember correctly I was wanting to check the dimensions of the wall in relation to it, the cavity and tunnel. I knew it had to be some sort of double wall, but probably a triple one, as part of the safety precautions. I went round by the canal pathway to look at the outside of the building but that told me nothing. On this particular side of the factory the pathway only goes along a few yards before narrowing and tapering out altogether, with the wall going straight down into the water.

There were quite a lot of things about it that bothered me at the time but nowadays it all seems hazy. But I think the main factor must connect to the idea of isolation, maybe bringing on a form of deprivation or something. It wasnt good when I had to sit by the black holes at first, some of my imaginings were horrible. I just had to stick it out and conquer myself. I had to succeed and I did succeed. It taught me a lot about myself and has given me confidence. Sometimes I feel a bit smug, as if I've reached a

higher level than the others in the factory; but I dont
speak to many of them, I just get on and do the job,
enjoying its various aspects.

The City Slicker and The Barmaid

I came to someplace a few miles south of the Welsh border and with luck managed to rent a tent on a farm. Not a camping site. I was the one mug living on the dump and could only stay on condition I completed certain set tasks such as painting barn walls or driving tractors. And whenever the farmer was away on business I had to guide his ramshackle lorry into the village.

I also received cash for these tasks.

The grass was long in the field where I had to pitch the tent. Closeby was a barn. Here big rats jumped about getting fat on the hay and feed stored inside. Sometimes I discovered paw marks on the grease in my frying pan. This proves the rats got into my tent though the farmer would never believe me. During the night I liked to sit at the top end with a bottle in my hand waiting for a thing to creep in. And the hedge surrounding this field was full of beetles and other flying insects. When I lit my candle they broke into the tent, perched on the roof till I was sleeping, then came zooming down on me, eating my blood and knocking their knees in my hair. I was always waking in the middle of the night scratching and clawing at my skalp.

The actual farm animals themselves did not worry me. Although after sundown a pack of cows used to try and sniff me; they came wastling along at my back without a sound

bar the shshsh of their smelly tails. And no comfort
entering the tent with my boots soaked through with dew.
I was obliged to take them off at the door, seated on the
groundsheet with the tent flaps wide open. A terrible tent.
Two inch walls and sagging everywhere. The kind of effort
a scoutmaster buys at christmas for his six years old son.
And the groundsheet was always covered in clumps of
grass, earwigs and spiders. Dung too at times when I had
thought my boots okay enough to walk straight in.

No sleeping bag. Terrible itchy exarmy blankets hired
from the farmer's wife at 30 pence a week. Of course my
feet stuck out at the bottom and I can never sleep wearing
socks.

The farmhands were continually cracking jokes in Oi Bee
accents at my expense. Sometimes I would laugh, or
stare – other times I replied in aggressive accents of my
own which got me nowhere since they pretended not to
understand what I was saying. Because I drove the lorry I
was accorded a certain respect. In the local den of a pub I
was known as Jock the Driver. The previous driver was an
Irishman who worked seven years on the farm till one
Saturday night he went out for a pish in the lavatory round
the back of the pub. It was the last they ever saw of him. A
man to admire. The men working beside me were yesmen
to the core. Carried tales about each other to the farmer
and even to me if the farmer was off on business. Whole
days they spent gossiping. I never spoke to them unless I
had to. The tightest bunch of bastards I have ever met.
Never shared their grub or mugs of tea. Or their cash if you
were skint. And they never offered you a cigarette. If you
bought them a drink they thought you were off your head
and also resented it because they felt obliged to buy you
one back. In their opinion city folk were either thieves or
simpletons. An amazing shower of crackpots the lot of
them.

The barmaid in this pub was a daughter of the village. I

think she must have hated me because I represented outside youth. And apart from myself there were no other single men of her age in the dump. She was chaste I think unless the Irishman ever got there which I doubt. I never fancied her in the first place. A bit tubby. Just that if I hadnt tried I thought the regulars might have felt insulted – the barmaid not good enough etcetera for a city slicker like me. The night I made the attempt was awful. It reminds me of B feature imitation Barbara Stanwyck films.

Once or twice the manager used to bolt his doors and allow a few regulars to stay behind after closing time. He must have forgotten about me. With the shutters drawn and the local constable in the middle of his second pint of cider I for some reason threw an arm about the barmaid's waist for which I was dealt an almighty clout on the jaw. What a fist she had on her. I was so amazed I tried to land her one back but missed and fell across the table where the constable was sitting, knocking the drink over him. I was ejected.

Long after midnight, maybe as late as two in the morning, I came back to apologize if anyone was still about, and also to collect the carry-out I had planked in the grass behind the lavatory. I had been wandering about retching for ages because of that country wine they had been feeding me. Powerful stuff. Inside the pub the lights had been dimmed but I knew they were there. I could hear music coming faintly from the lounge. I crept round the side of the building then up on my toes and peering in through the corner of the frosted glass I spied the barmaid there giving it a go as the stripper. Yes. Doing a strip show on top of the lounge bar watched by the copper, the manager and one or two regulars, including an unhealthy old guy called Albert Jenkinson who worked alongside me on the farm. And all silent while they watched. Not a smile amongst them. Even the drink was forgotten. Just the quick drag on the smoke.

I lost my temper at first then felt better, then again lost my temper and had to resist caving in the window and telling them to stick the countryside up their jacksie.

No one noticed me. I did not stay very long. Her body was far too dumpy for a stripper and her underwear was a bit old fashioned. Her father worked as a gardener in the local nursery and rarely went into the pub.

Once I got my wages the following week, and it was safe, I got off my mark and took the tent with me.

An Enquiry Concerning Human Understanding

During a time prior to this a major portion of my energy was devoted to recollection. These recollections were to be allowed to surface only for my material benefit. Each item dredged was to have been noted as the lesson learned so that never again would I find myself in the situation effected through said item. A nerve wracking affair. And I lacked the discipline. Yet I knew all the items so well there seemed little point in dredging them up just to remember them when I in fact knew them so well already. It was desirable to take it along in calm, stately fashion; rationalizing like the reasonable being. This would have been the thing. This would have been for the experience. And I devoted real time to past acts with a view to an active future. The first major item dredged was an horse by the name of *Bronze Arrow* which fell at the Last in a novice hurdle race at Wincanton for maidens at starting. I had this thing to Eighty Quid at the remunerative odds of eleven-double-one-to-two against. Approaching the Last *Bronze Arrow* is steadily increasing his lead to Fifteen Lengths ... Fallen at the Last number two *Bronze Arrow*. This type of occurrence is most perplexing. One scarcely conceives of the ideal method of tackling such an item. But: regarding Description; the best Description of such an item is Ach, Fuck that for a Game.

Agnes Owens

Agnes Owens

Arabella

Arabella pushed the pram up the steep path to her cottage. It was hard going since the four dogs inside were a considerable weight. She admonished one of them which was about to jump out. The dog thought better of it and sat down again. The others were sleeping, covered with her best coat which was a mass of dog hairs; the children, as she preferred to call them, always came first with her. Most of her Social Security and the little extra she earned was spent on them. She was quite satisfied with her diet of black sweet tea and cold sliced porridge kept handy while her children dined on mince, liver and chops.

The recent call on her parents had been depressing. Loyal though she was, she had to admit they were poor company nowadays. Her bedridden father had pulled the sheet over his face when she had entered. Her mother had sat bent and tightlipped over the fire, occasionally throwing on a lump of coal, while she tried to interest them in the latest gossip; but they never uttered a word except for the terse question "When are you leaving?" — and the bunch of dandelions she had gathered was straight away flung into the fire. Arabella had tried to make the best of things, giving her father a kiss on his lips before she left, but he was so cold he could have been dead. She had patted her mother on the head, but the response was a spittle which slid down her coat like a fast-moving snail.

Back inside her cottage she hung her hat on a peg and looked around with a certain amount of distaste. She had to admit the place was a mess compared to her mother's bare boards, but then her mother had no children to deal with. Attempting to tidy it up she swept a pile of bones and bits of porridge lying on the floor into a pail. Then she flung the contents on to a jungle of weeds outside her door. Good manure, she thought, and didn't she have the loveliest dandelions for miles.

"Children," she called. "Come and get your supper."

The dogs jumped out of the pram, stretching and yawning nervously. One dragged itself around. It was the youngest and never felt well. Arabella's training methods were rigorous. This had been a difficult one at first, but the disobedience was soon curbed — though now it was always weak and had no appetite. The other three ate smartly with stealthy looks at Arabella. Her moods were unpredictable and often violent. However, she was tired out now from her chores and decided to rest. She lay down on top of a pile of coats on the bed, arranging her long black dress carefully — the dogs had a habit of sniffing up her clothes if given half a chance. Three dogs jumped up beside her and began to lick her face and whine. The one with no appetite abandoned its mince and crawled under the bed.

Arabella awoke with a start. Her freshened mind realized there was some matter hanging over it, to which she must give some thought. It was the letter she had received two days previously, which she could not read. Her parents had never seen the necessity for schooling and so far Arabella had managed quite well without it. Her reputation as a healer was undisputed and undiminished by the lack of education. In fact, she had a regular clientele of respectable gentlemen who called upon her from time to time to have their bodies relaxed by a special potion of cow dung, mashed snails or frogs, or whatever dead creature was handy. Strangely enough, she never had female callers. (Though once Nellie Watkins, desperate to get rid of the warts on her neck, had called on her to ask for a cure. Whatever transpired was hearsay, but the immediate outcome of it was that Nellie had poured the potion over Arabella, threatening to have her jailed. But she never did. Arabella's power was too strong.)

The councillor's son, who had been the caller on the evening after she received the letter, explained that it was from the Sanitary Inspector and more or less stated that if she didn't get rid of her animals and clean her place up she would be put out of her home. Then he changed the subject since he knew it would be out of the question for Arabella to clean anything, that was one thing beyond her powers, saying, "Now we have had our fun get me some water – that is if you use such a commodity. I know soap is not possible." And while Arabella fetched the water lying handy in an empty soup tin on the sink, he took a swallow from a small bottle in his jacket pocket to pull himself together. Arabella did not like the tone of the letter. Plaintively she asked, "What will I do, Murgatroyd?"

"That's your worry," he replied, as he put on his trousers. "Anyway the smell in this place makes me sick. I don't know what's worse – you or the smell."

"Now, now, Murgatroyd," said Arabella reprovingly, pulling a black petticoat over her flabby shoulders, "you know you always feel better after your treatment. Don't forget the children's money box on your way out."

Murgatroyd's final advice, before he left, was, "Try your treatment on the Sanitary Inspector when he calls. It might work wonders."

After giving this matter a lot of thought and getting nowhere she decided to call on her parents again. They were rather short on advice nowadays, but she still had faith in their wisdom.

Her mother was still huddled over the fire and she noticed with vague surprise that her father did not draw the sheet over his face. Optimistically, she considered that he could be in a good mood.

"Mummy, I'm sorry I had no time to bring flowers, but be a dear and tell me the best way to get rid of Sanitary Inspectors."

Her mother did not move a muscle, or say a word.

"Tell me what to do," wheedled Arabella. "Is it chopped worms with sheep's dropping or rat's liver with bog myrtles?"

Her mother merely threw a lump of coal on to the fire. Then she softened. "See your father," she replied.

Arabella leapt over to the bed and almost upset the stained pail lying beside it. She took hold of her father's hand, which was dangling down loosely. She clasped it to her sagging breast and was chilled by its icy touch, so she hurriedly flung the hand back on the bed saying, "Daddy darling, what advice can you give your little girl on how to get rid of Sanitary Inspectors?"

He regarded her with a hard immovable stare then his hand slid down to dangle again. She looked at him thoughtfully and pulled the sheet over his face. "Mummy, I think Daddy is dead."

Her mother took out a pipe from her pocket and lit it from the fire with a long taper. After puffing for a few seconds, she said, "Very likely."

Arabella realized that the discussion was over. "Tomorrow I will bring a wreath for Daddy," she promised as she quickly headed for the door. "I have some lovely dandelions in my garden."

Back home again, Arabella studied her face in a cracked piece of mirror and decided to give it a wash. She moved a

damp smelly cloth over it, which only made the seams of
dirt show up more clearly. Then she attempted to run a
comb through her tangled mass of hair, but the comb
snapped. Thoroughly annoyed, she picked out a fat louse
from a loose strand of hair and crushed it with her
fingernails. Then she sat down on the bed and brooded. So
engrossed was she in her worry she forgot to feed her
children, who by this time were whining and squatting in
corners to relieve themselves. She couldn't concentrate
on making their food, so she took three of them outside
and tied them to posts. The fourth one, under the bed,
remained very still. Eventually she decided the best thing to
do was to have some of her magical potion ready, though
such was her state of mind that she doubted its efficiency in
the case of Sanitary Inspectors. Besides, there was no
guarantee he suffered from afflictions. Sighing, she went
outside. Next to her door stood a large barrel where she
kept the potion. She scooped a portion of the thick
evil-smelling substance into a delve jar, stirred it up a bit to
get the magic going, then returned indoors and laid it in
readiness on the table. She was drinking a cup of black
sweet tea when the knock came on the door. Smoothing
down her greasy dress and taking a deep breath to calm
herself, she opened it.

The small man confronting her had a white wizened face
under a large bowler hat.

"Please enter," requested Arabella regally. With head
held high she turned into the room. The Sanitary Inspector
tottered on the doorstep. He had not been feeling well all
day. Twenty years of examining fœtid drains and infested
dwellings had weakened his system. He had another five
years to go before he retired, but he doubted he would last
that long.

"Please sit down," said Arabella, motioning to an orange
box and wondering how she could broach the subject of
cures before he could speak about his business. She could

see at a glance that this was a sick man, though not necessarily one who would take his clothes off. The Sanitary Inspector opened his mouth to say something but found that he was choking and everything was swimming before him. He had witnessed many an odious spectacle in his time but this fat sagging filthy woman with wild tangled hair and great staring eyes was worse than the nightmares he often had of dismembered bodies in choked drains. Equally terrible was the smell, and he was a connoisseur in smells. He managed to seat his lean trembling shanks on the orange box and found himself at eye level with a delve jar in the centre of a wooden table. Again he tried to speak but his mouth appeared to be full of poisonous gas.

"My good man," said Arabella, genuinely concerned when she saw his head swaying, "I can see you are not well and it so happens I am a woman of great powers."

She knew she had no time for niceties. Quickly she undressed and stood before him as guileless as a June bride. The small man reeled. This grotesque pallid flesh drooping sickly wherever possible was worse than anything he had ever witnessed.

"Now just take your clothes off, and you'll soon feel better," said Arabella in her most winsome tone. "I have a magical potion here that cures all ailments and eases troubled minds." So saying, she turned and gave him a close-up view of her monumental buttocks. She dipped her fingers in the jar and tantalizingly held out a large dollop in front of his nose. It was too much for him. His heart gave a dreadful lurch. He hiccuped loudly, then his head sagged on to his chest.

Arabella was very much taken aback. Nothing like this had ever happened before, though it had been obvious to her when she first saw him that he was an inferior type. She rubbed the ointment on her fingers off on the jar, then dressed. The manner in which he lay, limp and dangling, reminded her of her father. This man must be dead, but even dead, he was a nuisance. She would have to get rid of him quickly if she didn't want it to get around that her powers were waning. Then she remembered the place where she had buried some of her former children and considered that he would fit into the pram – he was small enough. Yet it was all so much bother and very unpleasant and unpleasantness always wore her out.

She went outside to take a look at the pram. The dogs were whining and pulling on the fence. Feeling ashamed by her neglect she returned to fetch their supper, when the barrel caught her eye. Inspiration came to her in a flash. The barrel was large – it was handy – and there would be an extra fillip added to the ointment. She felt humbled by the greatness of her power.

Cheerfully she approached the figure slumped like a rag doll against the table. It was easy to drag him outside, he was so fragile. Though he wasn't quite dead because she heard him whisper, "Sweet Jesus, help me." This only irritated her. She could have helped him if he had let her. She dragged his unresisting body towards the barrel and with no difficulty toppled him inside to join the healing ointment. With a sigh of satisfaction she replaced the lid. As usual everything had worked out well for her.

Bus Queue

The boy was out of breath. He had been running hard. He reached the bus stop with a sinking heart. There was only a solitary woman waiting – the bus must have gone.

"Is the bus away missus?" he gasped out. The woman regarded him coldly. "I really couldn't say," then drew the collar of her well-cut coat up round her face to protect herself against the cold wind blowing through the broken panes of the bus shelter. The boy rested against the wire fence of the adjacent garden taking in long gulps of air to ease the harshness in his lungs. Anxiously he glanced around when two middle-aged females approached and stood within the shelter.

"My it's awfy cauld the night," said one. The well-dressed woman nodded slightly, then turned her head away.

"Ah hope that bus comes soon," said the other woman to her companion, who replied, "The time you have to wait would sicken ye if you've jist missed one."

"I wonder something is not done about it," said the well-dressed woman sharply, turning back to them.

"Folks hiv been complainin' for years," was the cheerful reply, "but naebody cares. Sometimes they don't come this way at all, but go straight through by the main road. It's always the same for folk like us. If it was wan o' these

high-class districts like Milngavie or Bearsden they wid
soon smarten their ideas."

At this point a shivering middle-aged man joined them.
He stamped about impatiently with hands in pockets. "Bus
no' due yet Maggie?" he asked one of the women.

"Probably overdue."

Her friend chipped in, "These buses would ruin your life.
We very near missed the snowball in the bingo last week
through the bloody bus no' comin'." The man nodded with
sympathy.

"Gaun to the bingo yersel' Wullie?"

"Naw. Ah'm away to meet ma son. He's comin' hame on
leave and is due in at the Central Station. Ah hope this bus
comes on time or Ah might miss him."

"Oh aye – young Spud's in the army ower in Belfast. It
must be terrible there."

"Better that than bein' on the dole."

"Still Ah widny like bein' in Belfast wi' all that bombin'
and murder."

"Oor Spud's got guts," said the man proudly.

The boy leaning on the fence began to sway back and
forth as if he was in some private agony.

The well-dressed woman said loudly, "I shouldn't wonder if that fence collapses."

The other three looked over at the boy. The man said,
"Here son, you'll loosen that fence if you don't stop yer
swingin'."

The boy looked back in surprise at being addressed. He
gradually stopped swaying, but after a short time he began
to kick the fence with the backs of his heels as if he was
obliged to keep moving in some way.

"You wid think the young wans nooadays all had St Vitus
dance," remarked the man.

The well-dressed woman muttered, "Hooligans."

It was now becoming dark and two or three more
people emerged from the shadows to join the queue. The

general question was asked if the bus was away, and answered with various pessimistic speculations.

"Hi son," someone called, "you'd better join the queue." The boy shook his head in the negative, and a moody silence enveloped the gathering. Finally it was broken by a raucous female voice saying, "Did you hear aboot Bella's man? Wan night he nivver came hame. When he got in at eight in the morning she asked him where hud he been. Waitin' for a bus, said he."

Everyone laughed except the well-dressed woman and the boy, who had not been listening.

"Look, there's a bus comin' up," spoke a hopeful voice. "Maybe there will be wan doon soon."

"Don't believe it," said another, "Ah've seen five buses go up at times and nothin' come doon. In this place they vanish into thin air."

"Bring back the Pakkies," someone shouted.

"They're all away hame. They couldny staun the pace."

"Don't believe it. They're all licensed grocers noo."

"You didny get ony cheap fares aff the Pakkies, but at least their buses were regular."

Conversation faded away as despondency set in. The boy's neck was painful from looking up the street. Suddenly he stiffened and drew himself off the fence when two youths came into view. They walked straight towards him and stood close, one at each side.

"You're no' feart," said one with long hair held in place with a bandeau.

"How?" the boy answered hoarsely.

"The Rock mob know whit to expect if they come oot here."

"Ah wis jist visitin' ma bird."

"Wan of oor team is in hospital because of the Rock. Twenty-four stitches he's got in his face – hit wi' a bottle."

"Ah had nothin' to dae wi' that."

"You were there, weren't ye?"

"Ah didny know big Jake wis gaun tae put a bottle on him."

"Neither did oor mate."

All this was said in whispers.

"Hey yous," said an irate woman, "Ah hope you don't think you're gaun tae jump the queue when the bus comes."

"That's all right," said the one with the bandeau. "We're jist talkin' tae oor mate. We'll get to the end when the bus comes."

The crowd regarded them with disapproval. On the other side of the fence where the youths were leaning, a dog which was running about the garden began to bark frantically at the bus queue.

"Shut yer noise," someone shouted, which incensed the dog further. One of the youths aimed a stone at its back. The bark changed to a pained howl and the dog retreated to a doorstep to whimper pitifully for some minutes.

"Nae need for that," said the man, as murmurs of sympathy were taken up for the dog.

"This generation has nae consideration for anyone noo-adays," a voice declared boldly.

"Aye, they wid belt you as soon as look at you."

Everyone stared hard at the youths as if daring them to start belting, but the youths looked back with blank expressions.

"They want to join the army like ma son," the man said in a loud voice. "He disny have it easy. Discipline is what he gets and it's done him the world of good."

"Ower in Ireland, that's where Wullie's son is," declared one of the women who had joined the queue early.

"Poor lad," said the woman with the raucous voice, "havin' to deal wi' the murderin' swine in that place. They should send some o' these young thugs here tae Ireland. They'd soon change their tune."

"They wid be too feart to go," the man replied. "They've nae guts for that sort of thing."

At this point the youth in the middle of the trio on the fence was reflecting on the possibility of asking the people in the queue for help. He considered that he was safe for the moment but when the bus came he would be forced to enter and from then on he would be trapped with his escorts. But he didn't know how to ask for help. He suspected they wouldn't listen to him, judging by their comments. Even if the bizzies were to pass by at this moment, what could he say. Unless he got the boot or the knife they would only laugh.

Then someone shouted, "Here's the bus," and the queue cheered. The blood drained from the youth's face.

"Mind yous two," said a warning voice as the bus moved up to the stop, "the end of the queue."

"That lad in the middle can get to the front. He was wan o' the first here," a kindly voice spoke. The well-dressed woman was the first to climb aboard, saying, "Thank goodness."

"That's O.K.," said the youth with the bandeau, "we're all gettin' on together," as both he and his mate moved in front of the other youth to prevent any attempt on his part to break into the queue.

"Help me mister!" he shouted, now desperate. "These guys will not let me on." But even as he said this he knew it sounded feeble. The man glanced over but only momentarily. He had waited too long for the bus to be interested. "Away and fight like ma son," was his response. In a hopeless attempt the youth began punching and kicking at his guards when everyone was on. The faces of those who were seated peered out at the commotion. The driver started up the engine in an effort to get away quickly. One of the youths shouted to his mate as he tried to ward off the blows. "Quick, get on. We're no' hingin aboot here all night." He had already received a painful kick which took the breath from him. The one with the bandeau had a split second to make up his mind, but he was reluctant to let his victim go without some kind of vengeance for his mate in hospital. Whilst dodging wild punches from the enemy he managed to get his hand into his pocket. It fastened on a knife. In a flash he had it out and open. He stuck it straight into the stomach of the youth. His companion who had not noticed this action pulled him on to the platform of the bus just as it was moving away.

"Get aff," shouted the driver, angry but unable to do anything about it. The other youth, bleeding, staggered against the fence, immersed in a sea of pain. The last words he heard when the bus moved away were, "Ah wis jist waitin' on wan number – " Then he heard no more. Someone peering out of the back window said, "There's a boy hingin ower the fence. Looks as if he's hurt bad."

"Och they canny fight for nuts nooadays. They should be in Belfast wi' ma son."

"True enough." The boy was dismissed from their thoughts. They were glad to be out of the cold and on their way.

Getting Sent For

Mrs Sharp knocked timidly on the door marked 'Headmistress'.

"Come in," a cool voice commanded.

She shuffled in, slightly hunched, clutching a black plastic shopping bag and stood waiting for the headmistress to raise her eyes from the notebook she was engrossed in.

"Do sit down," said the headmistress when Mrs Sharp coughed apologetically.

Mrs Sharp collapsed into a chair and placed her bag between her feet. The headmistress relinquished the notebook with a sigh and began.

"I'm sorry to bring you here, but recently George has become quite uncontrollable in class. Something will have to be done."

Mrs Sharp shifted about in the chair and assumed a placating smile.

"Oh dear – I thought he was doing fine. I didn't know – "

"It's been six months since I spoke to you," interrupted the headmistress, "and I'm sorry to say he has not improved one bit. In fact he's getting steadily worse."

Mrs Sharp met the impact of the gold-framed spectacles nervously as she said, "It's not as if he gets away with anything at home. His Da and me are always on at him, but he pays no attention."

The headmistress's mouth tightened. "He will just have to pay attention."

"What's he done this time?" Mrs Sharp asked with a surly edge to her voice.

"He runs in and out of class when the teacher's back is turned and distracts the other children."

Mrs Sharp eased out her breath. "Is that all?"

The headmistress was incredulous. "Is that all? With twenty-five pupils in a class, one disruptive element can ruin everything. It's difficult enough to push things into their heads as it is – " She broke off.

"Seems to me they're easily distracted," said Mrs Sharp.

"Well children are, you know." The headmistress allowed a frosty smile to crease her lips.

"Maybe he's not the only one who runs about," observed Mrs Sharp mildly.

"Mrs Sharp, I assure you George is the main trouble-maker, otherwise I would not have sent for you."

The light from the headmistress's spectacles was as blinding as a torch.

Mrs Sharp shrank back. "I'm not meaning to be cheeky, but George isn't a bad boy. I can hardly credit he's the worst in the class."

The headmistress conceded, "No, I wouldn't say he's the worst. There are some pupils I've washed my hands of. As yet there's still hope for George. That's why I sent for you. If he puts his mind to it he can work quite well, but let's face it, if he's going to continue the way he's doing, he'll end up in a harsher place than this school."

Mrs Sharp beamed as if she was hearing fulsome praise. "You mean he's clever?"

"I wouldn't say he's clever," said the headmistress cautiously, "but he's got potential. But really," she snapped, "it's more his behaviour than his potential that worries us."

Mrs Sharp tugged her wispy hair dreamily. "I always knew George had it in him. He was such a bright baby. Do you know he opened his eyes and stared straight at me when he was a day old. Sharp by name, and sharp by nature – that's what his Da always said."

"That may be," said the headmistress, taking off her spectacles and rubbing her eyes, "but sharp is not what I'm looking for."

Then, aware of Mrs Sharp's intent inspection of her naked face, she quickly replaced them, adding, "Another thing. He never does his homework."

"I never knew he got any," said Mrs Sharp, surprised. "Mind you we've often asked him 'Don't you get any homework?' and straight away he answers 'We don't get any' – "

The headmistress broke in. "He's an incorrigible liar."

"Liar?" Mrs Sharp clutched the collar of her bottle-green coat.

"Last week he was late for school. He said it was because you made him stay and tidy his room."

Mrs Sharp's eyes flickered. "What day was that?"

"Last Tuesday." The headmistress leaned over her desk. "Did you?"

"I don't know what made him say that," said Mrs Sharp in wonderment.

"Because he's an incorrigible liar."

Mrs Sharp strove to be reasonable. "Most kids tell lies now and again to get out of a spot of bother."

"George tells more lies than most – mind you," the headmistress's lips twisted with humour, "we were all amused at the idea of George tidying, considering he's the untidiest boy in the class."

Mrs Sharp reared up. "Oh, is he? Well let me tell you he's tidy when he leaves the house. I make him wash his face and comb his hair every day. How the devil should I know what he gets up to when he leaves?"

"Keep calm, Mrs Sharp. I'm sure you do your best under
the circumstances."

"What circumstances?"

"Don't you work?" the headmistress asked pleasantly.

Mrs Sharp sagged. She had a presentiment of doom. Her
husband had never liked her working. 'A woman's place is
in the home,' he always said when any crisis arose – despite
the fact that her income was a necessity.

"Yes," she said.

"Of course," said the headmistress, her spectacles
directed towards the top of Mrs Sharp's head, "I understand that many mothers work nowadays, but unfortunately they are producing a generation of latch-key children
running wild. Far be it for me to judge the parents'
circumstances, but I think a child's welfare comes first."
She smiled toothily. "Perhaps I'm old-fashioned, but – "

"I suppose you're going to tell me a woman's place is in
the home?" asked Mrs Sharp, through tight lips.

"If she has children, I would say so."

Mrs Sharp threw caution to the wind. "If I didn't work
George wouldn't have any uniform to go to school with – "

She broke off at the entrance of an agitated tangle-
haired young woman.

"I'm sorry Miss McHare," said the young woman, "I
didn't know you were with someone – "

"That's all right," said the headmistress. "What is it?"

"It's George Sharp again."

"Dear, dear!" The headmistress braced herself while
Mrs Sharp slumped.

"He was fighting, in the playground. Ken Wilson has a
whopper of an eye. Sharp is outside. I was going to send
him in, but if you're engaged – "

The headmistress addressed Mrs Sharp. "You see what I
mean. It just had to be George again."

She turned to the young teacher. "This is George's
mother."

"Good morning," said the young teacher, without enthusiasm.

"How do you know George started it?" asked Mrs
Sharp, thrusting her pale face upwards. The headmistress
stiffened. She stood up and towered above Mrs Sharp like a
female Gulliver. Mrs Sharp pointed her chin at a right angle
in an effort to focus properly.

The headmistress ordered, "Bring the boy in."

George Sharp shuffled in, tall and gangling, in contrast to
his hunched mother, who gave him a weak smile when he
looked at her blankly.

"Now," said the headmistress, "I hear you've been
fighting."

George nodded.

"You know fighting is forbidden within these grounds."

"Ken Wilson was fighting as well," he replied hoarsely,
squinting through strands of dank hair.

"Ken Wilson is a delicate boy who does not fight."

"He kicked me," George mumbled, his eyes swivelling
down to his sandshoes.

The headmistress explained to no one in particular, "Of
course George is not above telling lies."

Mrs Sharp rose from her chair like a startled bird.
"Listen son, did that boy kick you?"

"Yes Ma," George said eagerly.

"Where?"

He pointed vaguely to his leg.

"Pull up your trouser."

George did so.

"Look," said Mrs Sharp triumphantly, "that's a black and
blue mark."

"Looks more like dirt," tittered the young teacher.

"Dirt is it?" Mrs Sharp rubbed the mark. George winced.

"That's sore."

"It's a kick mark. Deny it if you can."

"Come now," said the headmistress, "we're not in a

courtroom. Besides, whether it's a kick mark or not doesn't prove a thing. Possibly it was done in retaliation. Frankly I don't see Ken Wilson starting it. He hasn't got the stamina."

"Is that so?" said Mrs Sharp. "I know Ken Wilson better than you, and he's no better than any other kid when it comes to starting fights. He's well known for throwing stones and kicking cats – "

The headmistress intervened. "In any case this is beside the point. I brought you here to discuss George's behaviour in general, and not this matter in particular."

"And bloody well wasted my time," retorted Mrs Sharp.

The headmistress's mouth fell open at the effrontery. She turned to the young teacher.

"You may go now, Miss Tilly," adding ominously to George, "You too, Sharp. I'll deal with you later."

George gave his mother an anguished look as he was led out.

"Don't worry," she called to him.

The headmistress said, "I don't know what you mean by that, because I think your son has plenty to worry about."

Mrs Sharp stood up placing her hands on her hips. Her cheeks were now flushed.

"You know what I think – I think this is a case of persecution. I mean the way you carried on about George fighting just proves it. And all this guff about him distracting the class – well if that flibbery gibbery miss is an example of a teacher then no wonder the class is easily distracted. Furthermore," she continued wildly before the headmistress could draw her breath, "I'll be writing to the authorities to let them know how my son is treated. Don't think they won't be interested because all this bullying in school is getting a big write-up nowadays."

"How dare you talk to me like that," said the headmistress, visibly white round the nose. "It's your son who is the bully."

Mrs Sharp jeered, "So now he's a bully. While you're at it is there anything else? I suppose if you had your way he'd be off to a remand home."

"No doubt he'll get there of his own accord."

The remark was lost on Mrs Sharp, now launched into a tirade of reprisal for all injustices perpetrated against working-class children and her George in particular. The headmistress froze in the face of such eloquence, which was eventually summed up by the final denunciation:

"So if I was you I'd hand in my notice before all this happens. Anyway you're getting too old for the job. It stands to reason your nerves are all shook up. It's a well-known fact that spinster teachers usually end cracking up and being carted off."

The change in their complexions was remarkable. The headmistress was flushed purple with rage and Mrs Sharp was pallid with conviction.

There was a space of silence. Then the headmistress managed to say, "Get out – before I call the janitor."

Mrs Sharp gave a hard laugh. "Threats is it now? Still I'm not bothered, for it seems to me you've got all the signs of cracking up right now. By the way if you lay one finger on George I'll put you on a charge."

She flounced out of the room when the headmistress picked up the telephone, and banged the door behind her. The headmistress replaced the receiver without dialling, then sat down at the desk with her head in her hands, staring at the open notebook.

Outside Mrs Sharp joined a woman waiting against the school railings, eating crisps.

"How did you get on?" the woman asked.

Mrs Sharp rummaged in her plastic bag and brought out a packet of cigarettes. Before she shoved one into her mouth she said, "Tried to put me in my place she did – well I soon showed her she wasn't dealing with some kind of underling – "

The woman threw the empty crisp packet on to the grass.

"What about George?"

Mrs Sharp looked bitter. "See that boy – he's a proper devil. Wait till I get him home and I'll beat the daylights out of him. I'll teach him to get me sent for."

Commemoration Day

Molly strolled through the gates of the big city park possessed by a mild sense of adventure after she had cashed her Giro and purchased twenty cigarettes instead of her usual ten. She walked over the grass to the pond and watched children throw bread at the ducks but the wind blowing over the water was too keen for comfort. She moved onwards, tightening the belt of her skimpy yellow raincoat that clung to her lumpy hips like orange peel. A stone thrown by one of the children skimmed close to her fat legs. When she reached the protective shrubbery of the gardens she allowed herself the luxury of a few puffs. She studied tags tied to foreign-looking plants and was none the wiser. When she pulled on a bud about to bloom into some mysterious flower, the stem broke. Guiltily she threw it down. Following a side path in the hope of finding someone to chat with, even if only about the weather, she almost collided with a young man running hard towards her. As they stood, nearly eye to eye, she saw he looked as startled as she felt, but when she stepped aside to let him pass he asked harshly, "What's the time missus?"

"Half-past two," she said, glancing at her watch and not liking the word 'missus' or anything else about him.

"Is that all?"

"My watch keeps good time," said Molly coldly.

"Got a match on you?"

"I have not." A right ignorant one, she thought, with his spiky hair and hollow-cheeked face. He stroked his chin nervously and she noticed a jagged cut on the back of his hand. She said, "You've a bad gash there."

He looked at it. "Must have caught it on barbed wire." He stared behind him.

She said, "Better get it seen to," and added, "Where does this path lead?"

He put his damaged hand in the pocket of his crumpled jacket. "I wouldn't go up there if I was you." His voice was threatening.

Molly retorted, "I can go wherever I like. It's no business of yours."

"Please yourself, but the north lodge is closed to the public. One of the upper crust, Sir Peter Carlin himself, is exercising his horses, as if the old bastard didn't have anything else to do."

"Perhaps he hasn't. Anyway," she added suspiciously, "how come you were up there?"

"I wasn't. They chased me."

She softened at the information. "Oh well," she laughed, "no doubt the rich have got their troubles, like the poor."

"Not quite the same though."

"Trouble is trouble, no matter who you are." She looked him over considering he was a poor-looking specimen, but that was the style of them nowadays, seedy and ill-mannered.

"True." He nodded his head.

"And I've had mine, I can tell you."

"How's that," he asked, twisting his head backwards.

"When you've lost a husband and a son in the space of a year, there's not much left to worry about." She was aware this fellow wasn't all that interested by the jerky look of him, but she was glad of the casual way she could say this now.

"Hmm," he muttered, then, "God, I wish I had a match."

She searched in her bag and threw him a box. He lit a half-smoked cigarette and returned the box, grunting something which could have been thanks.

"Better get that seen to." She touched his hand.

"It's only a scratch."

Fumbling again in her bag, she brought out a neatly ironed handkerchief. "Tie that round your hand anyway. It will keep it clean."

"It doesn't matter," he said, backing away.

Molly shrugged and shifted about to ease her aching legs. The young man drew fiercely on the butt end of the cigarette then stamped it into the ground and shivered violently. "Do you feel all right?" she said.

"I feel fine."

"You look cold. I just wondered – "

"I had a dose of the flu recently. It's left me dizzy. Is that O.K. with you?"

"It's no concern of mine," she said coolly and made to move onwards.

He tugged at the sleeve of her coat. "Sorry missus. No offence meant. It's just that I've had a rotten day."

She studied his thin hard face. If Tommy had lived he would have been about this fellow's age, otherwise there was no comparison. Tommy had been fresh-faced and handsome, though not at the end.

"That's all right. We all have our off days," but she kept on walking.

"You haven't a fag on you?" he asked, catching up.

She stopped and gave him one. He accepted it without any kind of thanks. His hand shook.

"Not in trouble are you?" she asked.

"Trouble?" he repeated.

"It's not unusual nowadays."

He regarded her with a blank expression, then smiled crookedly. He put the cigarette in his pocket.

"Aren't you going to smoke that?"

"Later."

Like a mother and son on an enforced outing they continued to walk together back along the path leading out to the open park.

"Working are you?" Molly asked by way of conversation.

"No."

"That's the style of things nowadays – "

"I expect I'll get something soon," he said. "I hate all this hanging about. It stinks." He mumbled this as if he was speaking to himself rather than her.

"I can understand."

"Can you?" he said bitterly.

Molly wished she was back home with a pot of tea on the boil. This young man's presence was worse than none at all. She'd be better off listening to the news on the radio, and that was bad enough.

"I don't think you do," he added.

"Listen," she said, stopping short, "don't talk to me about understanding. I've had enough of that. My husband and my son used to say, 'Keep out of our affairs – you just don't understand.' Well they're both gone. One died for nothing and the other from drink, and here I am, still not understanding." She quickened her footsteps out of anger but he kept pace with her easily.

"Sorry missus," he said.

"It wasn't only the drink though," she said, turning to her companion, "I've no doubt his heart was broken, my husband's I mean, after Tommy was gone."

"Tommy?"

She sighed. "I don't want to talk about it any more."

They walked on in silence. Molly judged that in another ten minutes she would be out of the park and on her way home – a pity the excursion had done nothing for her at all, and by the look of it, this one at her side was no happier than she was – poor sod, at his age too.

"I suppose you young ones have a lot to be bitter about – no work, no future, nothing to do," she said giving him a sidelong glance.

He shrugged, looked behind him, then asked again, "What's the time now?"

"Twenty to," she informed him, adding, "Meeting someone?"

"Maybe."

She thought possibly he wasn't all there in the head. People like that sometimes had a passion for wanting to know the time as if there was nothing else to care about.

"They might be looking for someone in Maloney's bar. If you like I'll put in a word for you. I used to work there. Maloney would listen to me." After a pause she added, "He liked my Tommy."

"I've heard of Maloney," he said, without enthusiasm.

"It's good money and free drink, within reason."

"I don't drink."

"It's not a qualification." Molly considered with the face he had, as sour as piss, he'd as much chance as a snowball in hell with Maloney, then she tripped over a stone embedded in the grass.

"Watch out!" he said catching her elbow.

She laughed to cover her distaste at the touch of him saying, "Swollen feet, that's my problem."

"Hold on to my arm," he offered.

Amazed at his decency she complied, but when she discovered she was being led towards the duck pond she said, "I'd rather go home now, if you don't mind. I can manage fine."

"Wait a minute. I've a fancy to see the ducks," but he looked backwards as if he'd more of a fancy to see what was behind him. They reached the pond before she could think of the right words to allow her to head for the gate. It was deserted except for the ducks bobbing up and down in the water like plastic toys. Straight away the young man turned his back on them and looked over to the park gate, breaking her hold. "What's the time?" he asked.

"Nearly ten to." There was definitely something wrong. He was either mad or – her mind swivelled away from other possibilities as she knelt down and dipped her handkerchief in the edge of the water. Avoiding his face she stood up. "Wipe that cut. It's starting to bleed." He wiped his hand carelessly and threw the cloth into the water as if its crisp whiteness offended him.

"Did you have to do that?" Molly said, angered by the sight of the spreading piece of linen with the blue initial T embroidered on the corner attracting the ducks, which turned away fastidiously on closer investigation. His face remained pointing towards the gate like a dog that smells wind of a rabbit.

"I really must go," she snapped.

"No don't."

"Why shouldn't I?"

"You're Tommy's ma, aren't you?"

Molly held her breath. Her head swam and she felt sick, a sure sign of blood pressure. She closed her eyes until the nausea passed. "My son is dead."

"I know." His thin face appeared less harsh, almost sympathetic.

"What has he to do with you?" She wanted to strike the insinuating look from him.

"I never knew him really," he explained with his half smile, "but we are keeping faith with him. You might say this is his commemoration day."

A spasm of fury shook her. "Commemoration day?" she shouted. "Dear Christ, will it never end!" She looked upwards for a second then faced him steadily. "I'll tell you something. I don't want no commemoration for Tommy from you or those others. As far as I'm concerned he wasn't my son at the end, dying the way he did – poisoned with hatred and half mad, just like you."

His face was hard again. "I'm sorry you think that way missus, but it's nothing to do with you."

"Nothing to do with me? You knew who I was didn't you, else why have you clung to me like a limpet, talking about commemoration day."

The young man's eyes swivelled to the gate then back to her. "I hadn't a clue who you were. I only needed you for the time on your watch. I lost mine climbing over the barbed wire and I have to be at the gate on the hour to get picked up, otherwise I'm done for." His voice harshened. "So, what's the time now missus?"

In an exaggerated fashion Molly lifted up her arm and studied the watch.

"The time missus – the time." He stepped forward as if to grab her.

She laughed. "The time is it? I'm afraid I can't tell you that exactly, because you see my watch is always slow, I should think by quarter of an hour roughly. I should have got it fixed long ago but I'm never too concerned about what the exact minute is. It suits me, especially now Tommy and his Da have gone. Why should I care about the time?"

There was a space of silence during which Molly could observe the whites of the young man's eyes enlarge around the green and yellow flecked irises. She had always admired green eyes, yet Tommy's had been deep blue with long eyelashes. Probably this young man with the green eyes was going to choke the life out of her since he was done for anyway, but he just sighed then sat down on the wet grass, reclining on one elbow, staring over at the ducks still bobbing up and down like plastic toys. He looked ex-hausted. It was time to get going, thought Molly. There was nothing to be done, but she couldn't resist asking, "I suppose old Carlin won't be exercising his horses any more?"

"I reckon not," he said with his lop-sided smile. He sat up and searched in his pocket and brought out the cigarette she had given him earlier. It was crushed and bent. He threw it in the water. The ducks swam over. Before she left Molly handed him her cigarettes and matches. It was the least she could do. Now she dreaded going out into the street to hear the fearful whispers, the jubilant shouts and see the gloating eyes. It was all going to begin again.

The Silver Cup

If you glanced in at Sammy's room when the door was open it seemed to be on fire. This was the effect of the flame orange paint which he had stolen from a garage. The room was really as damp and fœtid as an old shed and contained a sagging bed, a set of drawers riddled with small holes caused by darts (not woodworm) and a carpet tramped free of its original pattern. Sammy liked his room. It was his territory and a haven to his friends who shared it with him most evenings from five to ten o'clock. The message on the outer panel of the door, 'KNOCK BEFORE ENTERING', was directed at his parents. Sammy's Ma did her best to comply with it. His Da was inclined to kick the door open if enraged by the noise coming from within, but usually ordered his wife to 'see what that bugger's up to' rather than risk raising his blood pressure to dangerous heights. Sammy's Da was not a happy man. He was banned from smoking and alcohol, was on an invalidity pension due to a poor heart condition from over-indulgence on both counts, and saw little in his son to give him pleasure. Yet pinned above the mantelpiece, the faded photo of himself when a youth was the spitting image of Sammy.

"Why don't you take your dinner beside us?" asked Sammy's Ma, entering his room with a tray of food after knocking.

"His face wastes my appetite," said Sammy sitting on the edge of his bed, wrapped in a multi-coloured sleeping bag, twanging his guitar. Sammy's Ma sighed.

"What a sight you look. If the cruelty man could see you – "

"Close the door behind you," said Sammy, his face invisible behind a fringe of hair.

Back in the living room she lifted her husband's plate the second he had mopped up the final trace of gravy with a chunk of bread.

"Going somewhere?" he asked, with a touch of sarcasm.

"I think I've left a pot on the gas," she explained, dashing through to the kitchenette where she felt safe amongst the unwashed dishes. She focused her thoughts on the evening ahead. The western film on the television was not to her taste but it should keep her husband quiet. He always maintained he liked a bit of action, but none of that lovey dovey stuff, nor plays that were all gab, nor anything which related to female predicaments. Sammy's Ma had learned to keep her mouth shut about what she liked. After the film he was certain to go to bed with, as he described it, brain fatigue, prompted by 'certain persons', whom she took to mean herself. Then, alone, she would sit through the remainder of the viewing, her eyes flickering between the clock and the set, marking time until twenty-past eleven when she would make herself a cup of tea. By half-past eleven she was back at her post, cup in hand, leaning towards the screen, all attention to the preacher on 'Late Call'. She considered his sermon as good as a tonic. If she closed her eyes she could imagine she was in church. Not that she ever attended church. Her husband viewed darkly any mission which necessitated her being gone from the house for more than an hour. Besides, her wardrobe was lacking in the formality required for such an occasion. 'Late Call', brief though it was, gave her an impression of being

part of a congregation listening and nodding in unison.
Sometimes, in a more fanciful mood, she imagined she was
sailing down the Mississippi in a steamboat while an invisible choir sang "We shall gather by the river", which was
strange, since she had never been further than the town-
head in all her fifteen years of marriage.

"Have you seen my good ball-point pen?"
Her husband's voice broke into her thoughts, causing
her to drop into the sink a plate, which immediately
cracked.
"Not recently."
She turned on the water forcefully to hide the ruined
plate.
"I've looked everywhere!" he shouted.
Sammy's Ma shook her head in despair. His pen, his
screwdriver, his socks, his heart pills, were just a few of the
articles which he lost daily.
"Have you tried behind the clock?"
"Everywhere, I told you," then he added, "except that
bugger's room."
"I don't think Sammy's in his room."
She had been dimly aware of a door slamming a while
back, which could have meant anything.
"All the better," said her husband, and strode off.
Sammy's Ma suspected the pen was an excuse for him to
search her son's room. Once he had found a heap of empty
beer cans and a half-full box of potato crisps under the bed.
"Thieving – that's what he's up to," had been his cry at the
time. Sammy's staunch denials and assertion that one of his
pals' uncle owned a licensed grocer's had not impressed
her husband. She was placing the cracked plate in the bin
when the roar came. When she entered Sammy's room her
husband was holding aloft a large trophy in the shape of a
silver cup. Senselessly she asked, "What is it?"
"What does it look like?" he thundered, pointing to an

inscription on the base which said 'PRESENTED TO THE PENSION CLUB BY COUNCILLOR HOOD'. Sammy's Ma placed her fingers on her lips, unable to speak.

"He'll not get away with this," said her husband.

She sat down on the bed feeling giddy. To rob a pension club was unforgivable. A football club was more acceptable, when one considered the risks.

"He'll do time," her husband stated with satisfaction.

In a feeble manner Sammy's Ma said, "But he's not old enough."

"He'll go to an approved school then."

"Oh no," she whispered, while her husband peered inside the cup, saying, "This must be worth a few bob."

Blinking rapidly Sammy's Ma chanced the suggestion, "Maybe if you returned it there might be a reward."

His eyes bulged. "Me – return it?"

"You could say you found it in a field when you were out for a walk."

"The only place I'm returning it to is the police station," he replied, banging down the trophy on the chest of drawers.

Sammy's Ma almost bit through her lip. She could picture the neighbours in the street watching Sammy being led into a police van. They would snigger, and look up at her window, and shake their heads as if it was only to be expected. She knew they talked about her. Once from her kitchenette window she heard a woman in the back green say to another, "That one upstairs is a proper misery. Never has a word to say and runs along the road on her shopping errands as if she hasn't a minute to spare." She also knew they nicknamed her the road runner. Desperately she blurted out, "If Sammy gets lifted they'll only say we're to blame, and you most of all because you're his Da. They'll say – "

She broke off when her husband punched the wall in anger.

"Who'll say?" he demanded.

Sammy's Ma shrugged her shoulders and closed her eyes for a second. She had a great wish to stretch out and sleep on this sagging but quite comfortable bed of Sammy's and forget it all, but a groan from her husband snapped her to attention. He was rubbing the knuckles of his right hand.

"Are you all right?" she asked dutifully.

He sat down beside her breathing heavily. "I'm never all right in this bloody house."

Surreptitiously Sammy's Ma moved away from the proximity of her husband's body. She stared at the cup on top of the drawers. To her it had the look of a memorial urn on a grave. Moved by the association she suggested sullenly, "Perhaps we should bury it."

"Bury him is more like it," said her husband lifting the cup from the drawers now with a proprietary air, and polishing it lightly with the cuff of his sleeve. He appeared calm and breathed normally. "Could be worth a few bob," he said again.

"I shouldn't wonder," agreed Sammy's Ma without enthusiasm.

For some moments her husband continued to polish the cup with one cuff then the other. Finally he cleared his throat and said, "Our Perry could do something with this."

"You don't mean he could sell it?"

"I'm not saying he could, but," he looked furtively towards his wife, "he knows all the fences."

"Fences?"

"Somebody who handles stolen goods."

"It wouldn't be right."

Her husband shouted, "God dammit woman we didn't lift it in the first place, but it's one way of getting rid of it with some money to the good!"

"I'm not bothering about money," said Sammy's Ma primly. "Besides, it will be traced with that writing on it."

Her husband wiped beads of sweat from his forehead.

"Silver can be melted down," he said through clenched teeth.

To placate his mounting wrath she said dubiously, "I suppose it's not the same as stealing a purse, but all the same they'll miss it."

"It will be insured. They can get another one." Her husband jumped violently to his feet. The rebound from the sagging mattress threw Sammy's Ma across the bed.

"I don't care what you say!" he said. "I'm getting rid of this cup the best way I can, even if it's only to see the look on that bugger's face when he discovers it's gone."

He slammed the door hard as he left as if to shut her in.

Back in the living room Sammy's Ma looked down from her window to the street opposite where a group of women sat on the steps outside their flat, chatting and laughing and carelessly exposing their legs beyond the limits of decency. She clutched her husband's small bottle of heart pills, which she had found behind the curtains. She was thinking that for once she would have them ready on his command, when Sammy suddenly appeared.

"Who's been in my room?" he asked vehemently.

"If you must know it was your Da," she replied, placing the pills in her apron pocket.

"What? Why?" he queried in a high-pitched tone. She regarded him sadly, standing with arms folded.

"B-but," Sammy spluttered, "you know my room is private."

"Better tell him that."

"Where is he?" said Sammy, jerking his head about.

"Out." She added, "Seems he found a big silver cup in your room. Thought he'd better get rid of it. Thinks it's worth money, so he took it to your Uncle Perry. Appears he can get in touch with a fence."

When Sammy remained open-mouthed, eyes as usual concealed behind his fringe, unresponsive to the statement, she said, "Imagine anyone being called a fence."

"It's not his cup to get rid of," Sammy finally gasped.

Sammy's Ma sniffed. "It's not yours either. Donated to the pension club it read."

Sammy punched the air and shouted, "It was a pal who left it here! He was taking it to the jeweller's to get the inscription fixed! He just left it while we went out for a gang bang with the guys up the lane."

Sammy's Ma wrinkled her forehead. "Gang bang?" she repeated.

"What am I going to tell him?" demanded Sammy.

"Tell him it's probably being melted down," said Sammy's Ma with a nervous snigger.

For a second her son stood as if turned to stone, then he was out of the room in one long stride shouting, "He'll go to jail for this."

Two minutes later the sound of raucous laughter came from his room. Apparently Sammy's pals had a sense of humour.

She checked the time on the clock on the mantelpiece. It would be a long wait for her tea before 'Late Call'. She decided to waive the rules and make it now. In any case the prospect of the religious programme had lost its appeal after all this stimulation. She longed to speak rather than listen. At the window again she sipped the tea and noticed only three women remained on the steps. They no longer laughed. One yawned as if bored. The other two stared in opposite directions in an estranged manner. Clearly they sought diversion. Sammy's Ma became quite giddy with the notion that seized her, which was to join them on their steps. The story of the silver cup was too good to keep to herself. They would appreciate the humour and the irony of it. The difficulty lay in the approach, since a bare "good morning" or "good afternoon" was the most she had ventured to any of them. Then she conceived a great idea.

She dashed into the kitchenette and quickly brewed three
cups of tea, which she placed on a tray and carried down
the stairs of her flat. She was crossing the street towards
the women, flushed and smiling, when her foot caught on
the grating of a drain close to the pavement. The cups
shattered on the ground, followed by the tray. As she bent
down to retrieve the one unbroken cup the pills fell from
her pocket through the bars of the drain. Peals of laughter
resounded in her ears like the bells of hell going tingalinga-
ling as described in the song. But the mocking women were
not unkind. Two of them arose from the steps and led her
back across the street. They escorted her up the stairs to
her flat saying, "You'll be all right."

"It's about this silver cup," she began when they pushed
her gently inside the door.

"I must tell you about this silver cup," she said again.

"Yes, yes," they soothed, placing her down on a chair
inside the living room, while they looked around furtively.

"I really must tell you about the silver cup," Sammy's Ma
insisted.

"Do you think we should phone for a doctor?" one
woman asked the other.

"Is your husband around, dear?" said the other to
Sammy's Ma.

They decided to leave when Sammy's Ma began to laugh
hysterically. On their way out they heard the discordant
strum of a guitar from Sammy's room. One of the women
tapped the side of her head significantly while she gave her
companion a meaningful glance. Softly they closed the door
behind them to create no disturbance, and tiptoed down
the stairs.

Fellow Travellers

Jean boarded the train standing at the station and pulled at the top of the sliding door to the empty compartment. It was stiff and hard to move but she wanted a few moments' privacy to assemble her thoughts. She settled down in a corner and opened her bag to take out cigarettes, then changed her mind. Her throat was as rough as sandpaper with the concentrated smoking of the morning. She peered through the smeared window. By the platform clock there were still five minutes before the train left. Now she was undecided. Should she go back? Perhaps she had acted hastily. She rose and hauled upon the compartment door again. As she stood wondering, the electrically controlled outer doors of the train slid shut. She pressed the button, but they held fast. It was disgraceful. How were people to get in or out. She banged on the window, but the platform was deserted. The doors opened and she was confused again. To return now was to admit defeat. She went back to her corner. To her chagrin a man and woman of advanced years got on. They dithered in the doorway of the compartment. The woman smiled at Jean. Jean's eyes dropped. Subdued, the couple settled for the seat adjacent, and spoke to each other in whispers. Then the whistle blew like a sigh of relief.

Just before the outer doors closed a man hurtled
through the compartment and threw himself at the seat
opposite Jean, breathless and unpleasantly close. He
bumped her knee. "Sorry," he leered. She had a quick
impression of dark hair and brown eyes. Before she could
draw her breath he had thrust a packet of cigarettes
towards her. Hypnotized by his forcefulness she took one.
With similar speed he produced a lighter and held it under
her nose.

"Damned cold," he stated with a cigarette dangling from
his lips. He leaned back and crossed his legs. The tip of his
shoe prodded her calf.

She nodded and withdrew her leg. His gaze veered over
to the couple then back.

"I'm bloody frozen," he said confidentially.

He shivered in an exaggerated way and blew his free
hand. She took an instant dislike to him, but what was
worse she suspected he had been drinking. The prospect of
being confined with this person for the half hour's journey
was daunting, but to move away seemed drastic. Besides,
she was smoking his cigarette.

"The weather's bloody awful," he complained.

She grunted something unintelligible. Her throat was
dry and her tongue fired with smoke.

"Going to the city?" he asked.

"Not exactly." She considered getting off at the next
stop, but then she would be landed in a village with nothing
to offer except the Railway Hotel.

"I'm going to see my brothers," he confided. "City
lads."

"I don't care for the city," she said, hoping to discourage
him.

"City folk are the best." His eyes were bold and
disturbing. The old couple were staring openly at them.

She backed down. "I've nothing against city people."

He leaned forward. "My family come from the city –

great people." He added, "And my father was born in the
city. He's been dead for ten years."

He sighed. Jean's eyes were glazed with apathy.

"Do you know," he said pointing his finger, "they had to
hold me back in the hospital when they told me he'd
snuffed it. One of the best, he was."

"Hmm," said Jean.

"He gave us everything. It wasn't easy, mind you." He
shook his head sadly, and ground his cigarette end into the
floor creating a black smear near her shoe. The train sped
through the start of the built-up area. Jean tried to calcu-
late the stops ahead of her.

Unthinkingly she took out her cigarettes, then felt
obliged to offer him one. He took it without saying thanks.

"I could get off at any stop and I would be sure to meet a
relative." He smirked and added, "Where are we anyway?"

They gazed through the window to multi-storey blocks
of flats flashing by.

"My uncle lives up there somewhere," he said.

"Fancy," she said, looking out to a field of cows.

"Do you remember Dickie Dado, the footballer?"

She lied. "Uh huh."

"He was my nephew – great player wasn't he?"

"Er – yes. I don't know much about football though."
She gave a depreciating giggle.

He glared at her. "He died two years ago. Surely you
knew that."

"I'm sorry. I didn't know." Jean's face reddened.

"The team was never the same."

He looked over at the old couple and raised his voice.

"To think he died at twenty-three and some of these old
fogeys go on for ever."

Jean pulled hard on her cigarette. The old man stiffened.
She concentrated on the view but she could feel her
companion's eyes probing through her skin.

"You wouldn't think I've got a great family of my own – would you?"

She was forced to confront his sly smile.

"No. I mean, have you?"

"Two girls and a boy. Marvellous kids."

The information angered her. So what? she wanted to scream. Then to add to her misery the train increased its speed and caused them to bump up and down together in a ridiculous fashion. She pressed herself back against the compartment wall as he lurched about slackly, giving off a sour smell of alcohol. Her cigarette fell from her fingers and rolled about the floor. Mercifully the bumping stopped. Jean wiped the sweat from her forehead.

He began again. "The wife says I shouldn't show any favouritism. She thinks because I bought the boy a fishing rod he's my favourite. It's not true you know." His eyes pleaded for justice.

To stop his flow of words she began in desperation, "I've got a headache, would you mind – "

He appeared not to have heard her.

"I bought the girls a teaset," he went on. "You should see them with it. They make me drink tea out of the wee cups – simply marvellous." He shook his head, overcome at the image.

"I see," said Jean letting her breath out slowly. Her eyes wavered towards the couple, who were whispering intently. She pulled herself together and stated in a loud voice, "I find families a complete bore."

"Never," he said, taken aback for the first time. "The trouble with people nowadays is they don't care enough about their families. Pure selfishness, that's what's wrong with everyone."

He looked over to the old couple for support but they were staring ahead with blank expressions.

He continued, "Take my girls, they're just great, and the boy as well. Mind you I don't show any favouritism – the wife's wrong, but she can be a bitch at times." His lips curled and he repeated, "A pure bitch."

"If your kids are so wonderful, why didn't you bring them with you," Jean snapped and looked upwards to check the position of the communication cord.

He spread his hands out and whined, "The wife wouldn't let me. I told you she's a pure bitch."

Jean felt worn out. The train was slowing down for the next stop.

"I think this must be Duntrochen," she mumbled, toying with the idea of getting off.

"Not this place," he said with authority.

As the train pulled out she spied the signboard.

"It was Duntrochen," she accused, and closed her eyes to avoid any further involvement. Her eyelids flickered as his leg brushed against hers. She was obliged to move. Her companion was staring over the top of her head when she faced him with fury. To sever all contact she turned to the woman sitting beyond.

"Very tiring these train journeys," she gabbled. The woman looked startled.

"Yes, they are," she stammered.

"I was really intending to get off at Duntrochen," Jean added, hoping to establish a safe relationship with the dreary pair.

"It's a one-eyed hole anyway," her brown-eyed companion stated.

Jean was trapped into answering, "That's a matter of opinion."

"My mother died in Duntrochen hospital."

Jean was prepared to sneer at this disclosure, but the couple were looking at him with concern.

"That's enough to put you off any place," the woman replied.

"She was a wonderful person. Brought up ten of us without any complaint."

The couple nodded with compassion. Jean pictured with contempt a family album portraying a white-haired woman with ten leering faces looking over her shoulder.

"She couldn't do enough for us," his voice jarred on.

Jean coughed and began searching in her handbag. Anything to distract her from the creeping weight of his words.

"Mind you, she liked her drink now and then."

The couple were definitely attracted by this news. Their eyes blinked rapidly as the image of the saintly mother changed to one of a boozy hag.

"It was her only pleasure."

"Amen," said Jean under her breath.

But the subject was not finished. He touched her knee and said, "He was never off her back, my old man."

For a hideous moment she thought he was making a sexual innuendo.

"Gave her a life of hell," he added.

"Oh you mean," Jean spoke in relief, "a kind of persecution – "

The woman tutted. Her husband looked ill at ease. Jean rejoiced at their discomfort.

"Not surprising," she said, addressing the couple.

Her companion gave her a hard look, but he let the remark pass, and stated, "She was one of the best."

"But," said Jean, determined now to expose his inanity, "you told me your father died ten years ago, and he was one of the best."

"That's right," he replied, defiant.

"Now you say he gave your mother a life of hell and she was one of the best. I don't follow you." She bestowed a knowing smile on the old couple, but they looked at her uncomprehendingly.

"She never complained," he said with the quiet triumph of one who holds the ace card.

Jean wiped her clammy hands on her skirt. She judged she could be on the verge of a nervous breakdown. The word Valium came into her head. Her friend Wilma took Valium pills regularly and she was in charge of a typing pool. They must work wonders. She decided to get off at the next stop, no matter where it was, and head for the nearest chemist. She stood up and tugged at the compartment door.

"What's the hurry," he called, but she was transfixed by the thought that she might have to get a doctor's prescription for Valium. As the train pulled up she was flung back almost on top of the woman.

"Are you all right?" the woman asked with concern.

"Yes," said Jean, pulling down her skirt. To justify her erratic behaviour she explained, "I thought I was going to be sick. I haven't felt well all morning."

"I see," said the woman darting a considerate glance in the direction of Jean's stomach. Jean shot up like a jack-in-the-box. A tic beat on her cheek and her mouth twitched.

"I must get out of here," she gabbled.

"Don't upset yourself." The woman pulled on her arm. Her grip was surprisingly strong.

Jean fell back on the seat. She explained in a heightened manner, "Not morning sickness – just ordinary average sick."

The woman patted her hand. Jean rounded on her with venom.

"I'm not even married."

The couple regarded each other with dismay. The brown-eyed man blew smoke through his nostrils.

"Of course," said Jean, forcing herself to be calm, "I think you are all off your rockers."

"Really," said the old man. His wife shook her head as if in warning. The other man continued to blow smoke like steams of fury.

"I thought it was bad enough listening to that loony," she gestured towards the other man, "but you two appear to be in your dotage."

The couple cowered close to the window. The man tapped his head significantly.

"Thank goodness I'm getting off here," Jean uttered wildly and charged out of the compartment. She alighted from the train without a clue to where she was.

"Ticket please," said the collector when she scuttled through the barrier. "Always have your ticket ready," he reproved as she fumbled in her bag.

She moved out of the station in a distraught manner. She hesitated, torn between the beckoning brightness of Woolworth's and a telephone box on the opposite pavement. She braced herself and headed for the box. She dialled a number and held the receiver to her ear. Almost immediately the voice spoke. She cut through the querulous preamble.

"It's me — Jean. I'm sorry I rushed out like that — " She paused to listen as the voice gained strength. "I know, mother," she replied wearily, "but you must understand I have to get out sometimes for a bit of relaxation. I won't be doing anything desperate. After all I'm not a teenager."

Her reflection in the stained mirror on a level with her eyes verified the statement, showing the marks of the crow's feet.

The voice began again like the trickle of a tap. Jean interrupted.

"Yes mother I'm fine. I won't be gone for ever you know. I'll be back around tea-time."

She replaced the telephone and stood for a moment within the box feeling she had placed herself beyond mercy. In retrospect the man with the brown eyes became desirable. He had spoken to her and touched her knee. In his inept way he had offered her an association. She should have been flattered if not actually grateful and really he had not been all that bad-looking. It would have been something to boast about to her friend Wilma, who according to herself was continually exposed to such encounters. When she stepped out of the telephone box she was shamed by the memory of her neurotic outburst. She walked along the pavement, head downwards, hunched against the cold – going nowhere.

McIntyre

After fifteen years I could scarcely credit my eyes when I saw McIntyre again. I had come to the meeting because I was lonely. It would pass a little time and I would at least be warm. The issue would be boring, but members were always welcome. McIntyre looked older than the fifteen years warranted. I hoped the same did not apply to me. I thought I did not look my age though in the mirror the sight of criss-cross lines round my eyes made me wonder. His hair was now sparse and his once ruddy complexion had a jaded look, but his gaze was as direct as ever.

"How are you keeping?" he asked.

Tonelessly I replied, "Fine – and you?" but inwardly I felt an upsurge of pleasure at this chance encounter, wishing at the same time I had applied my make-up more carefully. After an awkward pause we drifted into the hall along with the others. It was the usual number of desultory figures waiting for the curtain to rise on the evening's business. He sat down at the table beside another shabby, younger man, and the six from our branch, including myself, sat opposite. The branch secretary spoke at some length on the matter of pay rises. I dreaded the moment for questions because I never had the courage to ask any, but I wanted to prove to McIntyre that I was still the same political enthusiast of old, though why, I don't know. We had gone our separate ways long since. Before any questions could be asked he had taken over.

"Five years ago," he informed us in his slightly nasal voice, "we were as poorly paid as yourselves, but we fought the management tooth and nail. We resisted their threats. We stuck together, and while I'm not boasting I am pleased to say we are one of the highest paid factories in the district. Don't give up. Don't be swayed and don't be intimidated. You will win in the long run. Yours is the power. Yours is the glory." He continued in this vein. I had heard it all before, but it still sounded authentic. Often it held good. Often, but not always. Fifteen years before he had been saying much the same.

"Let there be no increase in the rents. It is up to us, the people. We shall fight. We shall resist. We shall harass." And so we had.

My sister and I along with seven hundred or so council tenants had marched with McIntyre at our head to the Town Hall. We chanted "No increase in rents" until we were hoarse. It must have been difficult for the councillors inside to carry on with their business, which, McIntyre informed us, was the implementation of the new Rent Act. To us at that time it seemed the thin end of the wedge, calling for drastic measures.

The faces of the councillors peered anxiously out of the Town Hall windows while we all booed loudly. McIntyre turned to us, holding up his hands for silence. We quietened down, but not before Walter Johnson, normally an inoffensive simpleton, in the heat of the moment flung a full can of beer at Colonel Martin's car. This caused a large dent and some of the crowd were splashed. The Colonel was one of the few able councillors, but had no time for the tenant, so irrespective of the Rent Act we couldn't stand him. Still, we thought it was going a bit far flinging cans of beer around.

McIntyre looked angry. "I suggest the person who threw that can return home or I will call an end to this demonstration. There must be no violence."

He took it for granted that outside his commands we had no will of our own – which we hadn't, so we moved away from Walter, leaving him in a lonely circle. He shuffled about with a downcast face then finally slouched away from our midst.

A messenger emerged from the building in the shape of Daniel Smith, the town's well-known benefactor, who was always getting mentioned in the papers for his donations to natives in Moly Pololy or Chitinbanana. This charity cut no ice with us. We believed it should begin at home. McIntyre and Smith withdrew from our earshot. You could have heard a pin drop as we tried to listen, but apart from the nodding and shaking of their heads nothing could be gleaned. Then Smith retreated hurriedly and McIntyre conveyed the message. "I think we've got them worried. I am informed they are going to discuss all the implications of the Rent Act and will tell me first thing in the morning what the result is. I am confident they are impressed by the wishes of you, the people. So my friends, I would ask you to return home and await the verdict, which I think will be favourable."

We all cheered and broke up in good spirits.

In the morning the headlines of the local paper read, 'RENT ACT GOES THROUGH, DESPITE DEMONSTRATION BY TENANTS'. My sister, one of our revolutionary committee, was very angry.

"Who does that McIntyre think he is, trying to fool us last night that there would be no increases." Though McIntyre was the leader of our movement she had never liked him. I was disappointed too, but more on his behalf, rather than because we would have to pay a few shillings extra on the rent.

"Well, he tried," I said. "It's no reflection on him. He did his best."

"Thanks to him my husband is not speaking to me. He is fed up with my gallivanting to all those tenant meetings."

"That's not McIntyre's fault."

"You are infatuated with the man, and always have been."

I didn't answer. Infatuated was not the correct word, though I had never met anyone like him before. He spoke of little else but how to change the world for the benefit of the people – when his eyes would light up with a passion which would probably never be inspired by me or any other woman.

The first time I had had any contact with him was at a meeting my sister and I attended more out of boredom than anything else. He spoke against the council and the careless manner in which they spent the ratepayers' money. I admired his style and thought he had guts. Previously I had assumed the councillors were a bunch of well-meaning citizens, but he opened my eyes. On the way out I was close behind him wondering if I dare make any kind of an approach. Suddenly I was pushed against him with the surge of the crowd. He placed his hand on my shoulder to steady me and smiled. I wanted to say something intelligent, but before I could, he looked beyond me to someone he recognized. It seemed he was always looking beyond me.

"You won't get me to come to any more of his stupid meetings," my sister stated. She was wrong. Curiosity always got the better of her. Our next meeting was very much reduced in numbers, but the hardy few of us left apparently had another part to play. It was then I got the impression that McIntyre had forgotten that the Rent Act had gone through, because he ignored this point and carried on to tell us of the next stage of his campaign.

"As you know," he said, "Saturday is the opening of the

new Town Hall. We must be there to demonstrate how
we feel about this colossal waste of money and get as many
people as we can to turn up. I'll do some organizing and you
can do the same – get banners and slogans ready. We will
meet outside the cinema. Maybe", he added dreamily, "I
could get a band going – I've got contacts."

My sister was doubtful. "We haven't much time. It's a lot
of work. There's hardly any of us left – "

McIntyre smiled at her sweetly, "Of course you can do
it."

"We'll try," I said.

"That's right my dear," he said, patting my hand. "I know
you both will try."

On Saturday at the proposed time my sister and I along
with her kids set off, giggling nervously, and carrying our
banners self-consciously. But when we reached the busiest
part of the town without meeting any other demonstra-
tors, our faces became frozen with doubt, and we let the
kids carry the banners. Eventually they were trailed along
the ground until the brave slogan of 'No Rent Increases'
became unrecognizable with dirt. Outside the new Town
Hall, as perfect as a doll's house, we spied another committee member, Curly MacFadyen, the worse for drink, but no
sign of McIntyre or any kind of band. We peered through
the glass door and saw that the official opening had begun.
My sister looked at me bitterly. Always a woman of quick
decisions, though, she opened the door. We barged in,
right in the middle of a speech by an elegant lady in a floppy
hat. She broke off immediately she saw us. The kids rushed
in ahead of us perhaps thinking they were going to the
Saturday film matinee, and Curly, bringing up the rear, fell
on his back on the slippery polished floor. This should have
been funny but no one laughed. The local bigwigs and
officials were transfixed in horror behind draped tables.
Then an official came to life and moved in front of the

floppy-hat lady perhaps anticipating violence but we merely chanted in quavering voices, "Justice for the tenants –
down with the rent increase." For good measure the kids
aimed their banners at the table and upset an arrangement
of flowers. With crimson faces we caught hold of them and
marched them out by the scruff of the neck. Then we had
to go back and get Curly who was punching soundlessly at
the glass door. And still there was no sign of McIntyre.

"Don't ever mention that man's name to me again," said
my sister through clenched teeth.

She never forgave him. He explained to me later he had
come to the Town Hall, but we were gone. Apparently we
had been too early. Whether it was true or not I still
admired and loved him, but it was like banging my head
against a brick wall. It was only the cause he loved – any
kind of cause, or excuse for one. No matter how often I
accompanied him to drab halls where dedicated men and
women gathered together to fight against injustice, or
supposed injustice, I could sense he just tolerated me.
Eventually I gave up and drifted out of town. I had affairs
with other men but they always came to nothing. I think
McIntyre had ruined me. He gave me an inferiority complex from which I never recovered.

The meeting finished inconclusively, as usual, with an
optimistic call from McIntyre to keep going. He was
hurrying out of the hall with the shabby young man, the
latest disciple no doubt, when I caught up with him like a
body that runs on when the head has been chopped off. I
touched his arm. He turned – expressionless.

"Still carrying on with the good fight?" I questioned
foolishly.

He looked at me as if I was a troublesome heckler
then, after a moment's pause, asked, "Would you like a
drink?"

I had not the will-power to refuse. "All right."

He turned to the shabby young man. "I'll see you later John," he said with such contrasting warmth I could have wept. The young man shrugged and nodded towards me with a flickering glance of calculated understanding. Inside the lounge I clutched my glass of gin while McIntyre sipped his beer. He stared at me encouragingly. "You were saying?"

"Saying?" I strove to remember. "Oh yes – I asked you if you were still carrying on with the battle."

"What else is there?"

That was true. He had that at least. I had nothing. Spitefully I said, "Some people are betrayed in the battle."

He raised his eyebrows. "I never betrayed you. You betrayed yourself."

"It may have seemed like that to you, but you didn't really care what I did." My face flushed. I knew I was talking out of turn. I laughed to prove it didn't matter. "It's all in the past anyway. I was definitely one cause you lost."

"Sometimes I lose, sometimes I win, but I must keep trying," he said loftily, as if he was God.

"And old man river he just keeps rolling along," I replied.

He looked at me with dislike. I knew I had to get away.

"I really must be going. I've made arrangements – "

"I understand," he said. He finished his beer. I swallowed my gin, and we walked out together. It was ironic but before he left me he said, "Don't blame yourself too much."

I wanted to shout after him, "Your feet still smell." I had noticed that. McIntyre might be a great man but he never understood that from many people's point of view smelly feet are worse than capitalism. Only to me had it been a comforting fault.

I returned to my shabby flat which was not very presentable, but then there was no one to see it but myself. After fetching a bottle of cheap wine from the cupboard, I settled down as comfortably as I could in front of the one-bar electric fire, holding my glass high as though drinking a toast.

We Don't Shoot Prisoners on a Sunday

"We don't shoot prisoners on a Sunday."

I looked at César, suspecting a joke, but his face was straight.

"Only horses then?" My remark was flippant, under the circumstances, but I was tired of his arguments, his excuses, and most of all, his smell.

"Not even horses." He added "Señor" within a bubble of laughter. I stared at the floor of the cell and wished he would vanish, like the cockroach I saw slide into a crack in the stone, but I was obliged to respect his last wish to talk to me. In a flash he became serious.

"Here, we recognize Sunday as God's day."

"And how many have you killed, even if not on Sundays, including the priests?"

"How many have you?" He clasped me by the shoulder. I flinched. It was just like him to try to establish old bonds. "Besides," he added, "it was them or us."

"And the priests, was it them or us?"

"Before the treaty it was them, now after the treaty it is us." He added, "Or at least me."

He angered me, even now, with his one-track mind.

"Besides," he said, "priests are only men, and they must learn to die quickly too, otherwise they lose sight of God."

"A Sunday is as good a day as any to learn to die quickly."

My voice shook with strain and exhaustion. I hoped he wouldn't mistake it for weakness. "I don't give a damn about the day or the time, so long as the sentence is carried out in the name of retribution and justice for the village. Understand?"

"Yes – Señor."

"Don't start calling me Señor at this late date."

"Yes, Josetti."

"My gringo name is Joseph." There was a stench of sweat between us which could not be solely attributed to César.

"But you are wrong about Sundays," he said.

I shut my eyes for a second to banish the sight of him picking his teeth.

He continued, "It is a day to rest and reflect on our sins, and why if actions were right in the past they are wrong in the present, and we might consider that possibly today's decisions could be wrong in the future." Then he wiped his finger on his jacket and faced me with black eyes, his lips stretched to expose the decay caused by a poor diet. As always he looked happy.

"Why plead so hard for yourself?" I asked.

He squinted at me dangerously. "I do not plead. I only ask for this day so that you may consider your decisions. I have no cares or worries for myself, but I worry for you, because you are my friend, who may live a long time with a bad taste in his mouth."

I had no answer. His cunning was too deep to be defeated by words. I sat at the rough table and flicked through a greasy bible to distract myself from his pressure. The pages were scored and mutilated, perhaps by César himself, but I suspected they were older marks.

"A worthy book for those clever enough to read?" he questioned.

"It is badly written." I thought I should leave.

"Perhaps the priest can help us to understand it," said César quickly when I stood up.

"You are expecting one?"

"For me he will happily come."

I was forced to laugh. It was either that or strike him. We both laughed. The noise within the sombre stone walls was indecent, but I felt much better for it. Finally César slumped over the table and I collapsed into the chair. He fetched out a pouch and rolled me some tobacco which smelled nostalgically of old blankets.

I inhaled deeply. "So already they are creeping back for you?"

"Who, Josetti?" He spoke my name as tenderly as he would have done a whore's.

"The priests."

"Like the vultures they wait for death – even for yours."

"Not for me. I'm not one of the genuflectors." I looked at my watch. There was plenty of time yet – in fact, too much.

"You will have no choice – unless," his eyes narrowed, "you think to get away from here."

I crushed the tobacco stub into the stone floor. "One can hope."

He put his face close to mine, stinging my eyes with his peppery breath. "Josetti, if we become good friends again, I could arrange for you to leave here with much money."

"Where would you get it?"

He gripped my arm hard, as always when he was carried away with a stupid plan. He whispered, unnecessarily I thought, within the thick walls. "When the priest arrives we could hold him to ransom."

"Who would pay it? The village rots in hunger."

"The church. It stinks of gold."

"The churches are burned. Every bit of gold was taken."

He laughed, tightening his grip cruelly. "In the city there is plenty more: stored in the earth; in the walls; in the tombstones; in the graves with the dead. Anywhere they can think of to hide, and they will get it for a brave priest who has survived to give the last rites for a last peseta."

His grip loosened. I pushed him away and stared at the wall, the bars on the window, then finally at César who was breathing hard.

"Think of it Josetti – you could leave this place you hate and live the rest of your life at peace with yourself – eh?"

I considered his plan desperate, though not impossible, but I suspected one way or another I would never be at peace with myself.

"I can never understand you," I answered to avoid commitment.

"So," he continued, "normally we don't shoot prisoners on a Sunday to give everyone time to think matters over."

"Normally," I echoed, then, "Does it ever occur to you I could be tired of the gold, the tears, the killings? That's why we are in this situation."

"There will be no killing this time. The gold will be enough," but his tongue passed over his lips as if he could taste blood.

"I don't think you could resist it, the killing, I mean."

"I swear on that bible I will resist it." He reached for it but I shook my head and laid my hands over it.

"I will swear on my life."

"Your life?"

He saw the joke and laughed.

"Besides, who would keep law in the village afterwards?"

He shrugged. "Who cares – let them stew." A mosquito crawled up my arm and I brushed it off. It fastened on César's hand apparently unnoticed. "But someone must give the order to hold the priest," he shouted, as if the plan had been approved.

"I wonder who?"

He threw up his hands, disturbing the mosquito. "Should we ask that insect who sucks my blood without any great considerations?" His voice was menacing now. I knew he would become violent if he was not humoured. To play for time I crossed the room and peered through the small barred window. The view of the stains on the bleached wall outside was accusing.

"César," I asked, "why do you make it hard for both of us?"

Now he looked more sullen than dangerous. "Forget it then."

I tapped the bar of the window with my nail, goaded by images of green fields, wet streets and blonde women. "And how could you be sure of the gold?"

"I am sure of nothing." He blew a smoke ring into the air and it hovered above his head like a halo.

"Then the plan is not foolproof?"

"Who knows?" He was becoming more remote by the second, despite the sweat on his forehead.

"There is a place", he began, as if the subject oppressed him now, "where, for not too much money, you can buy a passage."

"It's too late," I started to say, but he had slid down the wall, falling asleep with his mouth open, grunting in a drunken fashion, because the tequila never quite left his system. I was reminded of a clown who, defeated for the umpteenth time, will leap up to be defeated again. His excuses for the cause were lost. I never had any, and the cause itself was a blood-stained memory better forgotten. To be fair, he had saved my life on a number of occasions, but then I had saved his on a similar number. The score meant nothing to me any more.

Now I was hungry and alert, but it was too early to call upon the guards. Doubtless they would rush in thinking it was time to carry out the sentence, and if this happened before the priest arrived the village would see it as a gross injustice, only to be expected from a gringo. César had a point when he said let them stew. Apathetically I fingered through the bible. The only statement worth reading was the name of the owner and the comment under it. "To Sancho, on his tenth birthday, in the hope he will follow the teachings of our Lord." I looked at this for a time, then closed my eyes in an effort to induce sleep and remained still within the sound of César's piggish grunts. Eventually the door opened and the guards slithered in on their bare feet. They seized César, who writhed and protested like a small boy called to face school. He struggled for a second then apologized. Carefully he arranged his hat and had actually turned to go with them, when he paused and looked at me saying, "About the plan. You have decided?"

"I have decided," I stated with deliberation, "to shoot prisoners on a Sunday if I am required to."

His jaw slackened. The pupils of his eyes dilated for a second, then shrank. He threw back his head and laughed, too loud, even for him. "So, you shall remain here?" he asked.

"Yes." Just then I wanted to kick the guards out and tell him it was all a bad joke, but a name held me – Sancho, whom I didn't know and who was likely dead, when someone had scored and mutilated his book. Someone, if not César, like César.

"Why?"

I wanted to give convincing reasons without appearing pompous, but failed. "Because there must be no more killings in the village."

He regarded me with distaste, then shrugged. "Goodbye Josetti," he said with one final flash of his bad teeth. The guards straightened and saluted me crazily. "Watch out for the priest," I warned them. "See he is not harmed."

A short time afterwards there were shots – too many for my liking, but you couldn't expect the guards, who were the poorest of dirt farmers, to be good marksmen. Some day they might learn.

A Change of Face

I was five pounds short of the two hundred I needed by Thursday, and I had only two days to make it up.

"Why do you need two hundred pounds?" asked Ingrid, my room-mate.

"Let's say I promised myself that amount."

"That explains everything," she said. "I once promised myself a holiday in Majorca, but things don't always work out."

"In your case things never work out."

"I think you're crazy," said Ingrid. "What good is money to you anyway?" Her fatuity was maddening, but I kept calm.

"Lend me a fiver. You won't regret it."

Her tinny laugh pierced my ear. "What me – with scarcely a bean!"

"Get out," I said, "before I cripple you."

She folded down her tartan skirt and walked out the door with a hoity-toity air, ludicrous, I thought, in a down and out whore. I waited a good five minutes to make sure she was gone before I fetched the briefcase from under my bed. I never failed to be impressed by the look of it. Good quality leather was more in my line than the trash Ingrid flaunted. The briefcase had originally belonged to one of her clients. I remembered his piggish stamp of respectability. Mind you that was ten years before when Ingrid was in better condition. He had left it by the side of the bed, complete with lock and key and containing two stale sandwiches, while Ingrid slept off her labours. I explained later I had found it in a dustbin. Once again I counted the money acquired in pounds and pence but it still totalled only one hundred and ninety-five.

In Joe's Eats Café I leaned over the counter. "Joe," I asked, "how's about lending me a couple of quid — five to be exact. Until the Giro comes on Saturday."

Joe kept his eyes on the trickle of heavy tea he was pouring. He breathed hard. "What for?"

"Oh I don't know. Who needs money."

"It don't pay to lend money. I should know."

"Of course, never a borrower or a lender be," I said, fishing for ten pence.

"I've been done before. No reflection on you."

I looked round, then leaned over and whispered. "You can have a free shot and I'll still owe you the fiver."

He recoiled then hooted with laughter. "You must be joking — not even with a bag over your head."

I shrugged and put on what passed for a smile. "It's your loss. I know some new tricks."

Joe patted my shoulder. "I know you mean well, Lolly, but you're not my taste — nothing personal."

We brooded together for a bit. Finally Joe said, "Ingrid might lend it to you."

"Not her."

"Oh well . . . " He turned to pour water into the pot.

"I've got one hundred and ninety-five pounds," I threw at him. His back stiffened.

"What's the problem then?"

I knew I was wasting my time but I explained. "I need two hundred by Thursday. It would alter my whole life."

He chortled. "You paying for a face lift or something?"

"Better than that."

He shook his head. "Sorry kid, you see – "

I took my cup of tea over to the table without listening. Ten minutes later I was strolling along a quiet part of the city occupied mainly by decaying mansions.

"I'm short of a fiver," I explained to the tall man in the black suit.

His eyes glowed with regret. "I'm sorry. Two hundred is the price. I can't accept less."

"Will it be too late after Thursday?"

"I'm afraid so." He could not have been more sympathetic.

"What should I do – steal?"

"I can give you no advice."

He closed the door gently in my face and left me staring at the peeling paint. A cat leapt on to the step and wound itself round my legs. I picked it up and forced it to look at my face. "Stupid animal," I said as it purred its pleasure. I threw it away from me and returned home.

I walked into the bedroom and grabbed Ingrid by her sparse hair as she lay splayed over Jimmy Font, identifiable by his dirty boots.

"Out," I shouted.

She pulled on her grey vest screaming, "I'll kill you."

Jimmy thrashed about like a tortoise on its back clutching his privates as if they were gold.

I towered above him. "Hurry!" He gained his feet, made the sign of the cross, grabbed his trousers and ran.

"May you burn in hell," moaned Ingrid, rubbing a bald patch on her head.

I tossed over a handful of hair. "Before you go, take that filth with you."

"Where can I go?" she sobbed.

"The gutter, the river, the madhouse. Take your choice."

She pulled on her dress. "I don't feel well." I didn't

answer. "Anyway," she added, "if you had let Jimmy stay I might have earned a fiver to lend you."

I was not swayed by her logic. A drink from Jimmy's bottle would have been the price. I walked out of the room to escape from her staleness.

At one time they had told me in the hospital, plastic surgery could eventually work wonders. I did not like the word 'eventually'. Civilly I had requested that they terminate my breath, but they merely pointed out how lucky I was to be given the opportunity. Suspecting they would only transform me into a different kind of monster I had left them studying diagrams. That happened a long time ago, but I still had my dreams of strolling along an avenue of trees holding up a perfect profile to the sun.

"Are you listening," said Ingrid, breaking through my thoughts with some outrageous arrangement she would fix for me to get five pounds. She backed away when I headed towards her. As she ran through the door and down the stairs I threw out her flea-ridden fur coat, which landed on her shoulders like the mottled skin of a hyena.

The Salvation Army Band on the street corner blared out its brassy music of hope. I settled down on the bench beside Teddy the tramp and spun thoughts of fine wire in my head.

"Nice?" commented Teddy from the depths of an abandoned army coat. He offered me a pale-green sandwich from a bread paper, which I declined.

"We have much to be thankful for," he said as he bit into the piece.

A body of people gathered on the far side. The music stopped. Everyone applauded. I joined the group, who courteously stood their ground when I brushed close. My eyes were on the Sally Ann coming towards us with trusting goodwill and the collection box in her hand. I slipped my hand beneath the other hands holding out donations, then tugged the string loosely held by the good lady, and ran.

Six pounds and forty-seven pence lay strewn over my bed in pence and silver. I blessed the kindness of the common people and the compassion of the Salvation Army who would never persecute or prosecute a sorry person like me. Tomorrow was Thursday and I had the two hundred pounds, with one pound forty-seven to the good. With a mixture of joy and fear I poured five pounds into the briefcase. Then I studied a single sheet of parchment, the words on which I knew by heart. The message was direct and unfanciful, and unaccountably I believed it, perhaps because of its simplicity, and also the power which emanated from the black handwriting. Even the mercenary demand for two hundred pounds strengthened my belief in a force much deeper than plastic surgery. I calculated there must always be a price to pay, which for effort's sake should go beyond one's means, to accomplish results.

All evening Ingrid did not return. I wasn't surprised or sorry. In my mind's eye I could see her tossing against dank alley walls in drunken confusion – her wispy hair falling like damp thistledown over her forehead, her eyes rolling around like those of an old mare about to be serviced. Not that I wished her to be any different. Her degradation had afforded me stature, though after tomorrow I hoped never to see her again. Fancying a bout of self-torture to pass the time, I began searching for a mirror, suspecting it would be useless since I had forbidden them in the flat. I peered at my reflection in the window. Like a creature from outer space it stared back without pity. Satisfactorily sickened I raised two fingers, then turned away.

"See your pal Ingrid," declared Maidy Storr when I passed her stall of old hats, shoes and rusty brooches.

"Not recently."

"She stole a bundle of money from Dan Riley when he dozed off in Maitland's bar last night."

"Never."

"Well she did. I sat on one side of him and she was on the other. I remember she left quickly without finishing her drink. Next thing he woke up shouting he'd been robbed."

"How much?" I asked.

"Fifty quid, he said. Mind you I was surprised he had that much." She added winking, "You'll be all right for a tap."

"Haven't seen her since yesterday morning."

"Done a bunk has she?"

"Couldn't say."

"Well she would, wouldn't she. The law will be out for her."

"For stealing from a pickpocket. I don't see Dan complaining."

Maidy frowned. "I see what you mean. It makes you sick to think she'll get away with it."

"Couldn't care less whether she gets away with it or not." I picked up a single earring. "Have you many one-eared customers?"

"Leave that stuff and get going."

I walked away quickly when Maidy threw a shoe at me, and headed towards Joe's for breakfast.

"I think I'd like something special today," I informed him.

"How about some weedkiller," he suggested.

"I said something special, not the usual." I considered his confined choices.

"Be quick and move to your seat before the joint gets busy." Being a liberal-minded fellow Joe allowed me in his place when it was quiet, provided I sat in the alcove behind the huge spider plant. I chose a pizza and a glass of tomato juice.

"Living it up," he sneered.

"Might as well. Anyway I'm tired of the little creatures in your meat pies."

I could see Joe looking anxiously at a neatly dressed old lady approaching. Hastily I moved to the alcove with my pizza and tomato juice. The old lady was having an intense conversation with Joe. I suspected she was complaining about me. I finished my pizza and deliberately took my tomato juice over to a centre table. At a table near by a couple with a child looked at me, aghast. The child wailed. I smiled at them, or in my case, grimaced. The child's wails increased in volume. Joe charged over and signalled for me to get out. The neat old lady appeared out of the steam.

"Don't you know this is a friend of mine," she said, looking hard at Joe then bestowing a loving smile on me. Joe looked unconvinced, but he was stumped.

"If you say so." He moved the couple and the child behind the spider plant.

The old lady sat down beside me and said, "I'm sorry you have to put up with this sort of thing."

I shrugged. "That's all right."

"Such a lack of kindness is terrible," she continued.

"I suppose so."

"Can I get you something?" she asked.

"A pizza, if you don't mind."

She attended to me smartly. I could feel her eyes boring through me as I ate. She cleared her throat and asked, "Are you often exposed to such er – abuse?"

"Don't worry about it," I said. "You'll only upset yourself." Her eyes were brimming over by this time and I couldn't concentrate on eating.

"Is there nothing that can be done?" she asked just as I had the fork half-way up to my mouth.

"About what?" I was really fed up with her. I find it impossible to talk and eat at the same time.

"I mean, my dear – what about plastic surgery – or something."

I threw down my fork. "Listen, if you don't like the way I

look, bugger off." I paid her no further attention when she left.

"That's another customer you've lost me," Joe called over. I told him to bugger off too, then hastily departed.

For the remainder of the day I kept checking on the time, which meant I had to keep searching for the odd clock in shop windows. I half expected to bump into Ingrid. In a way I would have been glad to see her, because even if she was completely uninteresting, in her vapid manner she used to converse with me. She was still out when I returned home, no doubt holed up somewhere, frightened to stir in case she met Riley. I washed my face, combed my hair, put on a fresh jumper, and looked no better than before, but at least it was a gesture. Then I checked the money in the briefcase and left without a backward glance. I headed slowly to my destination so that I would arrive on the exact minute of the hour of my appointment. Normally I don't get excited easily, for seldom is there anything to get excited about, but I must admit my heart was pounding when I stood on the steps of the shabby mansion. The tall man in the black suit received my briefcase solemnly. He bowed, then beckoned me to follow him.

"Are you not going to count the money?" I asked.

His sepulchral voice resounded down the corridor. "If you have faith in me I know the money will be correct."

I wanted to ask questions but I could scarcely keep pace as he passed smoothly ahead of me. Abruptly he stopped outside a door and turned. The questions died on my lips as I met his opaque glance. It was too late to have doubts so I allowed him to usher me into the room. I can give no explanation for what followed because once inside I was dazzled by a translucent orange glow so powerful that all my senses ceased to function. I knew nothing until I woke up outside the corridor holding on to the tall man. Even in that state of mesmerism I knew I was different. My lips felt rubbery and my eyes larger. Tears were running down my cheeks, which in itself was a strange thing, since I had not cried for years. The man carefully escorted me into another room and placed me before a mirror, saying, "Don't be afraid. You will be pleased."

I breathed deep, and looked. I didn't say anything for a time because the image that faced me was that of Ingrid. I leaned forward to touch her, but it was only the glass of a mirror.

"You are much nicer now?" the man asked in an ingratiating manner.

What could I say? I didn't want to complain, but I had been definitely altered to be the double of Ingrid. Certainly the face was the same, and we had been of similar build anyway.

"Very nice," I croaked. "Thank you very much."

His lips curled into what could have been a smile, then he tapped me on the shoulder to get going. I shook hands with him when I stood on the step outside, clutching my empty briefcase.

"It's a funny thing – " I began to say, but he had vanished behind the closed door.

It might have been a coincidence but Ingrid never showed up. This was convenient because everyone assumed I was Ingrid, so I settled into her way of life and discovered it wasn't too bad. Certainly it has its ups and downs but I get a lot of laughs with her clients and it doesn't hurt my face either. The only snag is, now and again I worry about bumping into Dan Riley. Sometimes I consider saving up for a different face, but that might be tempting fate. Who knows what face I would get. Besides, I have acquired a taste for the good things in life, like cigarettes and vodka. So I take my chances and confront the world professionally equipped in a fur jacket and high black boots, trailing my boa feathers behind me.

Alasdair Gray

Alasdair Gray

A Report to the Trustees of the Bellahouston Travelling Scholarship

I apologize to the Bellahouston trustees, and to Mr Bliss, the director of Glasgow art school, for the long time I have taken to write this report. Had the tour gone as planned they would have received, when I returned, an illustrated diary describing things done and places visited. But I visited very few places and the things I did were muddled and absurd. To show that, even so, the tour was worth while, I must report what I learned from it. I have had to examine my memory of the events deductively, like an archaeologist investigating a prehistoric midden. It has taken a year to understand what happened to me and the money between October 1957 and March 1958.

On learning I was awarded the scholarship my first wish had been to travel on foot or bicycle, sketching landscapes and cityscapes around Scotland, for I knew very little of it apart from Glasgow, two islands in the Firth of Clyde, and places seen on daytrips to Edinburgh. However, a condition of the scholarship was that I go abroad. I decided to visit London for a fortnight, travel from there to Gibraltar by ship, find a cheap place to live in southern Spain, paint there as long as the money would allow, then travel home through Granada, Málaga, Madrid, Toledo, Barcelona and Paris, viewing on the way Moorish mosques, baroque cathedrals, plateresque palaces, the works of El Greco, Velázquez and Goya, with Bosch's *Garden of Earthly Delights*, Brueghel's *Triumph of Death*, and several other grand gaudy things which are supposed to compensate for the crimes of our civilization. The excellence of this plan, approved by Mr Bliss, is not lessened by the fact that I eventually spent two days in Spain and saw nothing of interest.

On the 31st of October I boarded the London train in Glasgow Central Station. It was near midnight, dark and drizzling, and to save money I had not taken a sleeping car. The prospect of vivid sunshine, new lands and people should have been very exciting, but as the train sped south a sullen gloom settled upon me. I looked at my reflection in the rain-streaked carriage window and doubted the value of a tourist's shallow experience of anywhere. I was homesick already. I do not love Glasgow much, I sometimes actively hate it, but I am at home here. In London this sickness increased until it underlay quite cheerful feelings and weighed so heavy on the chest that it began to make breathing difficult. I had been in hospital with asthma during the three previous summers, but a doctor treating me had said another very bad attack was unlikely and a trip abroad might do me good. I had a pocket inhaler which eased difficult breathing with puffs of atropine methondrate, papaverine hydrochloride, chlorbutal and adrenaline; and for strong spasms I had a bottle of adrenaline solution and a hypodermic needle to inject myself subcutaneously. In London I slept in a students' hostel in a street behind the university tower. The dormitory was not large and held about fifty bunks, all occupied. I was afraid to use the inhaler at night in case the noise of it wakened someone, so used the needle, which should have been kept for emergencies. This made sleep difficult. At night I felt trapped in that dormitory and by day I felt trapped in London.

The main shops and offices in London are as large as ours, sometimes larger, but the dwelling houses are mostly of brick and seldom more than half the height of a Scottish sandstone tenement. Such buildings, in a country town surrounded by meadows, look very pleasant, but a big county of them, horizon beyond horizon beyond horizon, is a desert to me, and not less a desert for containing some great public buildings and museums. I visited these oases as the trustees would have wished, but had continually to leave them for a confusion of streets of which my head could form no clear map. Like most deserts this city is nearly flat and allows no view of a more fertile place. The streets of central Glasgow are also gripped between big buildings but it is always easy to reach a corner where we can see, on a clear day, the hills to the north and to the south. I know I am unfair to London. A normal dweller there has a circle of acquaintance about the size of a small village. Only a stranger feels challenged to judge the place as a whole, which cannot be done, so the stranger feels small and lonely. I visited several publishers with a folder of drawings and a typescript of my poems. I hoped to be asked to illustrate a book, perhaps my own book. I was kindly received and turned away from each place, and although I could not feel angry with the publishers (who would have been out of business if they had not known what was saleable) I turned my disappointment against the city. I grew more asthmatic and walked about refusing to be awed.

The least awesome place I saw was the government church, Westminster Abbey. This once fine Gothic structure is filled with effigies of landlords, company directors and administrators who got rich by doing exactly what was expected of them, and now stand as solid in their marble wigs, boots and waistcoats as the Catholic saints and martyrs they have replaced. Among them is an occasional stone carved with the name of someone who has been creative or courageous. A less pretentious but nastier place is the Tower of London. Built by the Normans for the enslavement of the English natives (who before this had been a comparatively democratic and even artistic people, judging by their export of illuminated manuscripts to the continent) this fort was used by later governments as an arsenal, jail and bloody police-station. Nobody pretends otherwise. The stands of weapons and the pathetic scratchings of the political prisoners on their cell-walls are clearly labelled, and folk who would feel discomfort at a rack of police-batons or the barbed fence of a concentration camp feel thrilled because these are supposed to be part of a *splendid* past. The tower also holds the Crown jewels. There were more of them than I had imagined, twelve or fifteen huge display cabinets of crowns, orbs, maces, swords and ceremonial salt-cellars. Most of it dates from the eighteenth century – I recall nothing as old as the regalia of the sixth Jamie Stewart in Edinburgh castle. I noticed that the less the monarchs were working politicians the more money was spent ornamenting them. The culmination of this development is the huge Crown Imperial, an art nouveau job created for the coronation of Edward the Fat in 1901, when the Archbishop of Canterbury placed the world's most expensively useless hat on the world's most expensively useless head.

Did anything in London please me? Yes: the work of the great cockneys, the Williams Blake and Turner. Also Saint Paul's Cathedral. Also the underground rail system. I found this last, with the H.G. Wellsian sweep of its triple escalators and lines of framed, glazed advertisements for films and women's underwear, and tunnels beneath tunnels bridging tunnels, and tickets which allow those who take the wrong train to find their way to the right station without paying extra, a very great comfort.

But I was glad one morning to get on a boat-train at
Liverpool Street Station and begin the second part of the
journey to Spain. I was in the company of Ian McCulloch,
who had arrived from Glasgow that morning. He is an artist
who received his painting diploma at the same time as
myself. He also wanted to visit Spain, and had saved the
money to do so by working as a gas lamplighter near
Parkhead Forge, Shettleston. We had arranged to travel
together and meant to share the rent of a small place in
south Spain. The boat-train ran along embankments above
the usual streets of small houses, then came to a place
where towering structures, part warehouse and part
machine, stood among labyrinths of railway-siding. The
little brick homes were here also, but the surrounding
machinery gave them the dignity of outposts. We arrived
at the docks.

The ship was called the *Kenya Castle* and long before it
unmoored we found it a floating version of the sort of hotel
we had never been in before. Our cabin was small but
compact. It held two bunks the size of coffins, each with a
reading lamp and adjustable ventilator. There was a very
small sink with hot and cold water, towels, facecloths, soap,
a locker with coat-hangers, a knob to ring for the steward,
another for the stewardess. In the lavatories each closet
contained, beside the roll of toilet paper, a clean towel,
presumably to wipe the fingers on after using the roll,
although there were washbasins and towels in the vestibule outside. (It has just struck me that perhaps the extra
towel was for polishing the lavatory seat before use.) The
menus in the dining room embarrassed us. They were
printed on glazed-surface card and decorated at every
meal with a different photograph of some nook of Britain's
African empire — *The Governor's Summer Residence, Balihoo
Protectorate, The District Vice-Commissioner's Bungalow,
Janziboola,* etc. The food, however, was listed in French.

Obviously some foods were alternatives to others, while some could, and perhaps should, be asked for on the same plate. We wanted to eat as much as possible to get the full value of the money we had paid; at the same time we feared we would be charged extra if we ate more than a certain amount. We also feared we would be despised if we asked the waiter for information on these matters. Our table was shared with two priests, Catholic and Anglican. Ian and I were near acquaintances rather than friends. With only our nationality, profession and destination in common we left conversation to the priests. They mainly talked about an audience the Anglican had had with the Pope. He addressed the Catholic with the deference a polite salesman might show to the representative of a more powerful firm. He said the Pope's hands were beautifully shaped, he had the fingers of an artist, a painter. Ian and I glanced down at our own fingers. Mine had flecks of paint on the nails that I hadn't managed to clean off for the previous fortnight.

After this meal coffee was served in the lounge. The cups were very small with frilled paper discs between themselves and the saucers to absorb the drips. There were many people in the lounge but it was big enough not to seem crowded. Darkness had fallen and we were moving slowly down the Thames. There were magazines on small tables: *Vogue*, *House and Garden*, *John O'London's*, *Punch*, the magazines found in expensive dentists' waiting rooms, nothing to stimulate thought. I played a bad game of chess with Ian and ordered two whiskies, which were cheap now we were afloat. I took mine chiefly to anaesthetize the asthma, but Ian felt bound to respond by ordering another two, and resented this. He had less money than I and he thought we were starting the trip extravagantly. The ship was leaving the estuary for the sea. I felt the floor of that opulent lounge, till now only troubled by a buried throbbing, take on a quality of *sway*. I was distracted from the

weight on my chest by an uneasy, flickering lightness in my
stomach. I left the lounge and went to bed, vomiting first
into the cabin sink.

While eating breakfast next morning I watched the
portholes in the walls of the saloon. The horizon was
moving up and down each of them like the bottom edge of
a blind. When the horizon was down nothing could be seen
outside but pale grey sky. After a few seconds it would be
pulled up and the holes would look on nothing but dark
grey water. The priests' conversation seemed unforgivably
banal. I felt homesick, seasick and asthmatic. I went back to
bed and used my inhaler but it had stopped having effect. I
took a big adrenaline jag. That night breathing became very
difficult indeed, I could not sleep and injections did not help
much. The impossibility of sitting up in the bunk, the
narrowness of the cabin and the movement of the floor
increased my sense of suffocation. I lost all memory of normal
breathing, and so lost hope of it. However, I could clearly
imagine how it would feel to be worse, so fear arrived. Fear
lessened the ability to face pain, which therefore increased.
At this stage it was hard to stop the fear swelling into panic,
because the more pain I felt the more I could imagine. The
only way to divert my imagination from its capital accumulation of fear was to think about something else and only
erotic images were strong enough to be diverting. Having
no experience of sexual satisfaction I recalled women in
the London underground advertisements.

Next morning I asked Ian to call the ship's doctor, who
entered the cabin and sat beside the bunk. He was an
elderly friendly Scotsman, straight-spined, red-faced and
silver-moustached. His uniform had several rings of braid
round the cuffs. His speech was all sudden, decided state-
ments interrupted by abrupt silences in which he sat erect,
gripping his knees with his hands and looking at the air in

front of his eyes. He felt my pulse, touched me with a stethoscope, agreed that I was asthmatic and went away. After a while a nurse came and gave me an intravenous injection which made me slightly better. Later that day Ian told me it was quite warm on deck and a whale had been sighted. The following day the doctor came back, sat erect beside me and asked how I felt. I said a bit better, I hoped to get up soon. He said abruptly, "How are your bowels?" I said I had no trouble with them. He sat in a tranced rigid silence for a while, then said suddenly, "Buy a tin of Eno's salts from the ship's store. Use them regularly," and left.

That night I developed an obstruction of the throat which coughing could not shift nor spitting reduce. Erotic images brought no relief though I tried to remember the most shameful parts of all the obscene things I had ever heard or read. Next day I asked again to see the doctor. He told me I had pneumonia and must be taken to the ship's hospital. He left and then the medical orderly came with a wooden wheeled chair. I panicked while being put in it, my mind crumbled for a few moments and I became quite babyish. I was not slapped but I was shouted at. Then I made my body as tense in the chair as possible in order to hold the mind in one piece. I was trundled along narrow corridors into the hospital where the nurse and orderly put me in a real bed. I was able to be calmer there. The hospital was a neat, bright little room with four beds and small flower-patterned curtains round the portholes. I asked for an intravenous injection of adrenaline. The nurse explained that this would not help pneumonia. She tied a small oxygen cylinder to the head of the bed and gave me a mask connected to it by a rubber tube. This helped a little. The orderly brought a form, asked several questions and filled it in. My religion puzzled him. I said I was agnostic and his pencil dithered uncertainly above a blank space. I spelled the word out but he wrote down "agnoist". Ian came and I

dictated a letter to my father to be posted from Gibraltar.
A radio telegram had been sent to him and I wanted to
mitigate any worry it might cause. I noticed nothing special
in Ian's manner but later he told me he had difficulty
restraining his tears. The doctor had diagnosed pneumonia
with probable tuberculosis, and said it would be a miracle if
I reached Gibraltar alive. While we were at work on the
letter the doctor entered with a man wearing a uniform
like his own. This stranger looked on with a faint embarrassed smile while the doctor spoke to me in a loud
cheery bonhomous Scottish way. "Aye, Alasdair, keep your
heart up!" he cried, "Remember the words of Burns:
'The heart's aye the part aye that maks us richt or
wrang'."
"Just so, Doctor, just so," I said, playing up to him. He told
me that I would be shifted to a land-hospital next morning
when the ship reached Gibraltar, meanwhile (and here he
looked at the dial on my oxygen cylinder) I'd better go easy
on the oxygen, I'd used up half a tube already and there was
only one left in the store. The two visitors went away and
the nurse told me the other man was the captain.

After that life was hard for a while. I finished one oxygen
cylinder and started on the last, which had forty minutes of
comfortable breathing in it. It was difficult to disperse
these forty minutes through the eighteen hours before we
reached Gibraltar, sleep was impossible and I was afraid of
becoming too tired to make myself breathe. During this
time I was well cared for by the nurse and the orderly. She
was a plain, slightly gawky, serious, very pleasant young
woman. She gave me penicillin injections and clean towels
to wipe away my sweat. The orderly was a blockily built
smallish sturdy man with a clumsy amiable face. He gave me
a large brandy at nine in the evening and another at
midnight. I felt these two were completely dependable
people. At one in the morning the doctor came in wearing

dress uniform. I had never seen a celluloid shirt front
before. He leant over the bed, breathed some fumes in my
face and asked, with an effort at cheeriness, how I felt. I said
I was afraid, and in pain. He indicated the oxygen mask, told
me to use it if I got worse and hurried out. The cylinder was
almost empty. When it was completely empty I rang the
bell behind my bed. The orderly ran in at once in his
pyjamas. I asked for more brandy, and got it. This did not
lessen the pain but made me unable to think clearly about
it. I may or may not have rung the bell for other brandies,
my subsequent memories are muddled. I remember just
one incident very clearly. The nurse entered wearing a
flower-patterned long dressing-gown and seeming very
beautiful. She looked at the empty cylinder, felt my brow
then went away and brought in another cylinder. I laughed
and shook her hand and I am sure she smiled. I felt an
understanding between us: she and I were in alliance
against something dismal. I don't know if she had disobeyed
the doctor in giving me the third cylinder. Maybe he had
very few and wanted to keep a certain number in case
someone else needed them on the voyage.

Later the ship's engine stopped and I knew we were at
Gibraltar. I think this was about five in the morning. I don't
recall who did it but I was shifted to a stretcher, wrapped
up as snugly and tightly as an Egyptian mummy, carried into
a bare kind of cabin and left on the floor. The stretcher had
little legs which kept it above the planks. My breathing was
easier now and I was beginning to feel comfortable. The
doctor, in ordinary uniform, stood nearby looking out of a
porthole. He was less drunk than when he had visited me in
the night but mellow and communicative. I saw now that
his erect abrupt manner disguised a wonderfully controlled, almost continual intoxication. I felt very friendly toward him and he toward me. He sighed and said, "There
she is – Gibraltar – under the moon. I never thought to see

her again, Alasdair, I forget how many years it is since I last
saw her."

"Were you in practice ashore?"

"This National Health Service is *rotten* Alasdair. Forms to
be filled, paperwork, the pen never out of your hand. In the
old days the doctor worked with a stethoscope in one hand
and a s,s,s, a *scalpel* in the other. How do you feel?"

"A lot better."

"You've come through a bad time, Alasdair, a very bad
time . . . . a Catholic priest told me I was a lost soul last
night."

He looked out of the porthole again then said, "I was
married once. The girl died a month after the wedding."

"Do you think I could have another brandy?"

"Would ye not like a whisky? I can give ye a good
Glenlivet."

I won't pretend the doctor used these exact words but he
referred to these things in the order I have recorded them,
and stuttered on the s of scalpel, making me imagine a
surgical knife vibrating in a trembling fist. Later we heard
the chugging of a small boat. He said, "That's the lighter,"
and went out and came in again with three seamen and a
Spanish doctor, a broad, duffle-coated, rimless-spectacled,
crew-cut, laconic man. He spoke quietly to the ship's
doctor, tested me with a stethoscope then left, refusing
the offer of a drink. I heard the chugging of the boat going
away.

I was shifted into hospital later that morning in bright
sunshine. I was still wrapped tightly on the stretcher with
only my face exposed. I felt comfortable, privileged and so
incurious I did not try to see anything not directly above my
eyes. I saw a section of the high side of the ship against a
pale blue sky. I heard a babble of voices and felt a hard cold
breeze on my cheek. I think I recall the top of a white mast
or flagstaff with a wind-taut flag on it. This must have been

aboard the lighter. Sometimes my upward view was irregularly framed by downward-staring faces: the doctor, Ian, customs officers and strangers. Once the lined dry face of a middle-aged lady looked down for a moment, smiled and said, "I say, you hev hed a bit of bed luck, you've come rathah a croppah, heven't you," and some other terse kindly things full of English-hunting-field stoicism. I liked her for her kindness, and for being so easy to classify. I saw the wooden ceiling of a customs shed, the low steel ceiling of an ambulance, and then, after a ten-minute sound of fast uphill car-travel, the cream ceiling of a hospital vestibule. In this way I arrived in Gibraltar without seeing the rock. Indeed, since leaving London, I had only once seen the sea, through portholes, during the first breakfast afloat. I was now put to bed under a suspended bottle of cortisone solution, which dripped down through a rubber tube into my arm. I was visited by the hospital chief, the laconic doctor who had examined me on board the ship. He said, "You are suffering, of course, from a bad but perfectly ordinary asthma attack. I was sure of that as soon as I saw you this morning, but could not say so. You understand, of course, that it is against professional etiquette to question the decision of a colleague."

The ward was three times longer than broad with eight beds to each long wall. The wall facing me was all window from pillow-level to ceiling. I saw through it a glassed-in veranda containing a few beds and beyond that the water of a wide bay. The hospital stood high up so steep a slope that I could see only the top of the building in front, two elegant towers faced with biscuit-coloured plaster. Far beyond and below these the bay had several sorts of ship moored in it, protected by long breakwaters with cranes on them. Distance made the ships look too small even to be useful toys while the breakwaters, exceptional bits of engineering to surround such a great body of water, seemed a few lines of forlorn geometry drawn upon it. The far side of the bay was all hills and small mountains with the whitish jumble of a town along the coast at their foot. This was Spain.

Although the head doctor was Spanish the routine and discipline of the hospital was British, the matron was a Scot, and of the three sisters two were English and one Welsh. The nurses were small plump Spanish or Gibraltarian girls, and most of the patients were Gibraltarian: that is, bilingual Spaniards who lived on the rock. They were inclined to be middle-aged and gaunt. There was a Velázquez-type dwarf called Paco with a calm, smooth, dignified face and slightly amused mouth. He would stand beside a bed resting his folded arms on it and talking quietly to the occupant in Spanish, or just leaning his brow on his folded arms. To my right was Major Mellors, elderly, gaunt and hawk-nosed. Facing me across the ward was Sigurdson, a taciturn humorous ship's mate from Lancashire. I learned the names and manners of these people gradually. The inmates of a hospital ward observe their neighbours closely but avoid, at first, contacting them, for each is too engrossed by their own illness to want the burden of sympathizing with someone else.

During my first week in hospital I was visited regularly by Ian, who had taken lodgings in Gibraltar, but after finding I was out of danger he set off into Spain. He was going to the village of Estepona a few hours journey up the coast, for he had heard good reports of it. He meant to find decent rooms there, settle in, and I would join him when I left the hospital. I made him take two pounds to compensate him for some of the money he had lost by the delay. The day after he left for Spain I was surprised to see him enter the ward. He sat by my bed and explained that he did not like Spain.

"It's so unhygienic, Alasdair. I got off the bus at Estepona and set out to find a place to stay, but the flies! I travelled everywhere inside this cloud of flies. I mean, it was ridiculous. And the children who kept following me, begging, were almost as hard to shake off. And everybody stared. I mean, they didn't do it sideways or behind your back, they stood still in the street and really looked at you. I found a place. I won't describe the sanitation because there wasn't any. I went out for a drink with a bloke I had met in the bus. We went into a bar and ordered wine at the counter. Before pouring it out the barman put down two wee plates each with a wee dirty bit of fish on it. I mean, we were expected to eat that. The counter was filthy – nothing was properly clean. I mean, outside the village you get these farm buildings with nice white walls, very picturesque. And when you go near you see the ground covered with little heaps of shit. They must just have squatted in the shadow to get rid of it."

"What was the countryside like?" I asked.

"Oh, it's picturesque all right. I mean, it's beautiful in a queer way. You get these low brownish hills in the dusk with a line of donkeys and their riders going along the top against a fantastic sunset. I mean it might grow on you. But I realize now that what I want to paint is in Scotland. I don't think I've wasted my money if I've discovered that. I think I'll use what's left to do some painting up the East coast, in Fife or Angus. Maybe I'll call in at Paris on the way home."

I won't pretend Ian used these exact words but he talked in that style and mentioned these things. Three days later he got on a boat which took him to France.

I was not unhappy in that hospital. The staff kept pain out of me with doses and injections. I was nursed, fed and allowed to live completely to myself. The homesickness seemed to have been burned out by my experience aboard ship. Sometimes a faint "Over the graves of the martyrs the whaups are crying, my heart remembers how" feeling drifted through my mind like faint smoke, but that was romantic nostalgia, nothing like the earlier sick hunger for Glasgow and those I knew there. This new equanimity came partly from the routine of hospital, which was familiar to me, but there was another reason.

A few years earlier I had begun work on a tragicomical novel and meant to write some more of it in Spain. In my luggage was a Cantablue Expanding Wallet, a portable cardboard filing cabinet shaped like an accordion and holding two complete chapters and the notebooks and diaries from which I meant to make the rest. I put this on my bedside locker and began working. I was slightly ashamed of this activity, which struck me as presumptuous and banal: presumptuous because, like Scott Fitzgerald, I believed the novel was the strongest and supplest medium for conveying thought and emotion from one human being to another, which meant that a novelist needed to understand great states of feeling, and although twenty-three years old I had never known carnal love and feared I never would; banal because one or two friends had also started writing a novel, and the rest had thought of writing one. So when the nurses asked what I was doing I lied and told them I was writing this report. But actually I was in Glasgow, the Glasgow of my childhood and adolescence and studenthood, and far more at home there than when I underwent these painful states, for now my mind hovered above the person I had been in perfect safety, without affection but with great curiosity. I found that person unpleasant but comic and was fascinated by the things and people it knew. My world was confused, shabby and sad, but had as much order, variety, good feeling and potency as any other. I tried to write an ordinary, easily-read language which showed the sadness and shabbiness but made the other things (which keep us alive) equally evident. While I worked at this writing I enjoyed the best happiness of all, the happiness which does not notice itself, until, stopping, we feel tired and see that an hour has passed like a minute, and know we have done as well as we can, and perhaps one day someone will be glad. I am sure this happiness is not rare. Everyone feels a little of it who makes or keeps something useful in the world, and does not just work for money and promotion. I suspect there is more of this happiness among skilled manual workers than in higher income groups, who have other satisfactions.

I was not shut completely into my head. I often looked out across the bay. Hospitals are generous with pillows to their asthmatic patients and I could see the coast of Spain without raising my head. On bright afternoons a few long wisps of white vapour would trickle up into the sky from wide-apart points on the sides of the mountains. Perhaps it was a memory of old fairy-tales that made me think this smoke came from the huts of charcoal-burners. I tried to imagine myself wandering there and totally failed. Gibraltar has one of the Mediterranean's moister climates and the view was often blotted out by low cloud. I also had an understanding with Major Mellors based upon definite but minimum communication. During the morning I might say, "Was it all right to tip the barber?"
"Yes. How much did you give him?"
"Ninepence."
"That was too much."
In the afternoon he might remark, on a wistful note, "I wonder how my garden's getting on."
"Is there nobody looking after it?"
"Oh yes, my servant Ali."
"Won't he look after it properly?"
"Oh yes, he's very good with flowers."
But the most sociable time was between the half-past-five cup of tea and the seven o'clock breakfast when Sister

Price sat at a table at our end of the ward. She was bright
and talkative, and Sigurdson and the Major and I would
interject and pass comments which seemed to us all
increasingly witty and humorous. Yet I cannot now recall a
single thing we said. The base of the conversation was four
very different people wanting to enjoy and please each
other and succeeding. For the rest of the day we were
friendly in a quiet way which later struck me as British, or
even European, when Mr Sweeney arrived.

He was the first mate of a big American ship and was put
in an empty bed beside Sigurdson. Had his flesh been firm
he would have been a broad tough middle-aged man, but
his cheeks were pouchy, he had a pouch under each eye,
when not talking his mouth drooped to the left as if his
muscles only kept hold of the right-hand corner. But he
was usually talking because he could only think aloud. We
learned he had a wife in America he seemed not to like
much, and a daughter called Baby, living with the wife,
whom he liked a great deal. "She's well over forty, she's
twice divorced, but she'll always be my Baby."
He was a Christian Scientist and said he had only come to
hospital because the company he served could take away
his pension if he refused. When disease or death was
mentioned he would shrug and say, "After all, what is the
body? Just fifty cents-worth of chemicalization."
If a silence lasted too long for him he sometimes broke it by
remarking, at random, "After all, the only realities are
spiritual realities."
Beneath his bed were three large cases from which he got
the hospital porter to produce, at various times, many
electrical gadgets connected with hygiene and grooming,
cigars, tissues, a radio, three ball-pens which wrote in
different colours, and a steel-barrelled pen filled with spirit
ink to which could be fixed several thicknesses of felt nib.
He did not converse. He might call one of us by name, but

his loud, even voice was clearly addressing our entire half of
the ward. Once he called out, "Say, Major! Could you lend
me just a small spoonful of that toothpowder of yours and
tomorrow I'll give you back a whole tin of it?"

"What's that, old man?" said the Major, maybe playing for
time.

"Could you lend me one little spoonful of that toothpowder of yours and tomorrow I'll repay you with a
whole big new tin of it? I got one in the case."

"Oh you mustn't give away all your pretty things like that,"
said the Major, gently.

"Major, when I'm tired of giving I'll be tired of living. If
people are grateful, well and good. If not . . . . "

He frowned, his mouth sagged into its expression of
slightly puzzled vacuity and for some minutes his eyes
searched the ward uneasily for something to think about.
At last they focused on a point beneath the table where the
sister wrote her reports. "Say!" he said, brightening,
"That's the saddest waste-paper basket I ever did see!
It's twisted, it's all to cock, it needs a new coat of
paint . . . . " and then he ran out of thoughts again and
eventually muttered that the only realities were spiritual
realities.

We were fascinated by Sweeney because he continually
presented himself, which none of us did. At first meeting
our accents had shown each other that Sigurdson was a
Lancashire seaman, the Major an English army officer and I a
well-read lowland Scot. The humorous prebreakfast chats
had confirmed this without adding detail. I knew the Major
had commanded the household troops of some Moroccan
or Algerian ruler, but had not heard it from his lips. He
must have noticed that I was writing something larger than
this report but my privacy did not disturb him. Mr Sweeney
gave us his whole childhood in half a minute.

"For the first twelve years of my life I was reared by my

mother and wow, you should have seen me. Blue velvet suit. Satin shirt and necktie. Curly hair down to my shoulders. She had just about made a little girl of me when my pa came and took me to sea with him. She didn't want it, I didn't want it, but he said, 'You're gonna cry your eyes out but one day you'll be grateful.' And I cried. I guess I cried myself to sleep almost every night for six whole months. But after a year I was tough, I was a man, and I was grateful."

He was not embarrassed by his sexuality. One day the Major asked what he thought of the Japanese.

"I like 'em. Collectively they're skunks but individually I like 'em. I remember my ship putting into Yokohama in thirty-six. The Mayor entertained a few of us. I like Japanese homes. They're clean. No furniture; you sit on mats on the floor. Nothing like that – " he pointed to the top of his locker which, like our lockers, was littered with many more or less useful objects – "All that stuff is kept in a smooth box in the corner of the room. And there's not much decoration either. But the room is built round an almond tree that comes out of a hole in the floor and goes out through one in the ceiling and the trunk and branches in the room have been given a coat of clear . . . . not varnish, but like varnish . . . . "

"Lacquer?" I suggested.

"Yeah. They're lacquered. Well, nothing was too good for us. They saw we didn't like their drink so without even asking they sent out for whisky. And when I went to bed, there she was. In a kimono. There are over fifty yards of silk in those kimonos. By the time she'd unwrapped herself I had almost lost my courage."

One day it was announced on the wireless that President Eisenhower had burst a small blood-vessel in his brain, his speech was impaired and he was confined to bed. Sweeney heard this with unusual gravity. He said, "He's sixty-two. My age." and was silent for a long time.

"After all," he said suddenly, "He's an old man. What can you expect?"

He complained of headache. The nurse on duty told him it would go away. "But what's causing it?" he demanded, "That's what I want to know. What's causing it?"

He called the sister, then the matron, who both told him a codeine tablet would cure it. "I won't take dope!" he cried, "You aren't going to dope me!"

He huddled silently under the bedclothes for over an hour. "After all," he said suddenly, "He's old. He's not indispensable, even if he is the president. He'll be replaced one day, just like the rest of us."

He clearly wanted to be persuaded that what he said was untrue. The Major and I kept glancing at each other with furtive, delighted grins, but we were glad when Eisenhower got well enough to make a speech and Mr Sweeney felt better. He was more entertaining when he was confident.

The trustees may wonder why I have spent so many words describing this man. I do so for reasons that would have made me describe Toledo, had I reached Toledo. He displayed a coherent kind of life. I admired his language, which was terse, rapid, and full of concrete detail. I realized this was part of his national culture and found an impure form of it in an American magazine he read each week with great seriousness. "Everything in this is *fact*," he explained, "It prints nothing but the bare facts. Other magazines give you opinions. Not this one."

I borrowed it and read a report of the British Labour Party conference. One of the leaders had tried to persuade the Party that bits of Britain should not be leased to the U.S.A. as bases for their nuclear weapons. Under a photograph of him looking pugnacious were the words "Number one American-hater, rabble-rousing Aneurin Bevan".

But I admired Mr Sweeney quite apart from his national style. With energy, skill, and a total absence of what I

thought of as intellectual reserves (a developed imagination, analytical subtlety, wide reading) he had managed
ships and men in two world wars and the Korean war. He
had worked and enjoyed himself and taken knocks among
the solid weights and wide gaps of the world I would not
face. Death worried him now that his body was failing, but
since the age of twelve he had never been embarrassed by
life. And by wrestling with the fear of death openly and
aloud he made it a public comedy instead of a private
terror. Aboard the Kenya Castle, when I was afraid of dying,
my fear did nobody any good.

Of course, I had to face the world in the end. Only
everlasting money can keep us from doing that, and mine
was being used up. Each day in hospital cost me twenty-one
shillings and I had been over three weeks there. When to
that was added the train fare to London, and cost of
lodgings there, boat fare to Gibraltar, ship's hospital fee,
the price of the ambulance journey and being X-rayed for
tuberculosis, and the small sum I had forced upon Ian, I
found I had spent, or else owed, more than half the
scholarship money. I recalled, too, that I had never been
discharged from hospital feeling perfectly well. It was
possible that something in the nature of hospitals pandered
to my asthma after the worst of an attack had been cured
by them. I asked to see the head doctor and explained that,
for financial reasons, I must leave next morning. He shrugged and said, "It cannot be helped." He advised me, though,
not to leave Gibraltar until I felt healthier, and even so not
to go far into Spain in case I had another attack, as in Spain
the hospital charges were extortionate, especially to tourists, and the medical standards were not high. This seemed
sensible advice. I asked the nurses for the name of a lodging
which was cheap, plain and good. I heard there was an
armed-forces leave centre in the south bastion which
usually had spare beds, was run by a retired Scottish

soldier, and easy to reach. Next morning I dressed, collected my rucksack, left the hospital doorstep and struck
with my feet the first earth I had touched since the port of
London.

I was on a road slanting up from the town of Gibraltar to
the rock's outermost point. The day must have been clear
because across the sea to the south I saw the African coast
looking exactly as Africa ought to look: a dark line of
crowded-together rock pinnacles, domes and turrets with
beyond them, when the eye had grown used to the
distance, the snowy range of Atlas holding up the sky. The
modern hospital behind me, the elegantly towered building in front (a lunatic asylum) stood on a great slant of white
limestone rock interspersed with small tough twisted
trees. I turned right and walked to the town, breathing
easily because I was going downhill. I came to a wall with an
arch in it just wide enough to take two cars, and beyond
this the road became the main street of Gibraltar. A small
lane leading to the left brought me almost at once to the
south bastion.

This was a stone-built cliff protecting the town from the
sea. The townward side was pierced by vaulted chambers.
The lower ones, which had been barracks, were entered
from a narrow piazza; the upper, which had been munition
storerooms and gun emplacements, were entered from a
balcony. All windows faced the town. High tides had once
lapped the other side of this bastion but now a broad road
ran here with docks on the far side. The guns and gunners
had shifted elsewhere long ago and the chambers were
used as a guest-house by the Toc H. The Toc H (I never
learned the reason for that name) developed in France
during the First World War, among British soldiers who
wanted spiritual communion and found the official army

priests too sectarian and not always near when things got tough. The only communion service was to light a brass oil-lamp in a dark place and pray that human pain would one day produce happiness and peace. Apart from that the organization existed to share extra food, clothing and shelter with whoever seemed in need. Jock Brown, formerly of the Highland Light Infantry in Flanders, was the Toc H man in south bastion. He was small, balding, mild-faced and wore a blazer with a white cross badge on the breast pocket and flannel trousers with bicycle clips at the ankles. His instincts were all turned to being mildly helpful. He believed that youth was a beautiful and noble state but was not surprised when young soldiers brawled, con-tracted venereal diseases and stole. He liked lending them cameras, books and records in the hope that they would come to enjoy using these instead. With the help of Isabel, a Spanish maid, he kept the hostel tidy and clean, the meals plain yet tasty, the general air of the place as mild as himself. I once heard him called "an old woman" by somebody who thought that a term of abuse. The critic was a man of Jock's age who had not been very useful to other people, so wanted to believe that everyday kindness was an unimpor-tant virtue.

On that first morning Jock led me up a ramp to the balcony and into the commonroom, a former gun-emplacement with a triangular floorplan. A hearth was built into the angle facing the door so that smoke left by the hole through which shells had been fired. The interior stonework was massively rough except for seven feet of smooth wall on each side of the hearth, and later I painted mural decorations here. Jock showed me to a dormitory next door holding four beds and introduced me to room-mates who had not yet risen. These were a private on leave from the Royal Surrey regiment, and an Australian and a German who would both be departing by ship next morning. I unpacked my things into a locker beside my bed then visited a bank in town where I uplifted the second part of the Bellahouston Scholarship money, the first having been received in Glasgow. I pocketed a few pounds and hid the rest in a plastic envelope containing my shaving-kit.

That night, to obtain sound sleep in a strange bed, I decided to become drunk and found a big crowded bar nearby where I would not be conspicuous. The customers were mostly soldiers and sailors but there were women among them. A small plump one approached and asked if I would like a compañera? I said I would. She sat beside me, called a waiter and ordered a glass of pale green liquid, for which I paid. She was Spanish and her English was too poor to tell me much else. She tried to be entertaining by folding a handkerchief into the shape of what she called pantalones and unfastening the flies, but I did not find this exciting or feel she wished to seduce me. With each green drink I bought, the waiter handed her a small brass disc. When she went to the lavatory I tasted what was in her glass and found it to be coloured water. I got the waiter to refill the glass with green chartreuse but when she returned and sipped this she grew thoughtful and depressed, then left me. Clearly the management paid her no commission on the real drinks I purchased. So I drank by myself and listened to a small, very noisy band. It played a round of tunes chosen to cause nostalgia in as many customers as possible: *Maybe It's Because I'm a Londoner*, *Men of Harlech*, *Galway Bay*, etc. The Scottish number, *I Belong to Glasgow*, was repeated every ten minutes. It is not a tune I normally like but in this place it induced an emotion so heartrending that I had to grapple with it as if it were a disease. However, I stayed drinking until I was sure my head would lose consciousness as soon as it touched a pillow, then returned to the dormitory (which was in darkness), undressed, put

the shaving-kit under the pillow, my head on top of it, and
did indeed lose consciousness.

I wakened late next morning feeling brighter and healthier than I had done for many weeks. I also felt guilty (the
straw mat beside my bed was crusted with vomit) but I
knew that a day of brisk sketching or writing would cure
that. The English private remained curled below his blankets, the Australian and German had already left to catch
their boat. I took my toilet things and the straw mat to the
lavatory and washed the mat and myself perfectly clean.
Then I dressed and breakfasted, then climbed by an iron
ladder to the esplanade on top of the bastion and sat on a
shaded bench planning what to do. I still owed money to
the hospital. I took my wad of notes from the shaving-kit
and found it contained twenty pounds. The rest had been
removed.

My instinctive reaction to a painful event is to sit quiet
for a very long time, and as I brooded on my position this
struck me as an intelligent thing to do. The thief must be
one of three people, two of whom were at sea. If I could
persuade the police to act for me, which was unlikely, they
could do little but spread to others a nasty feeling I had
better keep to myself. The thief had left me enough to live
on for a while. Although my father was not rich he had
some money banked. I wrote him a letter explaining all the
circumstances except my intoxication and asking for a loan
of the stolen amount, which I promised to repay by taking a
regular job when I returned home. He posted the money
to me as quickly as he could. The asthma returned. It
worsened and improved, then worsened and improved. I
remained in the hostel for my twenty-fourth birthday, and
the New Year of 1958, and another two months. I wrote
five chapters of my book and painted a *Triumph of Neptune*
on the commonroom walls.

I also made friends with some rootless people who used the hostel a lot. There was a student from the Midlands who had left Britain to avoid national military service and seemed to live by petty smuggling. There was a tall stooping bronchial man, also from the Midlands, who hovered around the Mediterranean for health reasons. There was a middle-aged American with a sore back who had been refused entry into England where he had gone to consult an osteopath of whom he had heard great things. He kept discussing the reasons for the refusal and wondering if a slight tampering with the datestamp on his passport would make entry easier if he tried again. There was Cyril Hume, an unemployed ableseaman with a photograph of a cheerful, attractive-looking wife in Portsmouth who "realized he needed to wander about a bit". I think it was Cyril Hume who learned that a ship would be sailing to the Canary Isles from a port on the African coast just opposite. Apparently the fare was cheap and the cost of living in the Canary Isles even less than the cost of living in Spain. My health was improving at the time so we all decided to go together. We took a ferry across the bay to Algeciras in Spain, and another ferry from Algeciras to Africa. There was a bright sun and a strong wind, the waves ran fast with glittering foamy crests. The jumbled rocky African coast and a steep promontory with a medieval fortress on it looked theatrical but convincing. Cyril Hume had bought us cheese, celery and bread. Standing in the prow of the ship it suddenly struck me that cheese, celery and precisely this chalky white bread was the best lunch I had ever tasted. Slightly breathless, I produced my medical hand-pump and inhaled from it. The surrounding crowd turned and watched me with that direct, open interest which Ian McCulloch had found upsetting. I enjoyed it. I liked being a stranger who provoked interest without even trying.

The port we reached was Ceuta, a Spanish possession. It looked just like Algeciras: whitewalled buildings and streets bordered by orange trees with real fruit among the leaves. The ship we wanted had left for the Canary Isles the day before so we returned to Algeciras and took lodgings there. Next morning, having slept badly, I decided to stay in bed. After my friends had left a maid entered the room and began making the other beds by shaking up the feather quilts and mattresses. I am allergic to feathers and started suffocating. I cried out to her but had no Spanish and she no English. In my notebook I hastily sketched a feather and told her it was *mal* – I hoped that the Latin root for evil was part of her language too. She smiled and repeated the word with what seemed perfect comprehension and then, when I lay back, relieved, she returned to violently plumping out the quilts. I gripped my hypodermic needle to give myself a big adrenaline injection but my hand trembled and the needle broke short in my flesh. The maid and I both panicked. She screamed and a lot of women ran in and surrounded me, jabbering loudly as I pissed, shat, and grew unconscious.

I wakened in a hospital managed by dark-robed, white-wimpled brides of Christ. A doctor came, gave me pills of a sort that can be bought cheap from any chemist, and charged dear for them. My friends arrived, discharged me, and escorted me back across the bay to Gibraltar and the Toc H hostel, where I stayed in bed for a week. I now had slightly more than ten pounds of money left: enough to buy a cheap boat fare back to London.

One day Jock Brown came to me and said that if I gave him my passport he would get me a ticket for an aeroplane going to London that evening. The ticket cost thirty pounds. Jock did not offer to lend me money. He took my passport, returned with a ticket and helped me to the airport. I crossed Spain at twice the altitude of Everest. It looked brown and as flat as a map. The only memorable feature was the white circle of the bullring in the middle of each town. London was foggy. I went to the University hospital and was given an intravenous adrenaline injection to help me reach Glasgow by overnight train. At Glasgow Central Station I took a taxi to the Royal Infirmary where I was drugged and sent home by ambulance. The morning was fresh and springlike but I felt no joy in homecoming. Glasgow was as I expected.

And now, to sum up, what good was the tour? What did it teach me? Not much about the world, but a lot about myself. It is evident that I fear to change. We are always changing of course. From the moment of birth we start the alteration and adaption called *growth*. Growth is usually gradual and foreseeable. Our surroundings don't change much and neither do we. But sometimes surroundings change radically and suddenly. A war is declared and we hide with neighbours in a dark shelter with queer noises outside. A mother dies, we must leave school and find a new way of living. We are awarded a scholarship and go to a foreign land in the belly of a posh liner. Such events should have made me grow into a different man. But I was afraid of losing the habits by which I knew myself, so withdrew into asthma. My tour was spent in an effort to avoid the maturity gained from new experiences. Yet in spite of the protective clutter of doctors in which I ended the trip that effort failed. We can accept maturity bravely or panic and kick against it, but eventually some form of maturity is imposed. Before going abroad the idea of teaching art to children appalled me. I have been doing it now for five months, and compared with partial suffocation in a Spanish estancia it is an almost painless activity. I will soon have paid Jock Brown what I owe him, and will then pay my father.

Also, since getting home I have had no more bad asthma attacks, and don't live in fear of them. So the Bellahouston Travelling Scholarship has done me good.

April 1959
11 Findhorn Street
Riddrie
Glasgow C3

POSTSCRIPT. Wishing to attach to this report photographs of my *Triumph of Neptune* I wrote to Jock Brown asking if he would take and send me some. He answered that this was impossible. Soon after I left the hostel it was visited by the wife of Gibraltar's governor. She felt the naked mermaids and nereids in the commonroom were a bad moral influence upon the soldiers using the place, so her husband asked Jock to paint them out. Jock, who liked my mural, wrote to the Secretary of State for War, Mr Jack Profumo, asking if he need obey the governor's request. Mr Profumo replied that "the man on the spot knows best", by whom he meant, not Jock Brown, but the governor's wife. So Jock, with rage in his heart, covered my mermaids with a coat of khaki paint. It is pleasant to imagine a more liberal age one day restoring them to light.

However, the town of Gibraltar needs room to
expand, and in a year or two the
south bastion will be
demolished.

The Answer

Late at night a young man entered a phonebox in the suburb of an industrial city. He put coins in the slot, lifted the receiver, dialled and waited a moment. Later he heard a girl's voice say, "Hello?"

"Hello Joan!"

There was no answer. He said, "This is Donald."

Silence.

"Donald Purdie."

Silence.

"How are you, Joan?"

Silence. He frowned in a puzzled way and said, "I'm just back from Loch Lomond – I've been boating with the McEwans. They asked me to give you their love."

Silence.

"Listen Joan, is anything wrong? . . . .

"Are you *all right* Joan? . . . .

"Joan, is this a joke? . . . .

"If you don't want to talk to me you'd better put the receiver down."

After a while he heard faint movements, then more silence.

He put the receiver down. He stood with heart beating loudly and a heavy weight in his chest, wondering what to do. He was too disturbed to go home to bed and it would be hard to live through the next days without knowing exactly what was wrong. At last he left the phonebox and walked through several streets to a place where two roads crossed. A taxi stood at a corner. He got into it and gave the driver an address on the other side of the city. He sat on the edge of the seat feeling excited and depressed. Sometimes the feelings in his chest got so big that he had to breathe deeply to quieten them. At other times he stared out of the window. The taxi passed through tenements, then the larger office buildings of the city centre, and after twenty minutes came to a district of bungalows, fields and petrol stations. It stopped before a bungalow with a garden sloping up from the road. Donald told the driver to wait and got out. The path to the door was made of granite chips and to make no noise he walked on the grass verge. The only light in the bungalow was at a side window, the kitchen window. Joan often stayed up late, reading in the kitchen. He stepped to the lit yellow oblong, struck the glass with a knuckle and called, "Joan! Donald here! Joan!" A moment later the light went out.

He walked heavy-footed on the crunching granite to the front door and rang the bell, waited ten seconds, rang again and kept on ringing. A light went on behind the door's thick rippled glass and it was opened by a girl who looked at him with a welcoming smile. She wore dressing gown and slippers, copious brown hair hung down loosely behind her shoulders, her eyebrows were strong and black, her nose long, her mouth large and humorous, her chin receded. She held the gown together at her throat with a big finely shaped hand and said in a pleased voice, "Donald!"
"Hello Joan."
"I've just been washing my hair."
He looked keenly into her face. She smiled back less broadly. He said, "Look, Joan, I phoned you about eleven.

You answered the phone but wouldn't speak to me. I've come to find why."

Joan looked worried and said, "Come into the hall."

He followed her into a narrow hall, shutting the door behind him. She said, "You phoned at eleven?"

"Yes, and you answered."

"But Donald I came home at quarter-past eleven. I've been to the farm all day. You must have spoken to someone else."

"I didn't. You said 'Hello'."

"Then you must have got the wrong number."

"No, I didn't. You said 'Hello' and I went on talking and you didn't answer. I listened a long time. You must have put the telephone receiver down and gone away . . . . "

He glanced down at a telephone on the hall table beside him. The receiver lay off its cradle on top of a telephone directory. She said quickly, "As soon as I came in I took the receiver off in case any of my mother's boring friends rang up."

Donald said heavily, "I don't believe you."

He put his arms round her shoulders and smiled sadly down at her face. She smiled and laid her hands flat on his chest in a gesture that stopped him pulling her towards him. He said, "Why haven't I seen you lately?"

"I'm sorry Donald, but it's been such lovely weather – I've been working for these friends on the farm and I've been so happy there that I haven't seemed to have time for other things."

Donald let his hands fall by his side and stared at her. After a moment she said uncomfortably, "Come into the kitchen for a little while."

The kitchen was small and cosy with a white tiled grate, an electric fire burning in the grate and a hearthrug before the fire. An open book lay on the rug, as if someone had sprawled there reading. Donald sat on the armchair by the hearth, his clasped hands between his knees, leaning forward slightly and looking at a piece of hearthrug. Joan sat at a distance on a chair by a dining table. Donald said, "You see I've come to feel . . . . rather emotional about you."

Joan said gently, "Oh, I'm sorry. I hoped that hadn't happened."

After a while she said, "You see we enjoy different things. You like books and jazz and ideas and . . . . clever things like that. When I was with you I thought I liked these things but I don't really. I like exercising horses and cleaning out hen-coops and living like a tinker. I realized that quite suddenly last week. Physical things are very important to me. I'm sorry, Donald."

"But I don't see why that should separate us! Most people who . . . . like each other a lot keep bits of life private from each other."

"I'm sorry, Donald. It's very neurotic of me but that's how I see it."

"You're not neurotic."

"Oh but I am!" said Joan anxiously. "I really am very neurotic! I often do the most silly things . . . . "

"Like not speaking to me on the telephone?"

She looked down obliquely and murmured, "Well, yes."

Donald stood up and said, "I'd better go."

"It was very kind of you to come all that distance."

"It was not. I had to find out what was wrong."

At the front door he said, "Goodbye, Joan."

She said kindly, "Goodbye, Donald."

He got into the taxi and gave an address in the city. He sat on the back seat in the posture he had taken in the armchair, and bits of thought passed through his head.

'Why did I say "rather emotional" when I meant "love"?'

'Why was I so meek and reasonable? I should have struck her. As I left I should have struck her face.'

'The last time we met we seemed to get on very well.'

The taxi stopped in a street of tenements with a theatre at one end. Donald paid the driver, entered a close and walked up flights of steps to a landing with a bright red door on it. He pressed the letterbox open with a finger and whistled through. After a while the door was opened by a young cadaverous man with a straggly red beard and wearing a coat over pyjamas. He stared at Donald, raised his eyebrows and said, "Well, well."

"Can I come in? I know it's selfish of me but I need to talk to someone . . . . "

"Come in then."

They crossed a lobby into a small room containing a bed, a chair, a dressing-table and a television set. The floor, dressing-table and television set were covered with untidy piles of books. The bearded man threw off his coat, lay on the bed, pulled blankets over him and stared at the ceiling, hands clasped under head. Donald said, "A bad thing has happened to me. If I don't tell someone I'll have to walk about all night brooding on it."

"All right, tell me."

Donald walked carefully about the room, talking in a slow, almost hesitant voice. Sometimes he said, "I may be mistaken about this bit . . . . " and sometimes, "She didn't say exactly that, she put it more subtly."

When he had finished the bearded man yawned and said, "That's very interesting, Donald. Were you very keen on her?"

"Oh yes. I thought we were going to marry. She's the one girl I know who didn't make me feel embarrassed when I wanted to be . . . . sexual with her. We were always comfortable together, she was so frank and pleasant and . . . . beautiful."

"No, Donald, not beautiful. Remember, I've seen her."

"Yes, beautiful! I know her face is so individual it's almost ugly, but her body is beautiful by any standard – slender, with wee steep breasts, and a very big backside (she said it made clothes difficult to put on) and fine long legs. And she could undress without looking self-conscious or coy."

"She *slept* with you?" said the bearded man, looking surprised.

"Once or twice. Twice, to be exact."

"I always thought her a quiet sort of girl."

"She is a quiet sort of girl."

"And . . . . what was she like?"

"Like?"

"Like in bed?"

"Oh, I never fornicated with her – we just slept. I wasn't in the mood for anything more urgent, and I didn't think she was either. She kept her underwear on. But I've never slept so sweetly as I did with her arms round me. I'm usually a poor sleeper."

After a pause the bearded man said, "Don't you think she might have felt cheated?"

Donald sat down, turned the pages of a book without looking at them and said, "It had occurred to me. It's one reason why I can't blame her for her behaviour tonight."

"Still, she could have broken with you more kindly."

"But you can't break kindly with someone who loves you! The right way is to break honestly. By a very honest little act she showed me she was done with me. She put my voice carefully down on the hall table so as not to disturb it, and went quietly away and washed her hair. Her meaning was pretty clear, but like a fool I went to her house and *discussed* it."

The bearded man said sleepily, "A pity you didn't play on her love of animals. If you'd galloped up to her door at the head of a troop of cavalry she would have found you irresistible."

There was quiet in the room for several minutes. Then Donald said thoughtfully, "Why don't I protest more? The last time I was in love and the girl broke with me (that was five years ago) I protested all the time. I did stupid things, like insulting her in public and praying God to kill her. I thought my condition was unbearable. Now I feel quite calm. I have this ache in my chest, but talking to you has made it less, and it will disappear altogether when I get to sleep. Tomorrow it will come back for a few hours in the evening, but it will be perfectly bearable. And during the coming weeks it will come for a shorter time each day, and in three or four months I won't have it at all. And that — " said Donald standing up, "is the sad thing. Joan will be nothing but an ache to me, then not even that, and in a few years it will be hard to remember her. I wish this ache would last as long as I lived, so I could always remember her. But even my memory of her will come to nothing and everything we did and felt together will be senseless and useless."

He looked at the bearded man as if hoping to be refuted, but the bearded man was asleep.

The Story of a Recluse

My father was the Rev. John Kirkwood of Edinburgh, a man very well known for the rigour of his life and the tenor of his pulpit ministrations. I might have sometimes been tempted to bless Providence for this honourable origin, had not I been forced so much more often to deplore the harshness of my nurture. I have no children of my own, or none that I saw fit to educate, so perhaps speak at random; yet it appears my father may have been too strict. In the matter of pocket-money, he gave me a pittance, insufficient for his son's position, and when, upon one occasion, I took the liberty to protest, he brought me up with this home thrust of inquiry: "Should I give you more, Jamie, will you promise me it shall be spent as I should wish?" I did not answer quickly, but when I did, it was truly: "No," said I. He gave an impatient jostle of his shoulders, and turned his face to the study fire, as though to hide his feelings from his son. Today, however, they are very clear to me; and I know how he was one part delighted with my candour, and three parts revolted by the cynicism of my confession. I went from the room ere he had answered in any form of speech; and I went, I must acknowledge, in despair. I was then two and twenty years of age, a medical student of the University, already somewhat involved with debt, and already more or less (although I can scarce tell how) used to costly dissipations. I had a few shillings in my pocket; in a billiard room in St Andrew's Street I had shortly quadrupled this amount at pyramids, and the billiard room being almost next door to a betting agency, I staked the amount on the hazard of a race. At about five in the afternoon of the next day, I was the possessor of some thirty pounds – six times as much as I had ever dreamed of spending. I was not a bad young man, although a little loose. I may have been merry and lazy; until that cursed night I had never known what it was to be overpowered with drink; so it is possible I was overpowered the more completely. I have never clearly been aware of where I went or what I did, or of how long a time elapsed till my wakening. The night was dry, dark, and cold; the lamps and the clean pavements and bright stars delighted me; I went before me with a baseless exultation in my soul, singing, dancing, wavering in my gait with the most airy inconsequence, and all at once at the corner of a street, which I can still dimly recall, the light of my reason went out and the thread of memory was broken.

I came to myself in bed, whether it was that night or the next I have never known, only the thirty pounds were gone! I had certainly slept some while, for I was sober; it was not yet day, for I was aware through my half-closed eyelids of the light of a gas jet; and I had undressed, for I lay in linen. Some little time, my mind hung upon the brink of consciousness; and then, with a start of recollection, recalling the beastly state to which I had reduced myself, and my father's straitlaced opinions and conspicuous position, I sat suddenly up in bed. As I did so, some sort of hamper tore apart about my waist; I looked down and saw, instead of my night-shirt, a woman's chemise copiously laced about the sleeves and bosom. I sprang to my feet, turned, and saw myself in a cheval glass. The thing fell but a little lower than my knees; it was of a smooth and soft fabric; the lace very fine, the sleeves half way to my elbow. The room was of a piece; the table well supplied with necessaries of the toilet; female dresses hanging upon nails; a wardrobe of some light varnished wood against the wall; a foot bath in the corner. It was not my night-shirt; it was not my room; and yet by its shape and the position of the window, I saw it exactly corresponded with mine; and that the house in which I found myself must be the counterpart of my father's. On the floor in a heap lay my clothes as I had taken them off; on the table my pass-key, which I perfectly recognized. The same architect, employing the same locksmith, had built two identical houses and had them fitted with identical locks; in some drunken aberration I had mistaken the door, stumbled into the wrong house, mounted to the wrong room and sottishly gone to sleep in the bed of some young lady. I hurried into my clothes, quaking, and opened the door.

So far it was as I supposed; the stair, the very paint was of the same design as at my father's, only instead of the cloistral quiet which was perennial at home, there rose up to my ears the sound of empty laughter and unsteady voices. I bent over the rail, and looking down and listening, when a door opened below, the voices reached me clearer. I heard more than one cry "good night"; and with a natural instinct, I whipped back into the room I had just left and closed the door behind me.

A light step drew rapidly nearer on the stair; fear took hold of me, lest I should be detected, and I had scarce slipped behind the door, when it opened and there entered a girl of about my own age, in evening dress, black of hair, her shoulders naked, a rose in her bosom. She paused as she came in, and sighed; with her back still turned to me, she closed the door, moved towards the glass, and looked for a while very seriously at her own image. Once more she sighed, and as if with a sudden impatience, unclasped her bodice.

Up to that moment, I had not so much as formed a thought; but then it seemed to me I was bound to interfere. "I beg your pardon — " I began, and paused.
She turned and faced me without a word; bewilderment, growing surprise, a sudden anger, followed one another on her countenance.
"What on earth — " she said, and paused too.
"Madam," I said, "for the love of God, make no mistake. I am no thief, and I give you my word I am a gentleman. I do not know where I am; I have been vilely drunken — that is my paltry confession. It seems that your house is built like mine, that my pass-key opens your lock, and that your room is similarly situate to mine. How or when I came here, the Lord knows; but I awakened in your bed five minutes since — and here I am. It is ruin to me if I am found; if you can help me out, you will save a fellow from a dreadful mess; if you can't — or won't — God help me."
"I have never seen you before," she said. "You are none of Manton's friends."
"I never even heard of Manton," said I. "I tell you I don't know where I am. I thought I was in — Street, No. 15 — Rev. Dr Kirkwood's, that is my father."
"You are streets away from that," she said; "you are in the Grange, at Manton Jamieson's. You are not fooling me?"
I said I was not. "And I have torn your night-shirt," cried I. She picked it up, and suddenly laughed, her brow for the first time becoming cleared of suspicion. "Well," she said, "this is not like a thief. But how could you have got in such a state?"
"Oh!" replied I, "the great affair is not to get in such a state again."
"We must get you smuggled out," said she. "Can you get out of the window?"

I went over and looked; it was too high. "Not from this
window," I replied, "it will have to be the door."
"The trouble is that Manton's friends – " she began, "they
play roulette and sometimes stay late; and the sooner you
are gone, the better. Manton must not see you."
"For God's sake not!" I cried.
"I was not thinking of you in the least," she said; "I was
thinking of myself."
And then Robert Louis Stevenson laid down his pen leaving
a fragment of perfect prose which has tantalized me since
the mid sixties when I read it in a little secondhand book
bought for one shilling from Voltaire and Rousseau's shop
at the corner of Park Road and Eldon Street. The cover is
soft black leatherette with a copy of the author's signature
stamped in gold on the front, a grove of three gold
palmtrees on the spine, and on the titlepage, in red, the
words *Weir of Hermiston: Some Unfinished Stories.*

Suetonius says that the Roman Emperor Tiberius enjoyed asking literary men awkward questions like, what
songs the sirens sang? What name Achilles used when
disguised as a girl? In the seventeenth century Doctor
Browne of Norwich suggested these questions were not
wholly unanswerable, so in our century the poet Graves
tested his muse by making her answer them. Can I deduce
how *The Story of a Recluse* would continue if Stevenson had
finished it?

I must first get Jamie out of this house which is so
miraculously like and unlike his own. By like and unlike I
mean more than the coincidence of architecture and
doorlocks, the difference of moral tone. In both the Rev.
Dr Kirkwood's manse and Manton Jamieson's Grange a
spirited youngster of twenty-two, one a boy, one a girl,
lives with an older man they are inclined to dread.
Stevenson had a habit of creating characters dialectically.

Perhaps every author works in this way, but Stevenson's antagonistic or linked opposites are unusually definite. In *Kidnapped* the cautious lowland Whig, David Balfour, contains a pride and a courage which only become evident when he is coupled with the touchy highland Jacobite, Alan Breck Stewart, who displays his pride and courage in his garments. *The Master of Ballantrae* is about two brothers, one a dutiful, long-suffering toiler who hardly anyone likes, the other an adventurous, revengeful waster with charming social manners. In *Weir of Hermiston* each character is the antithesis of one or two others, with the Scottish State Prosecutor, Lord Weir, maintaining unity by being the antithesis of everybody. In *The Strange Case of Dr Jekyll and Mr Hyde* a respected healer and detested murderer alternate inside the same skin. Manton Jamieson can only be the counterpart of the Rev. Dr Kirkwood if he is a dominant antifather, a strong lord of misrule. Since men drink and gamble in his house this has been already indicated, but if he too gambles it must be with no fear of losing. He must be formidable. No more need be deduced just now about this character. Several pages will pass before Jamie meets him, because Stevenson had already written a story about a young man blundering at night into a strange house containing a young woman and being caught there by a formidable older man.

The Sire de Malétroit's Door is one of his poorer tales. His imagination works best when he deals with Scotland, and this tale is set in the blood-and-thunder France of *The Three Musketeers*. A young nobleman, fleeing from enemies, escapes through a mysteriously open door at the end of a cul-de-sac. He finds he has got out of one trap into another, a trap set by a rich old man for the lover of his niece. The old man refuses to believe that the nobleman and niece do not know each other, and gives them till dawn to choose between being murdered or married. Stevenson had a deliberate policy of putting heroes into exciting positions for which they are not responsible. He expounds it in his essay, *A Gossip About Romance*, where he declares that most human life is a matter of responding to circumstances we have not chosen, and that "the interest turns, not upon what a man shall choose to do, but on how he manages to do it; not on the passionate slips and hesitations of the conscience, but on the problems of the body and of the practical intelligence, in clean, open-air adventure, the shock of arms and the diplomacy of life. With such material as this it is impossible to build a play, for the serious theatre exists solely on moral grounds, and is a standing proof of the dissemination of the human conscience. But it is possible to build, upon this ground, the most joyous of verses, and the most lively, beautiful, and buoyant tales."

The lively, beautiful and buoyant tales Stevenson wrote in accordance with this theory are *Treasure Island* and *Kidnapped*. The heroes of these are boys, but so obedient to ordinary, conventional promptings, and keen to be thought adult, and so trusting, and mistaken, and fearful, and capable of the rare brave act, that folk of any age or sex can feel they would be that sort of boy in those circumstances. And the circumstances are so interesting! *The Sire de Malétroit's Door* is a poor story because only the circumstances are of interest. The trap which closes on the young nobleman squeezes nothing out of him but a gallant speech about his readiness to die. This wins him the niece's affectionate respect and a marital conclusion which is meant to be triumphantly life-affirming but is actually servile. This hero is not believable.

But Jamie Kirkwood is believable; and at first sight, and to my mind, is a far more distinct person than Jim Hawkins and David Balfour. No wonder. These youngsters cheerfully leave home with a fortune in view, getting trapped for a few hours on the way to it by Long John Silver and Captain

Hoseason. But Jamie Kirkwood, a man of twenty-two, eats and sleeps inside the trap where he was born. His jailer is no 18th century buccaneer but a 19th century, rigidly respectable, damnably ungiving Edinburgh clergyman who offers his son a choice of three courses: servility, hypocrisy, or rebellion. But Jamie will not turn hypocrite to get a little of the freedom he craves. By honestly answering his father's home thrust of enquiry he brands himself – in his father's eye and in his own – as a rebel and a cynic, the last of which he certainly is not. A cynic would have lied to get more money. This is a moral story about human conduct and the passionate slips and hesitations of the conscience. The circumstances which drive Jamie are the circumstances of a father's overbearing nature pressing to a division his son's appetites for freedom and for truth. Truth wins, and drives the son to despair. Despair drives him to gamble and drink the winnings. It is now highly likely that a young man of his class, and city, and century, will impose himself on a strange woman in a disreputable house. Jamie's blackout, the coincidence of doorlocks and bedrooms, lets Stevenson cut whole pages of transitional scenery and present this likely outcome as an achieved fact, while screwing our curiosity to a new, surprising level. What now?

To hold our curiosity, to give Jamie's feelings time to develop through the exercise of his own curiosity, he must leave this house without learning much more about it. Of course, he knows the architecture. The back door opens into a kitchen and cellar region where at least one servant is waiting for guests to depart and the master to go to bed. Jamie must leave by the front door, opening and closing it in stealthy silence. His pass-key allows this. The danger is that someone may unexpectedly leave the gaming room and catch him creeping through the hall. The girl, with another sigh, tells Jamie that she will return to the company

downstairs, announce she has changed her mind about
retiring, and hold their attention for four or five minutes.
She seems in no doubt of her ability to do this. She fastens
her bodice, ignoring Jamie's thanks and apologies with the
look of someone about to lift a familiar, weary burden. She
descends the stairs. He follows her halfway, then waits. He
hears a door open, one boisterous shout of welcome, a
door firmly closed. Shortly afterward a piano strikes out a
tune by Offenbach. This is his signal to escape. He does.

But in the second paragraph of his story Jamie said, "I
came to myself in bed, whether that night or the next I
have never known." If this means that he never gets back to
the daily calendar of events in his father's home then he
must be caught by Manton and Manton's friends while
attempting, with the girl's help, to leave the Grange. Her
conduct shows that Manton is jealous and powerful. If he is
also intelligent, and the young people tell him the truth, he
will neither quite believe nor disbelieve them. If he is a kind
of 19th century de Malétroit, a touchy megalomaniac, he
could offer Jamie a choice between emigration or public
disgrace. Let Jamie depart at once for America, without
the girl, and Manton will pay him something more than the
fare out; otherwise Manton will hand him to the police on a
charge of unlawful entry. Stevenson certainly had the skill
to make such an operatic twist seem plausible, but why
should he? It would not bring the end of the story an inch
nearer, that end which has been announced at the very
start, indeed before the start. This is The Story of a
Recluse. Jamie will divide himself from humanity and have
no children of his own, or none he sees fit to educate. A
high-spirited young man who may be merry and lazy, but is
brave enough to be honest while in difficulty, will become a
deliberately lonely, coldhearted rake who cares less for his
children than his own harsh parent cared for him. If the
splendid interview in the study, and the debauch, and the

meeting with the girl, produce nothing but Jamie decamping abroad then they are trivialized, because many different stories could start like that. They are equally trivialized if Jamie is charged before a magistrate, reported in the press, expelled from university and disinherited by his father. If we are to feel more than some shoulder-shrugging pity for a very unlucky fellow we must see him develop before attracting the blows which warp him. He must whole-heartedly desire something, and fight hard for it, and be horribly defeated.

What stops him noticing the day of the week for a long time is a sudden, almost total lack of interest in his immediate circumstances. This begins a few moments after leaving the Grange. As Jamie strides along the pavement, each street lamp casting his shadow before him as he passes it and behind him as he approaches it, his feeling of delighted release is replaced by astonishment at his close dealings with an attractive, brave, interesting woman. Everything to do with her which embarrassed and fright-ened him is now a vivid, intimate memory. He has worn her night-dress, slept in her bed, seen her in a privacy allowed only to lovers and husbands. She has talked to him as an equal, conspired with him as a friend, and saved him from social ruin. He and she now share a secret unknown to anyone else in the world, yet he does not even know her name! He cannot believe that he will not meet her again.

He gets home, stealthily opens the door and closes it more stealthily behind him. He is perplexed to see that the hall, dimly lit through the fanlight window by a lamp in the street beyond, is exactly as it was when he last saw it – surely it should have changed as much as he has changed? And it is doubly familiar, for without the different arrangement of hats and coats on the hallstand he could be entering the house he left half an hour before. He tiptoes

across the hall and upstairs, so exactly reversing his recent
actions that he hesitates before his bedroom door, heart
thudding in hope and in fear that when he opens it he will
again see the girl's bedroom. However, this is no tale of the
supernatural. He undresses, puts on his own night-gown,
slips into bed and lies remembering what happened after
he last found himself in this situation. He recalls especially
the girl's sigh and her long, very serious look at herself in
the mirror. He is sure he knows what she was thinking at
the time: "Who am I, and why?" Although most young
people ask themselves that question the thought makes
him feel nearer her. And who is Manton Jamieson, this man
she lives with but dare not trust with the truth about
herself? Her husband? (The idea brings a touch of panic. He
dismisses it.) Her brother? Uncle? Step-father? (Few
women in Scotland, in those days, would call their own
father by his first name.) Whoever Manton is, he gambles
for money with his guests while providing them with
strong drink; no wonder the girl is discontent. (And Jamie,
who has so recently gambled and drunk, does not notice he
is viewing Manton from his father's standpoint.) In the
midst of these speculations he falls asleep.

And is roused as usual next morning by a housemaid
tapping his door, and lies for a while staring blankly at the
ceiling, knowing he is in love. I assume that Jamie's nurture
has depended so exclusively on his father because his
mother died young – perhaps in childbirth. Before what
now seems a dreamlike encounter with the girl Jamie has
met only two kinds of women: the mainly elderly and unco
good who belong to his father's congregation, and those
who drink in pubs and shebeens used by nearly penniless
medical students. Jamie cannot *not* be in love with the girl.
He feels no need, at this stage of his passion, to be more
than gloriously astonished by it. He dresses, goes downstairs and breakfasts with his father. This meal is usually

eaten in a taciturn silence broken only by his brief replies to infrequent paternal questions. These questions always take the form of remarks. His father never asks Jamie where he spent a day or evening, but says, "I am informed that you were seen last Thursday in Rose Street," or, "You did not come directly home from college last night." This morning his father makes several such remarks which Jamie hardly hears but responds to with a nod or a murmur of "Yes indeed." Near the end of the meal he notices that his father has risen and now stands with his back to the fireplace, declaring in firm tones that he fears Jamie is not attending properly to his studies; that man is born to earn his bread in the sweat of his brow; that a minister of religion is required to set an example to the community and that he, personally, has no intention of supporting a mere idler, wastrel and profligate. Instead of hearing these familiar words with an expression of sullen resentment Jamie nods a little, murmurs that he will give the matter thought, and absent-mindedly leaves the room and the house.

Thirty minutes later, pass-key in hand, he discovers himself about to enter the drive of the Grange. With a quickened pace he continues along the road, almost amused. He has been too busy mixing hopes and speculations with memories of the night before to notice where he is going. He spends most of that day and the next two or three days in the same walking dream. The Grange is a fairly new building so I imagine it in a line of prosperous villa residences, part of the western suburbs along the Glasgow road near Corstorphine hill. Twice or thrice a day he strolls past the front of it from a great distance on one side to a great distance on the other. More frequently, and taking great care not to be seen by servants, he prowls the mews lane at the back, for there he can see her high bedroom window. Sometimes, like someone shaking off a lassitude, he hurries into the city and wanders the city streets near the kind of fashionable shop she must occasionally visit, or sits on a bench in Princes Street gardens, watching the strollers in the comforting but not yet urgent knowledge that if he could sit there for three or four weeks he would certainly see her passing. He believes that the chance which brought them together will certainly, if he stays ready and alert for it, bring them together in a perfectly ordinary, social way which he will manage to build upon. He fears she cannot be thinking about him as much as he thinks of her, but is certain she thinks of him sometimes, and if it is with even a fraction of his own emotion he believes he can persuade her to break free of twenty Mantons. Meanwhile the notion of a strong, jealous Manton strengthens him. If the girl was wholly free or only slightly confined he might feel compelled to hurry, but he is sure that Manton can keep her for him. He is also fascinated by the kind of person he is becoming under her influence: patient, determined and steady. He has nothing now to say to the friends he met in pubs and betting shops. None are fit to share the secret he is nursing. He is close to monomania. All the loving capacities of a soul starved of love are flowing, silently, in one direction. The nearly unbroken silence in which he breakfasts and dines with his father no longer seems a gloomy oppression to be avoided. His spirit is grateful for it. This is fortunate. Days must elapse before his next small allowance and he lacks the means to eat elsewhere.

But if Jamie's obsession is not fed by a new occurrence he will be driven to keep it alive by some rash initiative which I cannot imagine. I have read, and so has Jamie, of lovers who further their intrigues by bribing and plotting with a servant, but Jamie is too stiff-necked to make a social inferior his confidant. He also assumes that even servants are inclined to honesty, so any approach he makes will be reported to the master of the house. Also he has no money for bribes. His love is doomed to fade and dwindle unless

providence – who in this story is me masquerading as
Robert Louis Stevenson – provides another useful coincidence, and why should I not? Nowadays the wealthier folk
of Edinburgh know each other very well; they were
certainly not more ignorant a century back. After a few
days Jamie, in mere restlessness of spirit, resumes attend-
ance at the university. He tries to hammer down his
memories of the girl (which are no longer pleasurable, but
frustrating) by concentrating on the demonstrations of his
lecturers. He tries to believe that everything which dis-
turbs him is located in a circulatory, respiratory, digestive
system animated by nervous shocks similar to those generated in the Galvanic pile or Wimshurst apparatus, but here
generated in a cerebral cortex reacting to external stimuli.
Later, feeling very dismal, he stands in the cold dusk on the
range of steps overlooking the great, grey, classically
pillared and pilastered, gaslit and cobbled quadrangle. Let
there be a haze of fog in it, seafog from the Firth tinted
brown and smelling of smoke from the Edinburgh lums, and
making opal haloes around the lamps, and making ghostly
the figures of the students hurrying singly and in groups
toward the gate, and making their voices very distinct in
the thickened air.

"Good night Charlie! Will I see you later at Manton's
place?" cries someone.

"Not me. I'm clean out of funds," says another. Jamie leaps
down the steps and overtakes the last speaker, who is
known to him, under the high arch of the entrance. They
turn side by side into Nicolson Street. Jamie asks, "Who is
Manton Jamieson?"

In answering this question I must describe the person
who does so, for Stevenson, like nature and like every good
storyteller, creates nobody to inform and change someone
else without giving them an equal fulness of life. Those who
appear most briefly speak for whole professions or com-

munities. See the doctor in *Macbeth*, the housepainters in *Crime and Punishment*, the itinerant barber at the start of *Kidnapped*. If they are a bigger part of the plot they often emphasize the main characters' obsession by lacking it while resembling them in other ways: thus Macduff is given the same rank, courage and royal prospects as Macbeth, but less ambition and a less ambitious wife; Raskolnikov's best friend is also a clever student in poor circumstances, one who works to get money by translating textbooks instead of murdering a pawnbroker. Stevenson frequently coupled young men in this contrasting way because (quite apart from his dialectical habit of mind) young men often do go in twos, and he was more fascinated by the beginnings of lives than by the middle and later periods. Since I have hinted that Charlie is a fellow student who has also lost money by gambling I will enlarge him by basing him partly on Alan in the novella *John Nicholson* and partly on Francie in *Weir of Hermiston*. He is more elegant and popular than Jamie and his guardian grants him a far larger allowance, but he has squandered it and will be poor for a while to come. Though in love with nobody but himself he greatly likes company. He has recently started avoiding his wealthy and fashionable friends because he owes money to some of them. He is shrewd enough to know that the casually superior manner which makes him acceptable to such people will make him obnoxious to those he considers their inferiors. Although Jamie is a very slight acquaintance, and not one he would normally want to cultivate, he is disposed to treat him, for the time being, as a kindred spirit. He assumes that Jamie's interest in Manton is the same as his own, and the most natural thing in the world: the interest of an outsider in a special sort of glamorous elite. It will soothe his hurt pride to instruct Jamie in the ways of Manton's world, and eventually lead him into it.

So what strong lord of misrule can preside in this douce, commercially respectable, late 19th century city where even religious fanaticism reinforces unadventurous mediocrity? Scotland had many wealthy landowners who were equally indifferent to gambling losses and bourgeois opinion but almost all these had shifted their town houses from Edinburgh to London a generation earlier, and the names of the few who remained would be known to the sons of the professional classes, especially if they had the same social habits as the Prince of Wales. Jamie has not heard of Manton Jamieson when the story starts. Despite Manton's Scottish surname he is a wealthy, recent incomer. Let him be the son of depressed gentry or educated tradespeople or a mixture of both. The death of his parents at an early age leaves him a little money, but not enough to buy an officer's commission or a professional education. He has no special talent but a deal of energy, courage and practical ability, so he takes these abroad to where they will best profit him. He is pleasant, tough, cautious, and whatever he does is done well, but for many years he keeps losing his gains by shifting to places where there are rumours of better opportunities. Let him eventually (though this is a cliché) make a pile of money in the Californian gold fields, not by prospecting but by selling necessities to prospectors. Let him take it to San Francisco where he manages to increase it on the stock exchange. He resides with, perhaps even marries (this is vague) the widow or mistress of a dead rich friend. She also dies, leaving him her money and making him guardian of either her daughter or her much younger sister – this also is vague. And now he tires of San Francisco. One reason for his many restless shiftings has been a secret desire for social eminence. He knows he can never shine among the millionaires of Nob Hill because their lavish expenditure would bankrupt him; it also strikes him as childish and hysterical. He is almost fifty, and because he has formed no strong attachment to any other place the memories of his native city are increasingly dear to him. He decides to return there. This is a mistake.

Since the days of Dick Whittington, the exile who returns transformed by foreign adventure is as common in popular fiction as in history books, and a lot more distinct. His earliest struggles are described in *Robinson Crusoe* and parodied in *Gulliver's Travels*. He arrives unexpectedly in Gaskell's *Cranford* to save his genteel old aunt from working in a sweetie shop, and in Galt's *The Member* he cheerfully uses a fortune made in India to make another in the corruption of British politics. Suddenly, in Dickens' day, his cheerful bloom quite vanishes. *Little Dorrit* has him sent to China by an unloving mother and returning, after years of clerical toil, to confront a land run by greedy rentiers, callous civil servants, venal aristocrats and shady capitalists. *Great Expectations* has him transported to Australia by an oppressive government and returning, after years of manual toil, to a land where he is a hunted criminal and an embarrassment to those he enriched. In Stevenson's day stories about prosperous, rather stuffy citizens suddenly shocked by intrusions from a dangerously unBritish past had become commonplace. They were plausible because although middle-class conventions had become more rigidly confining, the middle class was full of monied adventurers who adopted these conventions. Manton cannot adopt them because he never learned them. Like all returned exiles his memory of the homeland is out of date. The Edinburgh of his youth was dominated by free-thinking, hard-drinking lawyers and the remnant of a gentry who could still entertain themselves by using that demotic lowland speech which had been the language of the Scottish kings. Manton was sure that only poverty excluded him from this society. His notion of good living is to dine, drink and converse where his wide knowledge of life will receive attention, followed by some gentlemanly gambling where his superior skill will bring a profit. He knows this last amenity is enjoyed by many thousands in Paris, the German spas and Saint Petersburg. He finds it is now illegal in Britain and thought wicked and foolish in an Edinburgh whose social leaders belong to rival kinds of Presbyterian church. Manton is no churchgoer and his social chances are further reduced by the young woman he introduces as "My ward, Miss Juliette O'Sullivan, the daughter of a very dear friend". He jealously oversees all her actions but is silent (so is she) about her marriage prospects. In such a man, in an age when marriage is a respectable girl's only prospect, this suggests she is his mistress or his bastard. Only rakish bachelors, itinerant members of the acting profession and defiant youths of Jamie's age visit the Grange. Manton must feed his sense of eminence by teaching college students his own slightly vulgar notion of gentlemanly conduct.

The superficial part of all this is told by Charlie to Jamie as they stroll south along Nicolson Street, their breath adding puffs of whiter density to the haze of the fog. Jamie learns little more than he suspected already, but Charlie's suspicions of the girl's status in that household fill him with a queer sick excitement. He stands still and says, "Can you take me there?"

"Nothing easier," says Charlie. "You're a sort Manton would take to. The deuce of it is, I'm clean out of funds just now. Not that gaming is compulsory at the Grange, but it's the done thing. We'll be given all the champagne we want, so it's common decency that at least one of us hazards something on a game. How much have you got?"

"Nothing!" cries Jamie, staring at him.

"Not even a watch?"

Jamie hesitates, then detaches a watch from within his overcoat and hands it over. Charlie snaps open the silver case and brings it near his eye with something like the

professional regard of a pawnbroker. He says, "This is a good watch – we can raise quite a bit on it. Shall I show you where?"
An hour later, with coin in their pockets, they are received by Manton at the Grange.

He is a calm, bulky man with a quietly attentive manner. His heavy lidded, rather narrow eyes, and bushy, well-trimmed whiskers, and mouth half-hidden by a neatly brushed moustache, all convey amusement without definitely smiling. I am modelling him slightly on Edward, Prince of Wales, whom Stevenson found interesting enough to parody in two quite different ways, as the hapless hero of *John Nicholson* and as Prince Florizel of Bohemia in *The New Arabian Nights*. For this reason I will also have him playing baccarat when the young men call – roulette is kept for later in the evening. But first he introduces Jamie to, "My ward, Miss Juliette O'Sullivan, the daughter of a very dear friend."
The girl regards Jamie with a face as impassive as his own. Does she wear the black velvet gown he remembers? He is too full of whirling emotions to notice. It is her face he wants to gaze and gaze into so he tries not to see her at all, bowing deeply and turning again to Manton. He hears her murmur "Good evening" and on a louder, welcoming note greet Charlie with a "How nice to see you, Mr Gemmel." He is glad she knows how to dissemble. She is the only woman present and plays hostess to those not engaged by the cardplay. Jamie stands watching it, ensuring, by slight turns of the head, that she is always in the corner of his eye, never the centre of it. This is easy, for he can now see that the gown she wears is white satin. He is not jealous of those who chat with her, for they cannot know her as intimately as he does, and he is sure she is now as conscious of him as he of her. Meanwhile he watches the baccarat, a game unknown to him. It is a form of the games known nowadays

as pontoon and Black Jack. Manton, being host and the richest person present, is of course the banker. Charlie joins the game and wins a little, then loses a little, then wins more, then much more, then loses everything. Charlie suggests that Jamie takes his place at the table. Jamie refuses but gives Charlie money to play for him. In a pause for refreshment Juliette goes to the piano and accompanies herself in a song. Her voice is slight but sounds sweet and brave for she is clever enough not to force it beyond its range. If Jamie attended closely it would bring him to tears, so he stands beside the fire with his host, for it is from Manton that the girl must be won. Manton's conversation is entertaining, anecdotal, and polished by years of use. A bawdy element in it is not too heavily emphasized. He presents himself as onlooker or victim rather than cause of strange events, and seems as ready to listen as to speak. By occasional questions and an unmoving, attentive expression he usually draws from raw young men news of their families, college experience, hopes and opinions; but he draws very little from Jamie. Jamie sees that Manton is condescending to him, and dislikes it, but he still attends as closely to Manton as he did to the cardplay, and for the same reason – he wants to defeat him. So he notices what few others notice on their first visit to the Grange. Whether gaming or conversing, Manton's mind is only half occupied with his immediate company. As he and Jamie stand side by side with their back to the fire, both are keeping half an eye on the white figure at the opposite end of the room. Manton is less sure of her than Jamie is! The thought fills Jamie with a giddy foretaste of supremacy. Gaming is resumed. Again Jamie watches, but with greater understanding, and all at once his close-contained, highly stimulated, busily searching mind conceives a plan, a plot which will bring together himself, the girl, the Grange, Manton, cardplay, his father's tiny allowance and even Charlie in a single scheme of conquest. Throughout the evening Jamie (like Manton) has drunk almost nothing. The slightly tipsy Charlie is about to stake the last of the money on a new game. Jamie lays a firm hand on his shoulder and says, "We must go now."

He approaches his hostess, says "Good night Miss O'Sullivan," and is now bold enough to give her one steady glance. She turns to him the bright smile she has been bestowing on someone else, bids him good night and turns away leaving him disconcerted by her powers as an actress. Manton, perhaps flattered by the close attention of this taciturn guest, escorts both young men to the door, cheerfully commiserating with Charlie's misfortune and inviting both young men back with a particular nod to Jamie.

The cold night air slightly sobers Charlie. He says glumly, "I shan't be back there in a hurry. It's nearly a month till my next allowance and my brute of a governor won't allow me another advance on it. You are walking beside a desperate man, Kirkwood. You were wise to drag me away when you did. I usually hang on to the bitter end, because of Juliette, you know – the beautiful Miss Juliette O'Sullivan. But I've no hopes there. What do you think of her, Kirkwood? Isn't she a woman to die for?"

Jamie finds these remarks impertinent. He holds out his hand, palm upward, and with a sigh Charlie places the last sovereign on it saying, "Sorry I didn't do better for you, but luck was against me."

"Luck does not exist," says Jamie firmly. "Luck is superstitious nonsense. You lost to Manton like everybody else did, because he is skilful and you are idiots."

Charlie is inclined to be angry but is daunted by the small tight smile Jamie gives him. He says, "Could you have done better?"

"Of course not, so I did not play. When I go back there, Charlie – when *we* go back there, Charlie – we will play

and win because we will have made ourselves better than
Manton."

"How?"

"By study and practice. By practice and study. There are
books about cardgames are there not? Books by dependable authorities?"

"Well, Cavendish is considered pretty good, and two or
three French fellows."

"We'll work on them. A month just might be sufficient if
we apply ourselves hard. After all, you have nothing better
to do with your time."

And at breakfast next morning Jamie says to his father, "I
have a favour to ask you, sir. I believe I will do better in my
studies if I share them with a college friend, Charlie
Gemmel. Since this house is a quieter place than his
lodgings I want us to work most evenings in the privacy of
my bedroom. Would you object to him sharing our evening meal beforehand?"

The Rev. Dr Kirkwood looks at his son for a while. Jamie's
face flushes a hot red. The father says quietly, "I can have no
objection to that."

So each evening and for most of the weekends Jamie
shuts himself up with Charlie in that room which is so like
yet unlike *her* room. On the doorward side of a small table
they make a barricade of medical books high enough to
hide a card-pack and Cavendish's book on games of chance.
(This is mainly a guilty ritual, for the Rev. Dr Kirkwood is
not one who would enter his son's room unannounced.)
They play game after game, and catechize each other on
the details of the Cavendish strategy, and sometimes probe
a foreign work which gives other strategy and teaches the
techniques of foul play under the guise of warning against
them. But at this stage Jamie neither intends to cheat nor
suspects Manton of doing so. He is striving for purely
conventional mastery. His obsessions with the girl and with

the game are now identical. Each card dealt or lifted seems to put him in touch with her, with every petty victory he feels she is closer. Since Charlie does not share this erotic drive he is frequently exhausted, less by the games than by the intricate post-mortems which follow. He scratches his head woefully and cries, "We would soon be qualified doctors if we gave our medical studies this degree of attention."

Jamie smiles and shuffles the pack and says, "You're tired, Gemmel. Be banker this time."

So Charlie also becomes an obsessive player. The manse is a good place to evade his creditors and responsibilities. The meals there are well cooked, well served, and cost nothing. His only social life now is cardplay with Jamie. We can become addicts of almost any activity prolonged past the healthy limit. People have drunk themselves to death on water, the anorexic finds hunger intoxicating, some of the worst treated learn to welcome pain. The freedom of pushing faster toward death than our body or society requires is the essence of every perverse satisfaction, gambling included. Charlie, in the circumstances, is bound to get hooked on this cardgame, though not as absolutely as Jamie. When outside his room Jamie now plays imaginary games in his head. He no longer seems obstinately silent or fretful in his father's company, just thoughtful and deliberate. His step is firm, his manner composed, and though he eats as much as ever he has grown thinner. He never visits public houses, billiard rooms or betting shops. All pocket money is hoarded for the decisive game with Manton.

And one day, on the corner of the study table where a certain number of florins are usually placed for him, he finds as many guineas. He stares at his father with open mouth. The elder Kirkwood says, "I am giving you more, Jamie, because you deserve more. A while ago you asked for an allowance worthy of a gentleman's son while declaring that you would not spend it as a gentleman ought. You have changed since then, Jamie! When I look at you I no longer see an ordinary, thankless young drifter, I see a man determined to make his way in the world, a man I can trust."

Jamie continues to stare. His father is smiling at him with a futile expression of pride and approval and Jamie has a desolate feeling of loss. This is the first proof he ever received that his father loves him. He remembers once being a person who longed for such proof and would have been changed by it. That person no longer exists. Jamie would like to weep for him as for a dead brother, and also yell with laughter at the good money he has earned, yes, earned, by his love of a woman and devotion to a game his father would abhor. He sighs, whispers "Thank you sir," picks up the guineas and leaves the room.

For me that is the climax of the story. The catastrophe may be sketched rapidly and lightly.

That evening or the next Jamie suddenly grasps the nature of this baccarat which Cavendish so clearly explains. It is only partly a game of skill – anyone following the Cavendish system will play it as well as it can be played but, as in roulette, the main chances will always favour the banker: the banker has most money and therefore most staying power. Manton's superior skill merely maintains his lead in a game which is already on his side. Banks, of course, can be broken by *runs of luck*, but very seldom. Jamie knows that the chance which introduced him to Juliette will not wed him to her. With rage, then horror, then resignation, he sees that to win by skill he must win by cheating. He has now complete ascendancy over Charlie. They devise and practise signals which strike them as impenetrable, but are not. They decide to hazard all they can on a game: Charlie's quarterly allowance, Jamie's hoarded pocket-money, and

money borrowed at exorbitant interest from a professional lender, I imagine an evening at the Grange when the
whole company gradually gather round the table to watch
the play between Jamie and an increasingly grim-faced
Manton. Just before or just after Jamie breaks the bank his
fraud is exposed by the girl, who is Manton's accomplice
and supporter in every possible way. We have no reason
to think she ever found Jamie interesting. He was not,
perhaps, an attractive young man.

A Small Thistle

The Declaration of Independence by the United States' representatives in 1781 put the American episcopal church into great difficulty. It had no bishops, yet believed that bishops were essential to the making of new priests. Hitherto English bishops had consecrated American priests, but now the two countries were at war. The Church of England was headed by King George, who thought the U.S.A. an illegal organization. It seemed that the American episcopal priesthood must dwindle through senility into extinction, or turn itself into a wholly new kind of protestant sect. However, a third way was found. Although England's government had absorbed the Scottish one seventy-five years earlier, Scotland's legal system and churches stayed independent and intact. A leading light in the tiny Scottish Episcopal Church was the Rev. James Skinner, a poet whose *Reel of Tullochgorum* and *The Ewie wi' the Crookit Horn* are still found in anthologies. His son, William Skinner, was a man of liberal sentiments, and Bishop of Aberdeen, and would soon be episcopal Primate of Scotland. So in 1784 William Skinner and two other Scottish bishops laid their right hands on the head of Dr. Seabury, a Connecticut Yankee, thus turning him into a bishop too. The blessing which Jesus once bestowed on Saint Peter could now be carried across the Atlantic in a contagious form.

On Monday morning the 24th May 1973 Bill Skinner, a last descendent of the episcopal Skinners, died of heart failure in Gartnavel General Hospital, Glasgow, at the age of sixty-nine. The family fortune had trickled very thin by the time it reached Bill. His father, a robust but feckless man, had been educated at Heidelberg University and then lumberjacked and bummed his way across America before ending his days in the Town Clerk's office of Glasgow Corporation. When Bill left school he entered the shipyards as a marker-off, chalking points on steel plates where the rivet-holes were to be cut. Retiring with heart-disease in the 1940s he worked thereafter as a part-time laboratory assistant in a private college which crammed people for the University entrance exams. When that closed in the mid sixties he lived frugally on his National Insurance pension. He never married, spending most of his life with his widowed mother at their home in Otago Street, in what was surely the last gas-lit tenement flat in Glasgow. He had no children. His only surviving relative had been a distant cousin in America.

These are the bare statistical bones of Skinner's life, and one could be excused for thinking them bleak. The living reality was wonderfully different. Bill filled his life with such various imaginative activities – political, artistic, scientific, alchemical – that he became a source of delight and satisfaction to an unusually wide circle of friends. He was a member of the Andersonian Society, the Connolly Association, the CND, an American scientific correspondence society, and the Scottish-USSR Friendship Society.

His Otago Street home had a small laboratory where he did research into Particle Compression and the

Origins of Life, printing (at his own expense) a small pamphlet setting out his views on these subjects. Anyone who cared to make an appointment would be shown over the small museum he had constructed in his mother's front parlour, with its fossils, pressed plants, the head-phones powered by body electricity, the transparent seagull's skull and his exhibition of paintings. On average he produced two paintings a year: clear-edged, mysteriously coloured little symbolic works with names like "Scotia Aspires", "Tyro Wizard Town" and "Death of Death". I once heard him grow highly indignant with a critic who called him a Primitive. He thought this was a slur on his meticulous technique. Even in his last years, when badly crippled with arthritis, he produced, with the help of friends, two editions of the magazine *Anvil Sparks*, in which he wrote science, art and political notes, advertised the exhibitions of friends, and serialized the career of Henry Dwining, the alchemist in Scott's novel *The Fair Maid of Perth*, a character with whom he felt great sympathy.

Before illness confined him to the house he was an alert, quick, small boyish man with nutcracker nose and chin, and a mop of pale nicotine-coloured hair. Apparently it had once been bright red. When this faded he tried reviving the colour with a concoction of his own, but without much success. His pubs were the State Bar, the Blythswood Bar and the Pewter Pot before they were modernised. His favourite drinks were vodka with lime and High-Ho, another invention of his which he distilled from pharmaceutical alcohol. It was only brought out at Hogmanay, and a small glass of it diluted by three parts of water to one and flung in the fire could still produce dangerous explosions. He was cheerful, utterly inde-pendent, had many friends of both sexes and all ages, and not one enemy. He *succeeded* in life.

Some time in 1940, when working in the yards, he became a founder of a political party which drew its members mainly from the Anarchist, Trotskyite and Nationalist blocs. At the end of his life he was its only member, and he advanced its principles by fixing (with immense caution) small stickers to trees and lamp-posts in the quieter parts of the city near his home. The slogan on these stickers makes a good epitaph, and can be printed in full:

SCOTTISH
SOCIALIST
REPUBLIC

NEUTRALITY

To the left of "neutrality" is a small thistle.

Portrait of a Playwright

When Joan Ure was born in 1919 they called her Elizabeth Carswell. Her father was an engineer with Vickers-Armstrong. On both parents' side she came from three generations of small Clydeside shipbuilders and engineers, folk who had managed by hard work, thrift and steady, conventional behaviour to get free of the unemployment and poverty which threatened all parts, but especially the less skilled or more reckless part, of the Scottish work-force. An anecdote. Betty Carswell's grandfather, a fore-man, often spent an evening seated alone in the best parlour of his house, consuming a bottle of whisky in perfectly orderly silence. Had he drunk in a pub with fellow-workers he would have lessened his authority over them and perhaps lost the confidence of his employer. Had he drunk with his wife and family he would have lessened his authority over them and lost their respect. Betty was born into a culture which gave her good food, good clothing and a well-furnished home in return for self-suppression. In the nineteen-twenties bottle-parties and sexual daring were fashionable among wealthy people, but the lower-middle classes or respectable working classes (call them what you like) maintained a code of careful manners which recalled the world of Jane Austen. Betty then had a younger sister, Joan, and younger brother, John.

They went to family gatherings where their mother presented them to *her* mother for a clothes-inspection, and reported their behaviour in the previous week, and got approval and reinforcement for the rewards and punishments she had meted out. After a meal the men conversed on one side of the room, the women on the other, and the children by turns gave little recitations in the middle.

When Betty was twelve her mother entered hospital with tuberculosis, and Betty became her father's housewife and working mother to her sister and brother. Mrs Carswell came home after two years and thereafter managed the house from her bedroom. It was important for Betty to keep looking happy. Depression was construed as ingratitude to the mother who bore her, the father who nourished. How did she avoid becoming a neurotic drudge or empty-headed puppet? By imagination. By developing an inner world where, for a change, she had authority. It was not an exclusive world. When seven she had written a thirteen-page story and given it to her mother, thinking it beautiful. Mrs Carswell punished her for a misdeed by burning it, and was surprised by how much she cried. Before the days of television many literate children stocked their inner worlds with the help of books, but in the Carswell home it was thought bad of a girl to read for pleasure with so much dusting and tidying to be done. Betty liked school which positively ordered her to read poems, and good novels, and the plays of Shakespeare. Her English teacher wished her to continue to university. Her father did not. In 1933 there were no university grants, there was no national health service and an invalid in the family was a financial burden. Betty wanted to be a teacher, she would have been a splendid teacher, but she left school at fifteen then became a typist in Glasgow Corporation housing department. Two years later she met and married a businessman and became Mrs Betty Clark. The Second

World War began. Mr Clark was posted overseas and for
five years she lived alone in Glasgow bringing up her young
daughter.

By this time she must have appeared as she did in the last
twenty years of her life when I came to know her; small,
slender, fair-haired, with beautifully clear-cut features and
always very young-looking, though a little too bony — her
guilt about being supported by someone else, implanted in
childhood, lasted through marriage and led her to eat too
little. She made her own clothes and dressed very well. She
was eye-catching in a way that was too individual to be
merely fashionable, too smart to be eccentric. Her manner
upset some people at first, she was so ladylike, and polite,
and anxious to be helpful and understanding in every
possible way. And within this gushing manner was a gleam
of desperate amusement amounting to laughter, because
her intelligence was saying, "Yes, we must help and understand each other in every possible way all the time, which
can't be done. Yet it must be done." In later years this
manner greatly disturbed directors of her plays. She was
not afraid of authority but she knew people in authority
have delicate egos, and it distressed her to hurt them by
explaining how her work should be performed, and why
bits should not be cut out and others grafted in. It also
distressed them to find that, in spite of her eagerly submis-
sive manner, she could not be brushed aside.

But at the end of the war Betty had not committed
herself to being anyone but Mrs Clark. Her life so far,
though sad, and providing all the insights a writer needs,
had not been unusual for a woman. Then two extra hard
things happened. Her young sister Joan returned from the
Women's Auxiliary Air Force to live with her parents, and
entered a religious melancholy, though the family was not
particularly religious. Joan was found dead under a bridge

with her face in a stream, perhaps by misadventure, perhaps not. Then Betty entered hospital with tuberculosis. Lung-scars showed she had contracted it while nursing her mother.

Much later she wrote a story about a woman with a talent, who feels it is too small to matter, suppresses it, and faints. She is pleased, for that suggests the talent is genuine. To be absolutely certain she hides it again. "Very soon she coughed up the first gobbets of blood. And there she saw, brilliant at last, the brightness of the tiny talent she had." The woman dies rejoicing. She knows her talent is genuine, for it *was* death to hide it.

Betty used the materials of her life as much as any writer, but was seldom autobiographical. The people she presents are alternative forms of herself, the ends of roads she had only walked some distance along. She decided not to hide her talent. She signed herself out of hospital against medical advice and lived for another thirty years. In order to become a writer she took a pen-name: Joan Ure. It is a Scottish tradition. The authors of *Waverley*, *The House with the Green Shutters*, *A Drunk Man Looks at the Thistle* and *Sunset Song* did it, mainly to avoid embarrassing their relations. The lowland Scots suspect the creative imagination. John Knox, the man we love to hate, is usually blamed for this but the cause is poverty. The English middle classes know that imagination can be a way of managing things. Artistic wives and offspring can get jobs connected with publishing, television or education. But where there is little wealth respectable people fear the future and are sure that only *carefulness* will help them survive it. They feel that an active imagination excites the passions, especially sexual ones, and breeds discontent and extravagant actions. And indeed, for those with low salaries and positions, unimaginative carefulness is a way of avoiding pain, in the short run. In the long run it makes us the easy tools of people with high salaries and positions, and when they have no use for us they drop us in the shit. As in 1985 Britain. So an active imagination, though painful, is our only hope, and by imagination I do not mean fantasy. In Joan Ure's play *Something In It For Ophelia*, a young, energetic, slightly stupid girl has been to a performance of *Hamlet* and recognized in Ophelia (exploited and abused by a father and boyfriend who have no real interest in her) a possible form of herself. She is appalled. She feels such things should not be shown on a stage, and people should certainly not applaud them. After all, she has read in the *Scotsman* that the Scottish suicide rate is as high as the Swedish, only most of our suicides are women.

Joan Ure became the name of an imaginative intelligence pointing us to the passionate self-knowledge which can make us too self-governing and tough to be managed and dropped by other people. I am not particularly speaking of women when I say 'us'. She was a women's liberationist of course, but liked men too much to want the sexes divorced, and I doubt if she wanted a matriarchy. As a child she had lived under one. Her plays handle the commonplace facts: that hard housework, factory-work, office-work are unavoidable but freedom is essential; that we could all have more freedom with a fairer sharing of powers, but are everywhere in chains because we live unfairly, our love twisted by exploitation and warfare, men oppressing women and other men with their greater economic strength, women exploiting men and other women with their greater emotional insight. But Joan's plays are not dour, they are witty, moving, funny, and usually short. I'll speak of those I like most.

I See Myself as This Young Girl. 40 minutes, 3 actors.
A middle-aged woman, left to mind a baby by her brisk

student daughter, encounters a lonely sales-clerk who has "adventured out in his shorts". Each reveals the fantasies that keep them going. She imagines herself a young girl – not the actual daughter who exploits her, but someone more sentimental with nobody to help her. This is the one way she can allow herself the luxury of self-pity. The play is about the need to soar above our responsibilities without abandoning them. The tone of it is funny and melancholy.

Something In It For Ophelia. 40 minutes, 2 actors.
A Scottish Hamlet and Ophelia meet on Waverley Station platform while waiting for a train and reveal themselves as incapable of love. Ophelia is the tougher of the two but less admirable. She leaves the more sensitive Hamlet prostrate. Funny and harsh.

The Hard Case. 40 minutes, 1 actor.
A football fan, a small Glasgow businessman, is so appalled by the death of the children crushed at the end of that disastrous Rangers–Celtic game of 1970 that he deliberately smashes a shop window to get the chance of making a public statement about it. In the course of that statement he becomes his own judge, and binds himself over to keep the peace. At the time of writing it looked as if a new period of decency for Scottish football was beginning because the managers of both Rangers and Celtic had promised to abandon the policies which increased their gate money along with insensitive violence leading to stampede and killing. This is now forgotten. Rangers still refuse to employ Catholic players. Nowadays only Joan's play deals with Scottish football, and injustice, and that disaster, so openly yet delicately. No other writers have dared tackle it. Too big for them.

The Lecturer and the Lady. 40 minutes, 2 actors.
In this play Joan Ure is confronted by Betty Clark. An

ageing, conventional housewife approaches a young adventurous thinker, hoping she will receive the inspiration to leave the very dull husband she loves. She does not get it. The thinker who has abandoned her child and husband – "Two terrible things! And not been struck down dead!" – will not advise everyone to do as she did. When they part the brave thinker is sadder for having met the lady, the lady is a little braver for having met the lecturer.

Condemned for Ecstasy. 75 minutes, 7 or 8 actors.
This is a play about oppression and liberation, and is based on two peculiar historical events. In the late 17th century a pious, dutiful young woman, who kept house for her widowed father and bachelor brothers, found such consolation in reading about the sufferings of Jesus that she entered ecstatic states and coughed blood. She was tried for this by the local kirk session and told that her ecstasy was the work of the devil, and she should not submit to it. A hundred years later, at the time of the French Revolution, a remarkable Ayrshire woman got such ascendancy over her minister that he helped her found a matriarchal commune with herself as the Holy Mother. The stories of these women are introduced by a late 19th century "New Woman" of the Beatrice Webb type, who realizes that the outlandish failure and success of the earlier women is a form of her own.

The foregoing is a very partial list, and I realize it includes all her plays which I have seen well acted. *Take Your Old Rib Back Then* is a play I cannot read with pleasure, because the words on the page recall the gabbling voice of the only actress I heard play them. She was embarrassed by the long speeches and spoke too fast. Joan's plays had very few decent productions because: – she worked in Scotland where hardly any theatres used local writing; her plays were usually short, an evening would require two or three of them and the public aren't thought to like that; her plays were clever, and managements are uneasy with new, local work which is cleverer than themselves. They think it is probably stupid. Joan's characters hardly ever shout and always converse in clear, formal language. Restoration dramatists, great Irishmen and Noël Coward can do that, but surely not the Scots! We are a violent people. O.K.?

So to get her work seen Joan directed small productions performed by friends in an Edinburgh basement, sometimes acting in them herself. She made contact with amateur companies and worked hard, without pay, for organizations trying to change things, like the abortive Scottish Stage Company, and the more successful Scottish Society of Playwrights. Things are slightly better for local playwrights in Scotland today, and she is partly responsible for that, but the wear on her highly-strung nature was a punishing one. Most writers grow a surface to protect their nerves, rhinoceros hide or porcupine bristles or slippery suavity or facetious jollity. Joan Ure never did. What she showed you at any time was all there was of her, so even the company of close friends exhausted her after an hour or two. And apart from one year when she got a Scottish Arts Council grant she had always too little money. Her combination of intense drive and intense fragility led some colleagues to nickname her "the iron butterfly". Intellectually she was no butterfly and physically she was not iron. Instead of rusting and corroding like the rest of us she drove to breaking point. Her last months were painful and lonely. She refused to depend on friends, she loathed hospitals, but she had to enter them. At last her lungs completely failed her.

Luckily the value of a life is not in the end of it but in what a woman or man gives while able to give. Since I admire Joan Ure's art I find much in her life to mourn, nothing to wish undone. Joan Ure left several poems, an as yet uncounted number of short stories and essays, and over twenty-four plays and play fragments. Manuscripts and typescripts of these have been bought by Glasgow University Library. The Scottish Society of Playwrights has acting copies of most of the plays. It has also printed a volume, the first of its playscript series, Five Short Plays by Joan Ure, with an introduction by Christopher Small. Regrettably, Joan's bad luck still pursues her work. Through trouble with the printer the book, though readable, is unevenly inked, has obvious, irritating typographical errors, and contains The Hard Case in a mutilated radio version. But in the University and S.S.P. libraries her work is where directors, actors, scholars and anyone who enjoys writing can read it and obtain copies without much fuss or great expense. Her daughter, a doctor in Canada, and her brother John Carswell, in Newton Mearns, have her personal letters, diaries and tape-recordings. I hope one day to see a complete volume of all her plays, and another of her poems and prose pieces.

At her funeral in 1978 the family and friends of Betty Clark met the friends of Joan Ure for the first time. The second group were all writers and theatre people, and made a surprising discovery. We had thought Joan an amazingly young-looking woman in her late forties when she was a young-looking woman on the verge of sixty. In this matter our friend, whose life and art expressed more truth than most, had let us deceive ourselves. I don't know why this cheered me, a little.

Portrait of a Painter

The art of painting is in a poor way. The ambitious pictorial talents try for film and television while decent second-raters (the backbone of any industry) are lost to advertising. We needn't regret this. As Peggy Guggenheim said, the 20th century has already enjoyed more than its share of great painters. In the first fifty years of it Bonnard, Braque, Burra, Chagall, Kandinsky, Klee, Léger, Matisse, Mondrian, Munch, Nash, Picasso, Rivera, Rouault, Schwitters, Sickert, Soutine, Spencer and a dozen other fine artists were working contemporaries. If no such list of painters can be made today we can balance it with a list of creative film-makers. Paintings, of course, are still produced and sold for big sums. As a means of non-taxable banking, painting lags far behind the diamond industry, but it is still ahead of secondhand postage stamps. Our monetary system still has a use for an occupation which, since the big studio-workshops of Medieval and Renaissance times, has dwindled to a cottage industry. The galleries of the large dealers are close to the major stock-exchanges, and if such a dealer decides some new canvases can be propagated as sound investments, the maker of them has a chance of working in comfortable conditions.

Scotland, however, is a notorious low-investment area
and pictorially speaking we have never recovered from the
depression of the thirties. From 1880 to 1925 Scotland
supported a large population of full-time professional painters, the bulk of them living in the west. It is not coincidence that the Glasgow School of Painting throve when
Glasgow was the second biggest city in Britain and the main
supplier of the world's shipping. Dealers like Reid and
Annan were not only exporting local painting to England
and France, they were importing continental masterpieces
for the collections of magnates like Cargill and Burrell.
Scotland's art schools and municipal galleries were built in
this period, and built well. Things is nut whit they wur. In
1944 Sir William Burrell gave Glasgow Corporation the
best private collection of French, German, Italian and
oriental artifacts in Europe. The cost of housing this and
employing a sufficient staff of administrators, conservators
and security guards ensures that in the Scottish middle-
west little public money will be spent on local painting for
the foreseeable future. The Scottish dealers making a sure
profit nowadays are handling paintings of the 1830–1925
period, mainly for the London market where not only
Hornels and Laveries, but Houstons and Docherties have
become sound investments. Annan's lovely gallery in
Sauchiehall Street became an army recruiting office in the
sixties around the time that Upper Clyde Shipyards went
into liquidation. The Scottish export of machines, coal and
paintings has shrunk to a trickle.

It is not flippant to couple the health of a nation's art
with the health of its bigger industries. The drop in the sale
of newly made Scottish paintings since the start of the
century is sometimes explained by saying that photography
has ousted the portrait, that today's homes are too small
for big canvases, that modern art is so peculiar that only
very sophisticated people like it. All these explanations are

contained by the statement, "Most people can't afford to buy paintings." Quite true. Fine paintings always belong to rich private or public bodies, so the sales are happening where our prosperity moved to, near London. The number of commercial London galleries has multiplied by five or six since the start of the century. Prosperity is treating art as it treats other special skills, and drawing it south by feeding it best there.

Now, when prosperity (which is called Capital in the Free West) sailed south in the thirties it left Scottish painters clinging to their art-schools like drowning seamen to rafts. It is strange to think how unimportant the Scottish schools were to earlier masters. At the turn of the century art teachers were few, often foreign, and most Royal Scottish Academicians and members of the Glasgow Institute had nothing to do with them. Nowadays the greatest part of those who exhibit in the Royal Scottish Academy and Royal Glasgow Institute are dominies. Three-quarters of our painters work in the time left from educating people, so the dominie is our most obvious kind of artistic life. This may be a pity. In the present state of money-sharing it is inevitable.

I am sorry to spend so many words upon money when writing of an art-form. Nobody has more respect than the Scots for what can be measured by weight, volume and cash, but in softer moods we prefer to believe in the superior virtues of love, friendship, home, the church, a football team, the Orange Order and (if educated to it) Art. All the same, half the story of art is the story of who pays money for it. In Medieval days abbots and bishops hired stone-carvers and painters to do jobs as quickly as they hired weavers and builders, and a genius was one who did his work well enough to set a famous example. The city rulers of the Italian Renaissance spent new wealth raising

and decorating public buildings with a competitive exuber-
ance which our own rulers keep for weapon research:
artists of extra skill and imagination were given marble and
gold to work with, teams of assistants to direct, were
bargained for by competing governments. Painting became
an unstable industry when the rich stopped ordering art for
their community and started wanting it mainly for themselves. They began searching for completed work by
guaranteed, rock-bottom, gilt-edged geniuses, preferably
dead ones who couldn't spoil the market by flooding in
new pictures. However, despite the instability of their
profession nowadays, few painters kill themselves. Those
who can neither live by painting nor bear to lose touch
with it rarely put bullets into their skulls as Van Gogh did. In
Scotland, as I said, they usually become dominies.

Now, while it is possible for a good painter to teach
(Klee, Kandinsky and Cowie did it) there occur, even in
Scotland, painters who are unable to be anything else, and
unless, like Joan Eardley, they have an unearned income,
they need unusual toughness to survive. Modern artists'
early years are always a struggle because they are usually in
their thirties before they have hammered out a mature
style. But where Matisse, Braque, Bacon, Pollock finally
matured their style there were galleries to show it and a
public to buy. Where Angus Neil, Pierre Lavalle, Tom
McDonald, Bet Low and Carole Gibbons matured their
styles hardly anyone noticed. In public exhibitions their
work was swamped by the products of the dominies, and
there was no critical journalism to take note, no local
dealer to persuade wealthy citizens or the municipal gallery that here was good new work. Moreover, exhibiting
costs money which full-time painters can't always afford,
so they struggle to paint through thickening loneliness.
They grow touchy with prosperous friends and resentful
of the dominies, who can treat their touchiness as a joke.

Unluckily this resentment is not the healthy distrust expressed between Scottish writers, which is a robust gregarious activity, a way of flexing muscles and drawing attention to ourselves when we have nothing interesting or useful to say. The full-time painters' resentment is isolating, self-hurtful, and can lead to that rigid despair which unintelligent doctors try to clear from the brain with electric currents. They become hermits, and nobody is to blame: not the art schools, the Arts Council, the R.S.A. or the Scottish public. The force which turns artists into teachers or hermits is the force which shut the shipyard that developed the hovercraft. As a friendly member of the Arts Council once said to John Connolly, the sculptor, "You must be mad to do this kind of thing in Scotland." No no no no no! Not mad, just bloody unlucky. For in spite of the depressed state of local industry there are skilled workers among these part-timers and full-timers, these dominies and hermits. Why don't they take their skill south if they're any good? That's what the best Scottish tradesmen and technicians do. Artists do go south of course, but if there is more talent in Scottish painting and writing than in our other professions it is because nowadays workers in imaginative industries take longer to teach themselves their jobs, and when they've done it they sometimes find they've made unbreakable connections with a few houses and people, with a kind of life and kind of landscape. They have become natives.

Alasdair Taylor is a native artist, a full-time painter, and something of a hermit.

He was born in 1936 in the village of Edderton, Rosshire, where his father was station-master. His first profession was musical, for his mother was pianist in a small dance-band entertaining the Forces on leave, and at seven he began accompanying her on the drums. "When I felt tired they rolled me in a curtain at the side of the stage, I fell asleep and my father took over the drums. But he wasn't much good." In 1946 the family moved to Coalburn in Lanarkshire. He attended Larkhall Academy and Lesmahagow High School, grew keen on painting, but still drummed with small bands at balls and farmers' weddings. And at Glasgow School of Art he played with a student jazz group. He was also in the Student Christian Movement, where a meeting with a Franciscan inspired him to visit a monastery in England with thoughts of becoming a monk. I mention this because Alasdair Taylor is a lyrical painter: a painter whose colour, like a musician's sound, makes sombre and radiant feelings without showing (as many painters do and all good writers must) details of the social life causing them. Such an artist knows very well the feelings of hell, purgatory and heaven which were the material of religion before clergymen grew embarrassed by them. Alasdair Taylor rejected the Franciscans for the Presbyterian reason that he hated ritual. Since then he has experienced several religions and spiritualisms, but without desiring that fixed state of mind called belief. Belief in one system would put too narrow a box round his feelings.

In the third art-school year he came to London to look at Rembrandt etchings, and visiting an almost empty cinema one afternoon saw a beautiful girl some rows ahead. He spoke to her. She was a Danish au pair girl. They met several times and became firm friends. She returned to Denmark. On leaving art school he received a £50 painting prize, sold his drums, used the money to follow her to Silkeborg, and they were married. I give these details to show his jazzman's power: the power of acting spontaneously then building soundly on the result. Annelise is remarkable. She has calmness, strength, intelligence, and the love of painting not to nag her husband out of it when life is hard. She has prevented the usual despair and become the foundation of his art. One rare strong person who loves and supports your talent can outweigh a society which does not give a damn for you.

They returned to Scotland. He taught art for three days in a Dumbarton school then handed in his notice and got work as a midden man with Glasgow Cleansing Department while Annelise bore their first daughter. Six months later the Church of Scotland minister of Glasgow University made him caretaker of the Chaplaincy Centre. It was a busy place but for nearly five years it gave him room, time and security to work, and it was here I first saw his paintings.

He had two main sorts in that period, and the sort I preferred were the figures and portraits. The touches of pen and brush he used to show faces and bodies were amazingly free. An encounter with the Danish artist Asger Jorn had excited him to use paint richly and thickly. Rembrandt is said to have once painted a portrait so thick that, laid flat on the floor, it could be lifted by the nose. Sometimes Alasdair worked like that, building up the paint in jewel-like flakes. Yet he could still show whole characters and forms with a few quick nervous pen-strokes on paper. I was baffled and stunned by the other works, which the jargon of the schools would have described as abstract-expressionist-dadaist-symbolism with ingredients of pop-collage. They were full of outraged energy, outrage so strong that it sometimes incorporated swear-words. Why?

My answer is a banal one. Today urban life, like the art of painting, is in a poor way. Commerce and government are no more selfishly greedy than in other times but they are greedy in more versatile and quickly changing ways. Even in the prosperous sixties a work of popular sociology announced that modern happiness meant learning to accept, not only disposable* furnishings, clothes and cars, but disposable homes, friendships, marriages. Painters are forced by their eccentric position to look hard at the life round about them, and their products show it. Some see the communal world reshaped by advertising and have made art out of commercial pornography, soupcan labels, popstar photographs. Some, excited by the impossibility of seeing exactly what our highly calculating technology is doing to us, have painted unsensual abstracts intricately calculated to stop the eye of the viewer focusing on them. Others, who feel the world at its best is a succession of exciting shocks, make works which are quaintly or vividly shocking, but have little other content. A recent lot find their world so distasteful that they paint rural fairylands of little girls, flowers, rich country gardens, topiary lawns, parasols and Edwardian ballgames. However the two best-known British artists still paint modern people. Hockney makes his eye very cold and shows people as chalky-surfaced additions to modern furniture, bathroom fittings, swimming pools and glass-fronted banks. Bacon looks under the skin at our twisted loneliness and capacity for pain. And Alasdair Taylor, living in Glasgow, crucified an umbrella on a canvas and wrote swear-words under it, because his artistic gift was lyrical and nothing around him fed it.

In 1965 the job of Chaplaincy caretaker ended and the Taylors moved to Northbank Cottage, a small farmhouse near the tip of the Hunterston promontory. Behind it rises a high red cliff with a strip of ancient tangled woodland at

---

* *Disposable* used to mean *easily positioned*, and therefore *easily replaced*. The rapid manufacture and marketing of the sixties and seventies brought it to mean *for rejection after use*, with the implication that rapid wastage is efficient and carefree; then military logicians started using it to denote the part of a fighting force or population whose death will assist victory, or not prevent it.

the foot. The front faces the Firth of Clyde across a narrow field usually given to potatoes, and the view embraces three islands: Millport (a seaside village under a serrated green hill) the Wee Cumbrae (rocky terraces of golden bracken and heather) and Arran (a blue-grey mountainous silhouette). The nearest building is the atomic power station, half a mile along the coast to the north and partly hidden by a bend in the cliff. To the south the clachan of Portencross is hidden by a fault-dyke with an opening cut in it to let the track through. The cottage has an outhouse with a skylight which was once the studio of the landscape painter Houston, but is now used to store seed-potatoes. Alasdair's studio is in the main building, entered from a separate door at the back. The cottage, whitewashed and lit by oil-lamps, was the scene of a famous unsolved murder in the thirties. It has a plain, friendly feeling about it which is not purely why the Taylors moved there. The promontory is good farming ground, the landowners wanted an eye kept on the fields hidden by the cliff, so the cottage rent was a few shillings a week.

When Alasdair left Glasgow many people thought he would soon return. He had poured out such streams of conversation in their company that they thought him a mainly social animal. They forgot he had grown up in mainly country districts, and that social animals spend hours together without talking at all. The drummer in Alasdair felt that company should be stimulated and stimulating, so his conversation was always very quick, intense, crammed with insights and therefore exhausting. It drew off energy he needed for work, work which was best fed by reflections in the country near the wife and daughters who loved him and took him for granted. On coming to Northbank he collected small boulders and driftwood from the beach, weathered roots from old trees by the cottage. The stones moved him to mark them with enamel hieroglyphs. He

sculpted the wood into shapes suggested by its shape and
grain. Wood, even flat slabs of it, can be got more cheaply
than canvas, especially by a trained midden man, so his next
paintings were on wood. A sequence of abstractions based
on the life of Christ were painted on polished and varnished slices of a railway sleeper which was floated in by the
tide. The colour had a richness he had once used mainly in
portraiture.

Later a friend brought down in a lorry some backdrops a
theatre-group had thrown out, because they were a fire
risk. Alasdair cut them down, stretched them, and took
them into Houston's old studio, which was empty at the
time. He now had nearly forty big canvases, each stained
with blues, buffs, dull greens and pinks which had once,
across the footlights, seemed like skies, trees and mountains. These shapes began to suggest pictures to him, as the
tree-roots had suggested sculpture. Money was short;
these were his first canvases for many years; he decided
nothing must be wasted. He would touch these canvases
only when he felt exactly what to do. He worked with oils,
brushes and cans of spray-paint. These cans are a popular
medium with amateur muralists in the poorer parts of
Glasgow, but they cost nearly a pound each. Annelise, who
then worked in an Ardrossan youth centre, bought more
whenever she saw the supply run low. He left the choice of
colours to her. He expected the canvases to last a year or
two, but they were completed in a few weeks.

This was the first work of his artistic maturity. The surfaces were as energetic as before but with new variety,
depth and harmony. They hold many kinds of light and
colour; light in cloud, water and leaves, colour in seaweed,
pebbles, moss and rusty iron. Only the works themselves
can show the coolness and warmth, nearness and remote-
ness they contain, but I have said enough to indicate that

Alasdair Taylor is an abstract expressionist, one of the school containing most Kandinsky, much of Klee, all of Jackson Pollock, and in present-day England, Albert Irvin. This kind of painting, since it gives the beholder a shock which is not a shock of recognition, strikes most people as a chaos, a mere explosion of paint. Many abstract expressionist works strike me that way too. After the first shock of pleasure at what seems a great explosion of energy they get duller with each glance because they lack the variety, contrast and harmony which make a picture worth contemplating. But Alasdair's pictures abide contemplation. The shock of seeing one as a whole, at a distance, becomes at close range a pleasure in those strongly, subtly varied colours which are a main part of my sensual, visual delight in the airy, watery, rocky and growing world outside his studio.

From that time to this an abstract expressionist has lived and worked in a cottage on the Ayrshire coast, steadily painting, brooding, and painting again; sometimes visited by friends, a few of whom buy a picture from time to time; and partly unknown to, and partly ignored by, the official art world. For in Scotland, as elsewhere in Britain, a new official art world has come to exist, a separate one from art schools, institutes and academies. In the early seventies, by Arts Council subsidy and local government donation, new arts centres with exhibition galleries and salaried administrations came to most of the Scottish cities. The administrators are usually strangers to the cities where they work and are often English, because there are more highly qualified English than Scots looking for work in modern Britain. The administrations honestly wish to show the best in modern art, including local Scottish art, but how do they know what that is? By repute, and by experience. If artists exhibit once or twice a year with other artists, and have a single show of their own from time to time, administrations get to know them almost unconsciously, through an accumulation of tiny repetitions of names in conversations, invitation-cards and posters. They can also see the artists' product in galleries, in their absence, in a context of acceptance and appreciation, and can decide to exhibit it without meeting and judging a peculiar human being. Administrations, therefore, hardly ever meet the Scottish hermit painter, and only do so with discomfort on both sides. And nobody can help by approaching an administration, pointing to a distant figure and saying, "See him! Show him! He's great!" Those who do are the artist's friend, and prejudiced.

So in 1985 Alasdair is one of over 350,000 Scots whose work is not wanted and whose existence embarrasses administrations. He is not a tragic soul. He is not on the dole, his wife is the breadwinner, he labours at what he does best. He often feels lonely and useless, but we all have our troubles. Hardworking, salaried arts administrators and teachers have quite different troubles, and can dismiss him with a touch of envy. He creates what they are paid to promote. His work accumulates. One day more than five or six people will learn to love it.

The Grumbler

There is a sour taste in my mouth no matter how hard I brush my teeth, and though I change my underwear every morning and take a bath every night I am haunted by a faint, stale odour. Maybe the sourness and staleness is the taste and smell of myself. Is something rotting inside me? I have very little energy nowadays and often sweat for no apparent reason. My urine is the colour of very strong tea – I'm sure it used to be the colour of very weak tea – and I keep running to the lavatory and shitting almost nothing but wind and water. Last week, while shopping, the top half of my body suddenly felt too heavy for the bottom half and I got this pain round my middle, especially in the small of the back, a pain which made it hard to sleep at night. I saw two doctors: my General Practitioner who thumped me all over, said the pain was purely muscular and gave me a bottle of pills to reduce inflammation; and a chiropractor who said I had a slightly displaced vertebra then wrenched my thigh and shoulder before working on the inflammation with heat rays, massage and acupuncture. The backache remained. I went to bed and lay reading dull books I had read before and not enjoyed much, even then. I lacked the strength to read anything enjoyable.

It occurred to me that I was dying. I had a friend who once started dying. I saw him limping and asked why. He said there had been a pain in his knee the day before but it was much better now. For four years his leg was a bit worse every time we met but always much better than the day before, so he refused to see a doctor until he was unable to stand. Then, of course, he was taken to hospital where they diagnosed a heart condition and arthritis and psoriasis, and gave him treatment, and let him out a bit better than he went in, but not much. He hirpled around for another year getting worse and worse again, but always feeling better than the day before, till at last he was dead.

Well, as soon as I thought I was dying I felt a lot happier. I greeted visitors with a smile of patient tolerance. My voice became soft, slow and monotonous. When asked how I felt I replied that I was experiencing no pain, really – just a slight, continuous discomfort. Which was true. I felt magnanimous toward the world. "In a short year or two," I told it, silently, of course, "you and I will cease to trouble each other." However, I gave medical science one last chance. I went to the two doctors and told them there was no improvement. My G.P., with a touch of impatience, said again that my condition was muscular and I should keep taking the pills. The chiropractor frowned in a puzzled way and gave me more acupuncture. I still felt magnanimous. "There are some conditions medical science will never understand," I thought, "before it is too late," and I was about to put off all arrangements and appointments for the foreseeable future when the backache vanished! It suddenly did not exist. This hurled me into my former depression. I went out and got drunk and woke in bed next morning with no clear memory of where I had been the night before and with a huge bruise on my right shoulder which still hurts when I move my arm.

Why must I complain all the time? I have nothing nowadays to worry about except the state of the world as a whole. Especially the part where I live. It is a comparatively prosperous district but even here there is an increase of cracked pavements, rusty lamp-posts and litter in the streets, and women and children with aggressively ugly clothes and hair, and many more haggard, ill-dressed and mad-looking people. Britain grows fouler and fouler as it retreats from the full employment and social welfare it enjoyed when I was a student in the fifties. But I must admit that in the fifties, sixties and even seventies I spent a lot of time feeling like a lonely outcast. I had many friends, and saw them often, but they too felt like lonely outcasts. We grumbled a lot. We decided that our city was completely cultureless because it refused to blend imagination with political commitment. We hired halls and organized meetings to agitate and change things, but we were too poor and useless to do much good. When I say "poor and useless" I do not mean that I, personally, was ever penniless or unemployed, but I felt poor and useless because I had hardly any sex life and was getting older all the time.

When my marriage stopped a certain pub became the centre of my social life. Twice or thrice a week I drank with people I met nowhere else, university people, and Linda who was a dental receptionist, and her boyfriend who worked in a travel agency. One evening, when slightly drunk, Linda asked me, in a perfectly friendly way, why I hung about with people so much younger than me? Honestly, till that moment I had not noticed they were younger than me, but they were, by at least ten years. I sat with them because I enjoyed their company and supposed they liked mine, but when I thought about it I realized that their conversation bored me. What I enjoyed was exactly their youth, especially the youth of the women, though I had no hope of going to bed with one. I had become a harmless middle-aged lecher.

Several years after I had stopped visiting that pub I passed some other young people in the street, and an attractive girl left them and said, "Excuse me sir, may I kiss you on the mouth?"

"Of course!" I said, and embraced her, but she got embarrassed and broke away and ran back to her friends, who were laughing heartily. They must have dared her to say that because I appeared to be a very respectable, easily shocked old chap. It was a great relief when something similar happened which looked like ending differently. Around closing time one night a girl ran out of a pub door, slipped her arm through mine and said, "You look sexy. Will you take me for an Indian meal?"

I am sure she was not a prostitute. She looked dull, ordinary and overweight, but so do I, so I did not mind. I said, "Of course I'll buy you a meal," and led her to a place I know. I swear to God I did not expect us to make love that night. She was not a prostitute and I was not a fool. The most I hoped for was a flirtatious conversation with some double entendre and innuendo etcetera, and later we would separate with perhaps a slight squeeze and a kiss. I would also give her my telephone number, which might lead to something later if she learned to trust me. When we came to the eating place she halted and said, "This isn't an Indian restaurant."

It was not. It was dearer than an Indian restaurant, but I was friendly with the management, who allowed me credit, and as I had very little money on me there was nowhere else where I could get her a meal that night. I persuaded her to enter and we sat in a glass-roofed courtyard beside a waterlily pond and were served by some very friendly waitresses. She hated it. She ate fast with her face low over the plate. I kept filling her wineglass and she kept emptying it but she spoke not one other word till we were out on the street again, when she asked me to lend her money for the bus fare home. I gave it to her and she hurried off. That was typical of my sex-life in those days.

Why remember such miserable things? I lived for my work in those days and I was good at it, though a lot of folk said my methods were unsound. I suppose that is why the marriage stopped – I earned very little at first. My wife thought me a poor provider, so when she took a job of her own she didn't want to share anything at all with me, not even the children. But I knew I was right. I plodded straight on as if nothing had happened, and eventually some big men started referring to me in the trade journals. At the age of forty-five my bank manager allowed me to open a new account with a really gigantic loan. I left that bank feeling like a child of eight released from school by the summer holidays. Safety, power and freedom! At last all were mine again. Something tight and hard in me uncoiled, or maybe lay down and died. I was finished with love, sex, women. They had never wanted me, I no longer wanted them.

Shortly after, within the space of a week, I had an enjoyable time in bed with four different women, two of whom I had known for years and who had never shown the slightest interest in me. I don't know why this suddenly happened. I had not become a local celebrity. My reputation in the trade meant nothing to these women, and as for money, nobody ever got money out of me. Recently I read an article about Hollywood which said that if a woman there takes a lover, "all her best friends go through him like an express train". But these women were not acquaintances, so I was definitely not being passed around. There was a royal wedding that week, perhaps it inflamed some irrational passions, I can think of no other explanation. However, I found that I disliked casual sex. I started visiting regularly the only two who regularly want me. They are quite unlike each other, apart from being highly independent and not at all aggressive or malicious. They do not know each other but they know of each other, so I am not deceiving them. I am astonished by myself. I had thought this sort of luck was enjoyed only by aristocrats in improbable romances. I now have all I ever wanted or ever dreamed of wanting: professional respect, prosperity, independence and love.

At first it was very nice but I've got used to it and it's driving me mad. It feels like a happy ending. There seems nowhere to go but downhill. I've started drinking too much. Friends ask me what's wrong, but when I tell them I have everything I want they are unable to sympathize. My education is to blame. Two important things I learned at school were worry and boredom. My teachers, who were themselves usually worried and bored, seemed to think we would only become decent human beings if we were like that. Perhaps they taught me too well. I now turn everything I enjoy into worry and boredom in order to feel like a decent human being. This must stop. I refuse to be the creature of my education, a creature of habit. I will change myself tomorrow. Yes, tomorrow. Tomorrow.

I Own Nothing, I Owe Nothing

The mountain had two summits. One of them had been excavated to uncover ridges of rock around the main contours, ridges with flat upper surfaces and sheer cliff-like sides. I noticed that some ridges were not natural rock but reinforced with concrete.

The site manager and head ganger stood beside the workmen's huts staring hard at the second summit, a dome-shaped mass with granite outcrops. The site manager wanted to know if it could be concreted over by the following night? The head ganger was uncertain. The site manager said, "Let's take a closer look."
He turned and called to me, "Like to come?"
I followed them to a small vehicle used for inspection purposes. The driver was already seated, for there was one place available for me at the back. When I stepped in and sat down the tops of my thighs were as high as the vehicle's side.

From a state of rest we started straight up the mountain so fast that I was terrified of being jerked out backward by my inertia. I desperately wanted something to cling to but the only sure grip was on the edge of the vehicle's underside a few inches above boulder-strewn soil against which it continually banged and scraped without once reducing speed. I passed the journey in a state of fear while also feeling the amazement and exhilaration of flying over ground where folk normally only plod or crawl. We swooped up a curving path between the two summits. I expected us to turn a corner and crash into a rocky rampart, but when we reached one it was red earth and pierced by an arch. We ran through this into a huge quarry or amphitheatre enclosed by walls of scree curving up all round on to cliffs of vertical rock. The vehicle, powered by a strong four-wheel drive, ran part way up a slope of rubble, reversed faster down it, then sped up it even faster, the driver clearly building up momentum to take him on to the vertical. I shouted, "This can't be done!" but the vehicle rushed up an angle of the quarry wall and at the moment of reaching vertical twisted sideways on to the lowest point of a sloping cornice and we ran safe on to a rounded part of the second summit. The manager indicated it with a Napoleonic wave of the arm. "Tomorrow night?" he asked the ganger.

"We can try, anyway," said the ganger.

The site manager pointed at me, said, "This can't be done!" and chuckled. I saw he had asked me along so that my terror of the ride would emphasize his understanding and control, and make it easier for him to persuade the head ganger to attempt the impossible.

Later I was in a big crowded shed among the workmen's huts. Men were queuing in long lines before little booths fixed to the walls, booths containing oxygen masks. They were preparing to work in the thin air of the second summit by breathing deeply from these. Signs above the booths said that more than six minutes' oxygenation was bad for the health. I suspected that the whole business was bad for the health, a mere management trick to make the men believe their needs were being attended to. Having no intention of working on the second summit I went next door into a bleaker, emptier shed which was the restaurant. The only food was sandwiches in white polystyrene trays covered with transparent plastic. I knew the white bread of the sandwiches was as flavourless and un-nourishing as the polystyrene, but being hungry I chose an egg sandwich and a ham sandwich, and my mouth watered, anticipating with some glee the taste of the fillings. Since we had no better food we got great satisfaction from whatever flavour it contained.

As I lifted my sandwiches I was greeted by an old workman wearing spectacles and a dirty raincoat. He also was not going to work on the second summit. He said, "I'm getting a bit old for these impossible jobs. Mind you, I've nothing to complain about."
He pointed to a plastic table-top on which someone had scratched the words: *I own nothing, I owe nothing.* He said, "That's me too, yes. I can only manage the odd day's work now and then but I like to hang around the site and listen to the lads when they come back in the evenings. You hear a lot of different views of life if you keep your ears open. I hope I'm not boring you?"

The Domino Game

Two big men called A and B are discussing how to cut up a territory which is in contest between them. Their organizations, their cunning, their chances of success are about equal. The contest, if continued, will so weaken them that both will fall prey to X, a much bigger man who has hitherto held aloof. This is partly because he is doing very well in a distant territory where he has destroyed or absorbed every other competitor, and partly because he knows A and B will unite against him if he tries to destroy or absorb either. Their problem is that the disputed territory cannot usefully be cut in two. For geographical, religious and linguistic reasons, splitting it will more than wipe out the profit to be got by taking it over. Yet they cannot leave it alone. The disputed ground is occupied by small independent people who mostly want to stay small and independent, but some of the richer among them also want, with foreign help, to grow bigger at the expense of their neighbours. If A or B do not offer this help X will regard it as a sign of weakness and move into the territory himself. Of course, if A and B combined forces they could easily run the whole territory for the profit of both, but when B suggests this A says, "Combine under who?"

And the subject is dropped.

The discussion is a long one. They exhaust themselves trying to find a solution to the problem. At last A sighs and says, "Why can't we decide it by playing a game of dominoes? Winner take all." B laughs and says, "Why not? The winner will be a hell of a lot richer, the loser won't be one penny the poorer."

They relax by discussing the idea.
Neither has played dominoes since childhood and they suspect it is mainly a game of chance. A suggests that if there is any skill in it they had better play snakes-and-ladders, to equalize their chance. B disagrees. Snakes-and-ladders is played with dice, and dice, like card games, are associated with nervous tension, cheating, social ruin, knife fights and suicide. Domino is a game with friendly, jocular associations which harmonize better with the whole idea. They should play it in the dining-car of a train running through splendid scenery. They will invite X along as a guest and witness. It is essential that he sees they are good friends who trust each other before the game, and also during it, but especially after it. Yes, after it especially, X must see that although the game ends in a great acquisition by the winner, the loser is not sullen, humiliated, and keen for an ally who will assist him in a counter-attack. X must also see that the winner will not be made so greedy by his gains that he will do a deal with X to cut up the loser between them. And of course, the loser must see this too.
"What a surprise for old X if we settled it that way!" says B, chuckling. "He might even learn something from us."
"Yes!" says A, "if we did it that way we would be starting a new era in civilization. However — " and he shrugs, " — while I trust you, B, I certainly can't trust C, D and E."
These are members of B's organization. One of them, though nobody can yet say which one, will replace him

when he falls sick or retires.

"I know exactly what you mean," says B, who also has ambitious men under him, "We'll just have to combine forces."

"Combine under who?" asks A. "Will you agree to settle *that* by a domino game?"

And both laugh heartily. Each now knows the other will not serve under him. They also know that an organization cannot work with two heads.

So their contest continues to spread frustration and anxiety among their employees, poverty and fear among small independent people. It will continue until one of them is so weak that he accepts X as his ally, thereby winning a victory which will leave him, too, in the power of X. This future, which they see very clearly, pleases neither of them, but they have four consolations.

1 They are not young, the years seem to flash past them faster and faster, they will soon have to leave what they sense is an increasingly dangerous world.

2 Though not young, their conspicuous place in a well-reported contest makes them feel young.

3 They have private fortunes which the contest increases.

4 A contest which profits them is only natural.

Decision

I was ignorant when I was young. I didnae know that sex and children were connected — they seemed to belong to different worlds. My Mammy and her pals talked about sex in a queer oblique kind of way but they were quite open and direct when they spoke about children: "She's decided not to have a child yet," they said about a girl who had just married. I was sixteen when I married and I decided not to have a child either. I talked it over with my husband — he was a year older than me — and he entirely agreed. "Time enough for us to have children when we've a home of our own," he said, "and that won't be for a few years yet."
My Mammy thought it was a wise decision too. We were living with her.

Imagine my astonishment when my stomach swole up and the doctor told me I was pregnant. I said, "I can't be! I've decided not to have a child."
He said, "What precautions did you take?"
I didnae answer him. I don't take precautions when I decide not to have a cigarette, why take precautions when I decide not to have a baby? A woman in the bed beside me at the maternity hospital told me about birth control, but I was pregnant again a week after I came out.

Authority

I did struggle for it. By accident alone five older brothers
died before I took the crown of a thousand-mile-long
kingdom, founded by our grandfather, when the T'ang
dynasty could not hold China together. My handwriting
was excellent. I was not blatantly unfaithful to my wife. Like
a true philosopher I eschewed ambition and let landlords
and merchants run the country. The Sung empire
swallowed us whole. When ordered, I killed myself. Never
mind. I once wrote my name on a famous painting. I am
remembered, though my people are not.

Translation

The elder grandmother, or stipendiary magistrate, or rich
farmer's prodigal son scratches, or ignores, or perhaps
greedily enjoys the young slave-girls of the harem, or the
petitioners from an unimportant suburb, or the white
feathered-longnecked-furiously-hissing denizens of the
poultry yard: while in another continent and century and
civilization I turn a vertical row of pictograms into a
horizontal sentence of phonetic type, without spilling a
nuance.

Humanity

And one mild midsummer day, high among the rocky and heathery summits of Ben Venue, we found a small hollow brimful of perfectly smooth untrodden snow, and shouting "See the lovely white snow!" jumped into the middle of it with our great big boots.

Money

My ceiling admits no rain. I admire the movement of clouds over the city. Every weather, every season has its unique beauty.

Ending

Having beguiled with fiction until I had none left I
resorted to facts, which also ran out.

<

POSTSCRIPT for whoever likes lists of names and wants to know how the makers of this book came together.

In 1971 Doctor Philip Hobsbaum, who had recently started teaching English at Glasgow University, invited once a fortnight to his home a group of writers, mostly young and unpublished, to read and discuss each other's work. Scotland was the third British kingdom, or province, where he had conducted writing groups after leaving the Cambridge of Doctor Leavis. In London his circle included Peter Redgrove, Peter Porter, George MacBeth and Edward Lucie-Smith. In Belfast there were Seamus Heaney, Stewart Parker, Michael Longley and Bernard Mac Laverty. In Glasgow he brought together a number who lodged in the same square mile of tenements and terraces but, before entering his high corner flat on Wilton Street, had in many cases not seen or heard of each other. There was the American poet Anne Stevenson, the Skye poets Catriona Montgomery and Aonghas MacNeacail, with Liz Lochhead, Tom Leonard, Donald Saunders, Marcella Evaristi, Chris Boyce, Alasdair Gray and Jim Kelman. Kelman was in his twenties, had been born in Glasgow and usually lived there, though he had detailed knowledge of part of the U.S.A., Wales, the English Channel Islands and London. He had recently become a family man, a position he still holds. Gray was an older Glaswegian who lived by painting and by selling infrequent plays to broadcasting companies. These two at first were indifferent to each other's work. Gray was writing a novel which used the devices of fantasy to overlook facts which were essential to Kelman's prose.

An author who liked Kelman's work was Mary Gray Hughes, one of North America's best short-story writers. She visited the Glasgow group as a guest of Philip Hobsbaum and Anne Stevenson, and through her representations Puckerbrush Press of Maine published in 1973 Jim Kelman's first collection of stories, *An old pub near the Angel*. This book is now sought by libraries with an interest in Scottish fiction, but on first appearing it brought the author little money or fame. A first book by an original writer, issued by a small foreign publishing house which cannot afford expensive advertising and distribution, will not be reviewed by many big newspapers and magazines, and will be lucky to pay for its printing costs. Even so, *An old pub near the Angel* did good. It proved to those who cared for such things that Jim Kelman was a professional writer. Ten years passed before his next book of tales found a publisher, but single pieces appeared regularly in the annual Collins Scottish short-story anthology and such publications as *Words* magazine and *Firebird*.

In the middle seventies three former members of Philip Hobsbaum's group, Lochhead, Gray and Kelman, were tutoring part-time for Glasgow University adult education department. It was Liz Lochhead who first read and showed her colleagues the story *Arabella* which starts on page 113 of the book you now hold. She had been given it when visiting a class of writers in the Vale of Leven, a shallow valley of small factory towns along the river flowing from Loch Lomond into the Clyde at Dumbarton Rock. If you enjoyed that story you will know why Lochhead, Gray and Kelman were greatly excited. Most writing classes produce at least one entertaining story which might have been published in days when fiction magazines half filled the station bookstalls. *Arabella* was better than those. We learned that the author had come recently to storywriting, and worked as a clerk and shop-steward in a local electric clock factory. She was twice married, once widowed, with two self-supporting children and three still at school. Our first reaction was to call her a natural writer, which on second thoughts was silly. Nobody writes naturally. It is an art which is learned. Those who do it best have continued teaching themselves after leaving school, and the main teaching method is enthusiastic reading. Agnes Owens had obviously read enough, and read intelligently enough, to clear her language of the secondhand phrases used by ordinary writers to disguise their lack of ideas. When Gray and Kelman read more of her work (for eventually they also visited the small class in the Vale) they felt she sometimes used too many adverbs, and Jim Kelman has been unremitting in his efforts to make her like Chekhov more and Graham Greene less; but tutoring, where Agnes was concerned, had little to do with the quality of her writing. Being new to writing, in a district where nearly every sort of industry was closing down, her response to those who liked her stories was, "So who will print it? And how much will they pay?" They had to teach her that if she steadily posted her work to a certain number of small magazines, always with a stamped addressed envelope for return, she might get two or three stories published in four or five years and be paid thirty or forty pounds. They had to teach her that the magazines most interested in new talent were liable to cease publication before printing her. They explained that Scotland's really famous writers – those whose stories and poems were referred to by critics and lecturers – had either some sort of unearned income or did hackwork for education and publicity establishments. They told her that in Britain those who feed and house themselves solely by writing have to turn out two or three paperback novels a year, novels which critics and lecturers ignore. They said they knew she was a writer like themselves, but they could not welcome her aboard a sturdy ship called H.M.S. *Literature*. Such a ship exists, but is a work of communal imagination, and those who talk like captains of it are misleading or misled.

Agnes Owens's talent was too tough to be killed by learning that writing was not a full free life but just another sort of that daily life she knew like the back of her hand. In the next ten years she was paid thirty or forty pounds for a couple of magazine stories, and had a story accepted by an editor who vanished before printing it. She wrote radio plays which were returned by producers with letters expressing great interest in the next play she sent them. Her first novel, *Gentlemen of the West*, was returned by a publisher who said he might consider printing it if a famous Scottish comedian said something about it which could be used as advertisement. She posted the typescript to the comedian who put it on that pile of unsolicited correspondence which no famous person has time to answer. Industry in the Vale of Leven started closing even faster than in the rest of Britain. Westclox Limited went into liquidation and Agnes did what our dynamic prime minister would do if the Thatcher family had to go on the dole: she hunted for part-time cleaning jobs. She worked for a while in the house of the comedian who had received her typescript a few years before, and got it back.

Meanwhile Jim Kelman and Alasdair Gray, who had started writing ten and twenty years earlier than Agnes Owens, became luckier sooner. In 1983 Polygon Books, the Edinburgh University press, published Kelman's second collection of stories, *Not not while the giro*, and signed a contract for his second novel, *The Busconductor Hines*. Polygon is the only University press in Europe owned and run by the students. Perhaps because it does not need to make a profit it has recently become the most adventurous of small Scottish publishing houses, producing editions of native authors who are well known, but (from the viewpoint of publishers who will collapse if they make no profit) not well known enough. Kelman showed *Gentlemen of the West* to a Polygon editor who loved it, and Agnes's first novel was published in the spring of 1984.

By this time a collection of Gray's stories had been issued in hardback by Canongate of Edinburgh and bought for paperback by King Penguin. A director of a London publishing house asked him if he had enough stories to make another collection. Gray said no. There was a handful of stories he had intended to build into another collection, but found he could not, as he had no more ideas for prose fictions. From now on he would write only frivolous things like plays or poems, and ponderous things like *A History Of The Preface* or a treatise on *The Provision Merchant As Agent Of Evil In Scottish Literature From Galt To Gunn*. Even if his few unpublished stories were stretched by the addition of some prose portraits and poems they would still not amount to a book. The director asked Gray if he could suggest two other writers who would join him in a collection. And now you know how *Lean Tales* was made.